W9-CAE-626

THE GOD WE SEEK

THE GOD
WE SEEK

Paul Weiss

Southern Illinois University Press · *Carbondale*

For F. S. C. Northrop

A GREAT MAN, A FINE COLLEAGUE
AND A NOBLE PHILOSOPHER

PREFACE

SOME TIME AGO I sent a multilithed draft of this work to a number of philosophers, theologians and friends. What I there presented has been considerably changed, partly because of what I learned from their criticisms. Much of it has now been rewritten, some has been eliminated, and the whole reorganized and re-structured.

I am most grateful to Richard Bernstein, Peter Bertocci, Fr. Norris Clarke, S.J., James Collins, Robert Ehman, Ellen S. Haring, Charles Hartshorne, Iredell Jenkins, I. C. Lieb, Alvin Plantinga, Andrew Reck, Calvin Schrag, Richard Sewall, Eric Walther, Robert Whittemore and Jonathan A. Weiss for much needed advice, direction and help. I am sorry to say that I did not always succeed in assimilating what was urged. No one but I must be held accountable for any of the confusions or mistakes the book still contains.

This book is the last of a series of works started some twenty-five years ago. In them an attempt is made to deal with basic problems of knowledge and being both from an abstract and an experiential point of view. Though each was written as an independent study, each supplements and thereby, I think, strengthens the others. As I look back at the earlier writings, I see that they gain considerably from the later increase in perspective and from the outcomes of the later detailed examinations. There can be little doubt that the present work benefits from what was learned earlier in studies of the nature of being, the good and the known, but I think it too can stand alone.

Paul Weiss

New Haven, Connecticut
May 1964

CONTENTS

THE GOD WE SEEK

Introduction

ALMOST ALL MEN have been helped and subdued by family and society in the name of God, the being who remains steadfast when all else gives way. Speech and act soon overlay what was early absorbed by the child. Sometimes they correct, sometimes they skew, sometimes they pervert, but they never wholly deny to the child what had once been impressed on it. All of us speak of God in ways which reflect something of what we once were taught, almost unaware.

Some men become associated with particular institutions — church, synagogue, temple, mosque. These provide means for disciplining and educating them. Occasionally they provide the men with companionship, or food and drink. Men understandably become loyal members of, and sometimes apologists for such religious institutions. They live in terms of quite specific creeds, rituals, books, prophets and Gods. Some even make institutional life into a career, turning their backs on other types of life to give theirs to its defense, support or enhancement.

Such men are often hard to distinguish from others who try to make effective use of God. God, these believe, is the awesome being, all-powerful. If they could control Him, channel His vast power, what wonders might they not perform! No one perhaps is altogether free from a desire to make some use of God's power. Many prayers are but plaintive requests or petitions for favors. A good deal of behavior is kept within confines in the hope of a divine reward or in fear of God's awful wrath.

If we believe that we or others can dictate the way in which God's power will be manifested, we believe in magic. If instead we vitally hope that what we are or do will make a difference in

3

what God does, we are religious. The religious man grants
autonomy to God; the magician thinks he has Him under
control.

Most men, perhaps, are interested in God primarily as the
being who will strengthen, purify, sanctify or forgive them,
who will make good their failures and add to their achievements.
God is their salvation. Their interest in Him is a personal one.
They add individual notes to the God they learned about when
they were young. That a number of these men have somewhat
similar reasons for being interested in God does not, unfortunately, preclude them from acting toward Him and toward one
another in distinct and sometimes opposing ways. The very
intensity of their desire to remain within the outlook of family,
society or church, to use His power, or to achieve salvation,
keeps them in distinct religious groups. Thereafter they live
within the orbit of some particular religion.

The religions rarely bring God into clear focus, being content
to make Him present in communal worship, and to point to
Him as still beyond the dedicated community. The plurality
of religions testifies not only to distinctive estimates of God but
to a plurality of ways of acting and believing, and to various
relations supposed to connect man and man, man and God, man
and the world, and God and the world. The members of the
different religions, because they usually make little effort to
understand what God in fact is like, differ not only in practice,
but in their values and their justification, and ultimately in what
they say and do about their God.

One religion may focus on God better than others do, but
each, if it deserves the name of religion at all, must deal with
God somehow and to some degree. At the very least God is a
referent of each and every one of them. If He is pointed at by
one religion, He is pointed at by all. He is more than and other
than that which any group takes Him to be. How can we discover what He is like?

One way, some men hold, is through theology. They start
committed to some one religion, and then try to clarify and
explicate what it is that they and their fellow worshippers do,
assume and know. Inescapably they carry into the intellectual
arena the parochial concerns and special pleadings characteristic
of their own particular religion. They cannot therefore know

God as He truly is, for He surely is not wholly confined within
the bounds of any one religion.

To avoid parochialism a more neutral position must be taken
toward God than that characteristic of the practitioners or the
theological defenders of a particular religion. A study might be
made of all religions in the hope of isolating a single common
core in them all. The results of such an enterprise, not sur-
prisingly, have in the past proved to be small and thin. The elements common to all religions are not plentiful, and in any case
do not tell us about those aspects of religion which excite,
transform and penetrate men, or about a God who is above the
strife of those who claim to have Him wholly within their
charge.

We cannot discover what God is by adding the assertions
of the various religions to one another. The assertions are not
always compatible. The different religions make conflicting
claims. Each denies that the others do as much justice to God's
nature or demands as it does. God is not the least common
denominator of the objects of various forms of worship; He is
richer in being and meaning than any religion can express.

There are a great number of ways in which contact can
be made with God. We can find Him everywhere. We can
move to Him from anywhere. And our movements can traverse
many different types of routes; from act to thought, from fear to
faith. Apart from all special revelation, message, or miracle, there
are no less than fifteen ways of making contact with God.

God is an undifferentiated part of an ultra-natural domain of
which we become aware, when in terror or surmise, we look
beyond the conventional world in which we daily live (ch. 1).
We also make contact with God in a religious experience (ch. 3).
Here, severally and together, we ignore the categorizations of
the daily world to attend to immediately encountered content,
bearing the marks of His presence. Sometimes through the
fissures (ch. 3) of that experience it is possible to glimpse God,
the being who makes that experience possible. Sacred objects
provide a fourth way of making contact with God (ch. 4).
These are objects and events in the common-sense world, cut off
from their practical use and seen to express a divine power. Such
sacred objects also relate us (ch. 4) to the God which lies
beyond them, in somewhat the way in which a work of art

enables us to make contact with a reality external to it. Still
another way of making contact with God is through the production of an adequate idea of Him (ch. 5). God is also publicly
participated in; He is immanent in the dedicated community
(ch. 6). An eighth way is ours when we turn away from the
world and attach ourselves to an Other (ch. 9) which is more
appropriate to us and steadier than any the world could provide.
God is also immanent in every act of faith, satisfying it to some
degree from the very start (ch. 10). He is a transcendent as well
as an immanent being, referred to by the dedicated community
(ch. 6), reached by faith (ch. 10), enjoyed in worship (ch. 11),
lived for in service (ch. 12), arrived at by various proofs (see
Modes of Being, ch. 4), and mystically lived with (passim).

Not all these ways — e.g., the first, the ultra-natural, the
eighth, the act of attachment, and the fourteenth, the proofs,
have much direct religious import. The ultra-natural is available
to children, well before they can be religious. The other two
presuppose maturity, but one of them precedes a mature faith,
and the other is too unemotional to have religious weight. However, they are not without value. The ultra-natural provides
many with their first and sometimes their last intimations of the
existence of God. We must attach ourselves to God in order to
become religious. And we need proofs if the religious life is to
be well focused and stabilized, and if its claims are to meet the
challenge of a critical reason. God is enjoyed in experience,
sacred objects, our idea of Him, in the dedicated community, as
our Other, in faith and in worship. We reach to Him ultra-
naturally, through the fissures of experience, and by means of
community, faith and proofs. We re-present Him (and thereby
reveal His nature) in sacred objects and in service to Him. And
if we are mystics we will have direct access to Him. In all these
ways we become acquainted with God, but neither severally nor
together do these ways provide us with a rationally sustained
knowledge of Him.

To obtain a rational knowledge of God, recourse must be
had to speculation, systematic and dialectical. We will not know
what God is like until we engage in such a free study of Him.
It is one of the tasks of a philosophic system to tell us through
the agency of speculation and dialectic about the nature of God,
in independence of all religious commitment, and in abstrac-

tion from all restrictive conditions which family, society, church, personal desire, and need have imposed on our understanding of Him. I have tried to deal with God in this way in my *Modes of Being*, arriving at Him through the agency of multiple proofs, and analyzing His nature in the light of what else is known about reality. Something like the results of that work, I am convinced, must be assumed by all apologists for a given religion. God is a reality and unless one knows what that reality is like one will be in no position to know which religion does most justice to His nature and activities.

Strictly speaking, though, we need more than a speculative knowledge of God, if we are to properly grasp what and that He is, and how He is involved with what lies beyond Him. We can be sure that there is a reality to be reached only if speculative knowledge (with reaching and re-presentation) are matched by an enjoyment of and an access to God. Otherwise it might merely point to what might have no other reality but that of being the end of various acts of ours. Conversely, the content of an enjoyment and the outcome of a mystical access are too immediate to make it possible for one to know that it is God who is involved in them. Our knowledge, our reaching and our re-presentations must be supplemented by enjoyment and access if we are to confront a being who is at once intelligible and existent.

God in and of Himself is the objective unity of the termini of our approaches to Him and of what we obtain through a contact with Him. But since no one of us has both followed and united all these approaches, no one of us can be said to have an adequate grasp of what God is in and of Himself. For the same reason, though, no one of us can be said to have grasped the nature of anything whatsoever as it is in and of itself. Everywhere in this space-time world and in what lies beyond it, we are faced with realities toward which we adventure from only a few of many possible angles; only occasionally do we use the various outcomes to guide and check one another. Only rarely do we try to express creatively what all of them together presuppose. We are and perhaps ought to be content with accepting as final whatever fits in with most of what we have learned in other disciplines, at other times and in other ways. It is at any rate all that we apparently can today comprehend and use.

The major topic of the present work is the experience of
and concern with God in privacy and in a community. It does
not offer a report of personal experiences, except those which
are so rudimentary that they are shared by everyone. It is essentially a phenomeno-analysis, which is to say an account of the
nucleal, normative dimensions of private and public religious
life. Starting from the data open to everyone, it makes use of
the creative imagination in order to reveal the primary nuances
and distinctions essential to an adequate grasp of the nature of
religion.

contra ✓
in terms?

    The present work seeks to isolate the pure, undistorted rela-
tion men have to God; a relation which is diversely ritualized
and specialized by the various religions. This, which it seeks, is
no distillate, no abstract dessicated element, but something at
least as rich and as concrete as the specialized forms of experience and concerns exhibited in particular religions — but without
their bias. The experience and concern which men exhibit in a
particular religion distort the form of the religion they ideally
could have had and always have implicitly.

    The present work, though independent, takes advantage of
results I have previously obtained, using them as guides, corrections, suggestions and encouragement. It is aware that if God is
not everywhere He is nowhere; that, if there is evidence for Him
anywhere, there is evidence of Him everywhere; that, if anything whatsoever exists, He too must exist; that, if He does not
necessarily exist, He is not possible; that, if His existence can
be proved once, it can be proved an endless number of times;
that, if anything at all can be known, proved or encountered,
He can be known, proved or encountered; that, if He does not
give Himself to all beings, He gives Himself to none; and that
that religion is to be preferred whose God conforms most closely
to what is discovered in an impartial, detached, self-critical,
dialectical, speculative, systematic inquiry into the nature of
what is real.

    It would be good for men in the West to rid themselves of
Aristotle's unmoved mover, even when He is decorated with
Hebraic, Christian, and Muslim virtues. It would be no less good
for men in the East to free themselves from the idea of a God
who was forever self-centred, without involvement with this
world and us, an emptiness possessing no features. It is time

we asked ourselves whether we ought not to abandon the comparatively late idea that God is the creator of everything, that He has no needs, that He cannot be known in this life, and that He spends His energies thinking about us. We should call an end to special pleadings, and try instead to see what God is like, and how any man, anywhere, might turn to Him, move toward Him and encounter Him.

A religion rightly judges philosophy; telling it that its account of reality must have room for a being as rich as that which is religiously experienced. Conversely, a philosophy rightly judges religion, telling it that neither its account of God nor its aspirations and claims should require the denial of realities discovered in other ways, nor the denial of properties in God, learned through speculation. From a religious point of view the proofs of God which a philosopher provides are but instances of faith, just as, conversely, from the standpoint of philosophy, faith has a systematic, rational justification.

Religion begins with the awareness that there is a distance between man and God that can be bridged by us, or by God, or by the two of us together. It tries to deal with man's being and activities in terms of divinely grounded standards. A man is religious, whether inside or apart from a particular religion, only if he lives in terms of a final, loving, just (that is divine) assessment of all there is. Not every man is religious in this sense. All have a relation to God, but not all are concerned with what He might do to or for them now or later.

Religion has grades ranging from idolatry to mystical self-abandonment. Idolatry is the error of taking some item, itself requiring assessment, to be the final assessor of all there is. Those who look to some thing, animal, man, nation, state, to human history or to nature for their final assessment are idolators. Such men are religious in somewhat the sense in which a carpenter is an artist. They might exhibit the same concern for excellence, the same degree of devotion and sacrifice that a truly religious man (or artist) does, but the objective and the result of their efforts falls short of what a full religion (or art) requires.

The genuinely religious man, the truly religious man, he who is unequivocally religious, has attached himself to God deliberately and unreservedly in an act of faith. He is confident that there is an excellence he will attain because he attends to God.

If he is a religious mystic he loses himself in God or in the search for him. One can, however, be truly religious or mystical only occasionally and then only for short spans of time. Like everyone else, the religious man is constantly beset by doubts. He is not always sure just what God is, does, or wants, or whether he is rightly geared to God. While he struggles with these doubts he will continue to have a religious *interest*, but, strictly speaking, he will no longer be a religious man in the sense he was before. Were he to live in terms of the new outlook he had achieved through the act of faith, he would take a religious *perspective* on what he sees and does. No longer attending to God, no longer concerning himself with religious problems, he would then be an habituated religious man, not actively religious. If, instead, he turns back into the world and spends time and energy on some program which had been religiously grounded, he will fulfill some religious *duty*. He then may or may not also be a religiously *guided* man who allows his relation to God to be defined by a community, or who accepts on authority what he is to do in that community or outside it.

Religiously guided men make up the multitude of those who call themselves religious, though they are poles apart from men with an active faith in God. Only the latter are genuinely religious. They are few in number and have that dignity only episodically.

Yet the word "religion" is so loosely used today that one can, with propriety, speak of all those with religious interests, perspectives, duties and guides as being truly religious. No harm would come of this, were the differences in their grades kept in mind. After all, all of them in some way live for the love of God. It would conduce to clarity, however, if one were to speak of all of them as "having religion," and were to reserve the expression "being religious" only for those who deliberately turn to and give themselves to God's loving assessment, and perhaps control and correction.

God is experienced by men in their privacy. He is also experienced by them when they together constitute a religious community. Both individually and collectively they make contact with God and yet continue to seek Him. From beginning to end, sometimes clearly, usually obscurely, torn between doubt and confidence, they hope for the continued love of God.

Like almost every theologian and student of religion I have spoken of God in two senses. Both have many names: JHWH, ultimate Being, Deity, Nirvana, God beyond God, God the Father, the Hidden God, the Absconding God; the God of Israel, the God of Wrath, Lord, Jesus Christ, the God of History, the Savior, the Savored God, God the Lover. And like almost everyone else I surely slip unknowingly every once in a while from talking about Him in one of these guises to talking about Him in the other.

Religious men know that God in the first sense is unknowable to them, but they then often make the mistake of supposing that He is as such not knowable at all. But it is He who is the object of proofs; it is He who is one of the ultimate realities of the universe to be dealt with in a metaphysics. Philosophers know that God, as having this or that particular role, is God under a limitation, and beyond the reach of speculation, but they also often make the mistake of supposing that He is therefore not knowable at all. But it is He who is the direct object of a religious encounter in experience, faith, worship and revelation. The two divine realities are related as ground and consequence, whole and subdivision, being and role (persona). Their unity is sensed by the mystic and explicated by the systematic philosopher.

It is possible that I have overstressed the isolation of the detached individual in Chapter nine; it is surely proper to observe that when I separate myself off from the world I sometimes find myself suddenly affiliated, brought into a sympathetic rapprochment with other actualities, and thereby have immediate evidence of the effective presence of God. Just as private individuals are made publicly contemporary by the forces of existence, are forced into groups by being subjected to the prescriptions of common prospects, and are placed on a footing with all other actualities because with them they are rooted in a single Actuality, so they, in their privacies, are affiliated with other actualities through the compelling mediation of a spiritual force. That effective spirit and I are relative others of one another. It is only God, the ultimate Being, and I, as representative of whatever else besides that God that there be, who are absolute others of one another.

God as an ultimate being is outside the scope of the religious effort, and apparently of its interest, though it is possible to reach and to know Him in other ways, as I have tried elsewhere to show. My present concern is primarily with God the effective being with whom we all can be involved privately and publicly.

God is at once outside all of us, singly and together, ennobling all that is, and immanent, qualifying whatever there be. Here and now He provides evidences of His existence, and agencies by which one can come closer to Him. But it is no easy thing to attend to those evidences, and no easy thing to make use of the agencies He has made possible. We are about to start on a tortuous and troubled journey.

I. Experience

1. The Ultra-Natural

LANGUAGE HAS NOT yet been learned by the infant, concepts have not yet been forged, the will has not yet been exercised. All the infant has are pleasures and pains, a tincture of anxiety and sudden relief, some fear and perhaps a little hope. These emotions are faintly structured as they escape in the form of sounds and movements. They become more firmly structured by being caught within the mesh of the world. As a consequence the infant soon comes to face the world as partly qualified by its emotions. For the rest of its life it will respond emotionally to what had already been structured emotionally.

Family training and family life soon make the infant categorize the world in the ways a limited number of other humans do. Neighbors, common work, the need to interchange products, the intrusions, claims and demands of others make it function as part of a group, and eventually enable it to occupy some position in a society. It is sane and reasonable only so far as it lives in consonance with the sanctions, tolerances and commands of its society.

For the most part all of us deal with the world about in socially acceptable terms. Only occasionally does any one of us make use of steadier, more inclusive characterizations reflecting the spirit of our culture or the needs of mankind. Our daily world is overrun with conventions. Anticipations, memories, beliefs structure it and us. It is a mixture of the true and false, the foolish and the wise, the superstitious and the sound. Occasionally wellfocused, clear and inescapable, it also has much in it that is dim, blurred, and avoidable. Not as clear or as ultimate a realm as ordinary men suppose it to be, it is still not wholly unreal, though some philosophers claim that it is so.

The world of common sense is at once real and artifactual. The objects in that world are in part the termini of sound perceptions and successful practice and in part the products of social opinion. It would be foolish to dismiss it. It would be equally foolish to accept it without question. It is a world that is neither clear nor wholly controlled. No one of us understands it entirely nor knows how to fully master it.

When in the course of daily life we are faced with confusions and errors, conflicting attitudes and judgments, the bewildering and unexpected we are wrenched off our usual course. If we are alert to what is happening, we marshal our forces and see whether or not we can re-enter and remain in that world more effectively than we had before. We try to observe more carefully, try to adjust ourselves better, or we make use of the methods and results of various disciplines in the effort to extend our knowledge and controls.

Heavy bodies fall faster than light ones. A pencil and a piece of paper fall at different rates. Every man of sense knows this. Aristotle was right to insist on the fact. It can be empirically confirmed at any moment. Yet to refuse to go beyond such an ostensible fact is to preclude a satisfactory grasp of the course of projectiles or the movements of heavenly bodies. Since the time of Galileo we can explain why the paper descends more slowly than the pencil, and yet understand the fall of both, as well as the movement of the stars, in somewhat similar terms. The descent of the paper we can now say is a complex occurrence in which gravitational forces are intersected by others. We now understand the fall of paper and pencil in ways far superior to those at the command of common sense.

The arts, sciences and humanities tell us about the world faced in daily life, but in a refined, purged and somewhat formalized way. None of these disciplines knows a world completely separated from that of daily life. If it did, all evidence would have been left behind and there would be no place at which a man might safely alight after having lived in one of their worlds. Even a philosophy which seeks to achieve a perfect neutrality and objectivity in a systematic account, must start from common sense and can never wholly cut itself off from it. However, none of their worlds is ours until we have lived for quite a long while. Long before that time we find ourselves cut off from the common-sense world again and again in rather sudden and uncontrolled ways.

ii

SHOCKED, suddenly uprooted, or disturbed, faced with the unusual, we look about us with wild surmise. Occasionally we are beset by shapeless fears; through us rush feelings of fright and terror. We feel threatened, and frantically look for what will prevent us from being hurt, grievously.

All threats are nameless and amorphous, even those which are addressed to us by particular men, or which are expressed through particular things. It is not the thug but the irrational power at his disposal that weakens our knees and chills our blood. It is not the gun but the negation it commands that reduces us to helplessness. The awareness that we might become nothing is inseparable from a confrontation with an insistent but indefinite power, an assertive nothingness in which we are about to be lost. We are threatened, we never really know by what. That is why we do not know where to look for what will remove all danger. But we do try to look. We do not simply cringe before the threatening; we also seek for what could counter it.

When we are torn from the familiar, the reliable and the stable, we face a vast unknown. At one and the same time we shrink before it and look for some protection against it. Both the cause and the protection are often taken to be deep within ourselves, but sometimes they are taken to be quite outside. When both are felt to be within us, we take ourselves to be creatures of passions that are to be overcome by self-knowledge and self-control. When the cause of our dislocation and the protection against it are set outside us, we take ourselves to be puny members of a controlling cosmos. When the cause is attributed to ourselves and the protection is sought elsewhere, our fears testify that we are not properly attuned to what is objectively the case. When the situation is reversed, and the cause is located outside us but the protection is sought within, we tend to speak of ourselves as men who, through reflection and courage, can make ourselves into counterweights of what at first seemed tremendous and supreme.

The locating of causes and protections reflect a highly sophisticated attitude. Both the cause and the protection pervade a single fearsome totality which has no place for a sharp distinction between what is inside and what is outside us. If we place the cause of our terror in the lowest reaches of our selves, we move no less distant from empirical reality than we would have had we located the cause in nature or in God.

Threats have various colorations; they constantly shift in stress and direction. Irregular, criss-crossed with power, values, and awesomeness they characterize an entire ultra-natural region outside the world of common sense.

It is because we are aware of the ultra-natural that we are so sure that, no matter how much we now know, we do not know everything; that, no matter how strong we are, we know that we are weak, inadequate and transient; that, no matter how deeply immersed we are in daily affairs, we know that our daily world does not exhaust reality.

We are alert to the ultra-natural in our tragedies; we speak of it in our metaphysics; we look to it in our religions. He who denies its existence must content himself with accepting as ultimate the conventionalized world of common sense and what he can abstract from this. He will be unable to criticize his society or state, and unable to grasp the import of art. He will be unable to understand how history is possible, how he can be subject to the same laws that govern animals and things, how he can live in a cosmos, and what it is that frightens and lures him.

Following the lead of Descartes and Leibnitz, some modern thinkers take the common-sense pole to be a confused version of the other. Existentialists, such as Sartre, and Intuitionists, such as Schopenhauer and Bergson, take the world of common sense to be an appearance or expression of it — the Existentialists supposing that the real is ultimately individual while the Intuitionists take it to be cosmic in nature and reach. But the world of common sense is social, much larger than the individual and much smaller than the cosmos. Both Existentialists and Intuitionists do less than justice to the reality of the evidences on which their own theories depend. Not only do they push the works of engineering, economics, politics and education into the limbo of illusion, but they inevitably do this to the reading and writing of their own books.

Their opponents, the modern Analysts and Language philosophers, reverse this stress. It is their desire to treat what is outside the area of common sense as derivative from it; as secondary, unintelligible or trivial. It is no surprise to find these thinkers baffled when they try to understand what is meant by obligation, worship, dispositions, possibilities, substance and the like, for these not only refer to what is outside the reach of common-sense methods or interests, but are presupposed in any understanding of what common sense comprehends and does. The desire to know the truth, the willingness to submit to the outcome of disciplined inquiry, the capacity to learn or to construct theories, the ability to read and write books, and, as was already noted, the surety that no one knows all there is or knows anything existent with absolute certainty, depend on the at least tacit acknowledgment that there are powers not now manifest or evident in common-sense actions, meanings or beings.

Most of the towering figures in the history of thought have insisted on the reality of both dimensions — the commonsensical and the ultra-natural — and most have analyzed or qualified one or the other to produce such combinations as the Platonic Receptacle and a realm of Forms, the Aristotelian substances and a First Mover, the Kantian phenomenal world and a kingdom of ends, the Hegelian theses and the Absolute.

Both dimensions need analysis and clarification. Our daily thoughts and speech are, through habit and convention, kept fairly well in gear with common-sense things, but we find it hard to have equally adequate ideas or discourse for the other dimension. Eventually, though, we can come to see that its fluctuating ineffable nature is a product of the interplay of a number of distinct realities. Sometimes one of these realities stands out so sharply against the others that it almost obscures them. Most thinkers of magnitude have, therefore, taken some account of at least one of them, but have supposed that the others are only facets of it. Thus, some, with Hegel, speak of an Absolute, or with others of the ground of all being, in which they locate a providence and even a spatio-temporal dimension. Some, with Peirce, stress a concrete reasonableness, or with others the goal of history, or an ideal Good; they suppose that the structure, the law-abidingness of cosmic reality also controls the world and provides a ground for time and space. Some instead, with Spinoza, speak of nature, or with others of a realm of matter, or a physical universe. They suppose that only the extensional world is ultimate and purposive. The three — a final ground, an ultimate rationale and an environing nature — are all present. All are vaguely sensed in every threat.

A threat is perhaps most often felt as being directed at our continuance. By adjusting ourselves to the course of nature, we find something like an answer to it. We then recognize ourselves to be in a cosmos, in part tragic, in part benign. Sometimes, though, we sense a threat to what is meaningful to us or to what we cherish. All seems about to be reduced to irrationality or to triviality. It is then that we try to grasp hold of a still more distant, nobler good, enabling us to act as men of duty and character. But sometimes we feel that we are being abandoned, and try to save ourselves by clinging to something final which we take to be perfectly steady. When we do this we become dimly aware of God, the being who at once challenges and saves us. Though He forever flees from us we then are confident that He still is nearby.

The most common and primitive of all the ways in which God is apprehended is through an uncalculated response to the disturbing. But this apprehension is interlocked with one terminating in the remorseless course of nature and in a final good. When terrified we consequently are never really sure from what we are withdrawing and by what we are being sustained.

If we wish to distinguish nature, the Good, and God properly, we must have recourse to speculation. This enables us to discover the concepts and principles in terms of which an adequate understanding of what at once pervades, defines and heals us, can be obtained. But, if we do not also find a sound base in experience for our speculations, they will be hard to distinguish from fictions, and our fears could well prove to be just private ungrounded disturbances. It is experience, therefore, to which we ought now to turn.

2. The Dimensions of Experience

EXPERIENCE encompasses the unmediated aspect of whatever is confronted by a conscious being. It includes content externally met no less than content privately gone through; whether vague or clear. Across it dart the remembered, the imagined, and the expected. It is flavored with feelings of ease, fear, joy and terror. It can have any number of tonalities — brittle or tough, gay or sad, vital or dull. Usually, though, it has these and others intermixed in fluctuating ways. It spreads out backwards, forwards, sideways, toward the past, the future, to what is remote as well as to what is near. It may be interplayed with, yielded to, overcome, responded to; it can be utilized, suppressed, judged. And it makes a distinguishable difference to both consciousness and practice, affecting their natures, changing their rhythms and directions, altering their tonality.

We experience much that we rarely note. All that we sense is experienced; though most of it is not thought about, not deliberately attended to, nor distinguished in practice. The clock ticks throughout the day, but we do not attend to it. Nevertheless we are not entirely unaware of the ticking, for we quickly note when the clock stops. The tip of my nose is always visible, but I do not look at it, any more than I look at most of the items at the periphery of my vision. Experience evidently includes much more than that to which I am now attentive. But it also embraces much less than that which now affects me. I do not experience cosmic rays or what is now coursing through my bloodstream.

Dewey justly remarked that the experienced is not merely

something private or psychological, the creation of man. He thought, though, that it embraced "all subject matters," "the history of this earth," "death" and "transcendental systems." But these, like the microscopic, are surely beyond the reach of experience. Dewey evidently made "experience" include many items which exist beyond the reach of any man. In apparent compensation for his generosity he tended to exclude from experience the realities in which he was not interested. He did not seem to find a place in experience for our feelings of alienation, for our encounters with ethical or logical prescriptions, or for our awareness of the brute compulsions of existence. Like others, Dewey thought that experience extended to, but never went beyond, the borders of his philosophic system. I think he erred in both directions.

Experience exhibits many stresses and strains; it has thick and thin areas, regions of high and regions of low intensity. There are areas in it where all seems muddled or undifferentiated, though it itself is not chaotic or amorphous. It is complex, modulated, variegated, with an evident foreground and background, heights and depths. Since it does not include what we do not encounter, it obviously stops short of the beings which sustain it, and which define its opportunities. Fortunately, we occasionally feel ourselves pulled toward these through the fissures of experience.

Experience does not encompass the realities referred to by means of concepts, intentions or signs. It does not reach to what we surmise when we are suddenly wrenched from our common-sense moorings. Atmospheric pressure, many germs and parasites regularly condition us, but they are not experienced. We of course not only experience the use of our concepts but often their referents as well. But we do not then experience the external beings in which those referents are resident. Some reality always remains unexperienced.

Experience connects us with other realities. It terminates at them, but it does not reach into them. No matter how much of them it embraces, it stops short of them in their full concreteness, as independent entities having their own careers and rationales.

Our experience has two ends — ourselves, the experiencers, and the content experienced. It also has two supports — ourselves and a reality beyond us and the experience. We can be so deeply immersed in an experience that we are oblivious of ourselves. Nevertheless the experience is possible only because we are not entirely swallowed up in what we then encounter. On the other hand, no matter how singularly private and intimate our experienced content may be, it stands over against us who experience it, only so far as it is carried by external realities.

Sometimes we think about ideal entities — numbers, triangles, equations, virtues, peace. We experience the thinking of them as well as the content they allow to be caught by that thinking. They yield up content to the thinking and thereby qualify that thinking. Conversely, the thinking abstracts from them and thereby obtains a referent, makes them the object of the thinking. Numbers and shapes have a rationale of their own, apart from and over against the thinking of them, and over against and apart from what that thinking terminates in. They are not creations of ours to do with as we like.

A mathematician engages in a distinctive type of thinking, directed at a distinctive type of object. He does not experience numbers or shapes, but a way of thinking about numbers and shapes, terminating in abstractions from numbers and shapes. His thought, if it is to be reliable, must keep in accord with the relations which the mathematical entities have to one another. These he can discover in one of two ways. He can note how the confronted content dictates to his thought, compelling it to move in one direction rather than another, thereby revealing that content to have a power lying outside the control of the thinking. Or he can reflect on what it is that enables a particular content to become the object of thought. The outcome of his reflection is the object of a second thought which shows it to have a nature which, as standing apart from that thought, makes possible the abstraction at which the first thought terminated. Critical, constructive thought seeks to relate and eventually to adjust these two ways of dealing with what lies outside confronted content.

Remembering, too, is an experience. It stops with content which is inseparable from our act, falling short of the external, independent past realities which yielded that content. The remembered is something now experienced, now grasped as that which is related to something past, outside the reach of memory.

Since most of what we experience has a ground outside the experience which it presupposes and in which it is oriented, and since we do tend to look to the termini of our experiences to tell us something about the nature of that counterpart, we do not usually use "experience" to refer to the termini of our feigning or imagining. An experience requires that there be something actually interplayed with, felt, suffered, met. It, therefore, not only involves an experiencer, an experiencing, and something experienced; it presupposes someone who *can* experience, and something which *can be* experienced.

A man's experiencing is but one of the ways in which he is related to entities distinct from himself. His being is not exhausted in his career as an experiencer. And the content he experiences rides on the surface of beings which are as ultimate, as irreducible, and as independent as he is himself. But though he and the other beings are outside the field of experience, they are not completely cut off from it; nor do they have a meaning or being altogether alien to it or one another.

Experienced content is the real transposed, put into another context, given new affiliations, new neighbors, or subjected to new conditions. It is not the real, but it is also not an appearance replacing or perverting the real. Yet it has often been said to be A. illusory, B. derivative or adventitious, to be dispelled or replaced by something more ultimate, or C. final and all-inclusive, precluding the presence of anything outside its confines, and therefore warranting the denial that there are any selves or external substantial realities. An examination of these views should make it possible to see whether or not there can be ways of going beyond experience, and to learn what a religious experience is and what it can reveal.

A. A rather common view in the East is that what is sensed or known in daily life is an illusion. This position cannot be maintained. Since the illusion is recognized to have a being distinct from the supposed reality beyond it, it must have some reality of its own. Also, it must be related to the reality supposed to be beyond it; otherwise it would provide no warrant, no premiss, no evidence, and no occasion for leading one to move from it to that reality. And because the rejection of daily experience would have to occur in the realm of supposed illusions it could not, according to the theory's own argument, be effective in getting us to the real. Since common sense, perception, politics and even religious institutions (not to speak of the instruction on how or why one should free oneself from illusions) are known in part through the aid of the senses and in the course of daily life, the theory that all we daily experience is illusory also would, strictly speaking, make us reject almost everything we know. And it would evidently also stand in the way of our seeing how the theory could be true or could be used.

The experienced, to be sure, is to be distinguished from what is real, in and of itself. But this does not make the experienced unreal, nor disconnect it from a reality beyond it. It is not wise to put all we encounter aside, particularly since the encountered can lead us to know what is beyond it.

A good deal of what we daily confront is confused and dubious; it is also brute, compulsive, and effective. Were it sheer error, it would provide evidence that we had distorted the real and therefore had made some contact with it. This would not be true were experience solely man's creation. But were experience wholly a creation of man's, it would be indistinguishable from fiction. Then mathematics and mythology, football and fantasy would be on equal footing.

But might it not be the case that experience is partly created and partly given, and that it is not evident which is which? Yes. Ought we not then turn away from experience to pursue some more reliable guide to reality? Yes, it is desirable, I think, to try to reach the real through avenues other than experience. Inference and dialectic enable us to know the real in ways experience does not. But this contention does not demand that we abandon experience altogether — not even when we find that different parts of it bear no clear marks testifying to their degree of trustworthiness. Various reliable and revelatory facets of experience can be sifted out through the aid of what one has discerned of the real in non-experiential ways.

B.   It is better to view the experienced as a consequence or product of something more real than it is, than as an illusion to be dismissed or cancelled. The experienced has a centre of gravity outside the experience of it. It is not adventitious, unilluminating; it offers us evidences, lures, guides and clues to the nature of that on whose being it partly depends. Not only can it never be made to vanish entirely, but it tells us much about the real. We reach more and more of the real by extending and deepening our experience.

We learn from experience, we learn by attending to facets of experience, we learn by reflecting on experience, and we learn by peering through and by thinking about what lies outside experience. What we learn in one of these ways neither necessarily conflicts with nor compromises what we learn in the other ways. Each yields distinctive data and each requires the use of different criteria and "languages."

I have an experience when I stub my toe. I then come up against a brute resistance and feel a pain. I learn from such experiences that there are resistant, pain-productive areas all about me. I learn too to attend to them, to watch my step. If I speculate about the powers resident in them, I may come to understand what they are like as existing over against me. Encountered resistances, awareness of resistant areas, an understanding of the nature of things, and a knowledge that the things exist outside me, all deserve to be brought together in a single integrated account. No one of these items exhausts the universe. None makes reference to the others unnecessary. No one of them disqualifies the others. Each in fact helps us either to discover features, otherwise not discerned, or provides further content to make possible a systematic, critically achieved knowledge of their sum, and more.

c.   Phenomenalists, empiricists and pragmatists sometimes speak as though everything that exists is experienced. Were they to persist in holding to this strange opinion, they would be forced to deny that there are any hidden powers, any mysteries, any dimensions of being lying outside observation or the promise of it. But then they would also have to grant that there can be no action, no motion, no making in their world, since these are possible only because there are potentialities in things, capacities to exhibit new features at subsequent moments. They could speak of regions where there is flux and regions where there is none, of areas of quiet and of noise, but never of what makes these be, or what could replace them with something else. This fact is frequently overlooked because the advocates of the position so concentrate on what they confront that they tend to overlook the suppositions they make regarding the nature of the knower. Their entire procedure silently rests on the assumption that the knower is a substance with multiple powers. But sometimes they even go so far as to speak explicitly of his habits or of his capacities to associate ideas, to infer, to interact and to plan. In either case they allow that there is at least one being, the knower, who is more than he is experienced to be. Whether or not those who take this position go on to affirm that there are other substances which also have capacities not exhaustively expressed in what is experienced, they have given up the position that whatever is, is experienced, or even necessarily experienceable.

He who seeks to remain with experience has no right to say that he *can* know of the know*able*, or the experience*able*. These "cans" and "ables" require him to look outside an actual experiencing, to attend to what is not in fact experienced. And he would still leave undetermined the relation of the experienced to whatever was outside the being, and beyond the control of the knower.

Peirce, James and Dewey, in opposition to the traditional empiricists, affirm that the experienced is not subjective, inert, or merely sensed. They recognize and clearly say that it is extended, dynamic, variegated. They do not make it sufficiently clear, though, that it has its own insistent rationale, requiring us again and again to change our pace and direction.

Experienced content is not passively perceived, nor is it given as something intelligible with a rationale of its own. We are forced to submit to it and to whatever else it makes possible. Its features lure us to hold ourselves apart and thereby acknowledge the presence of external realities other than ourselves, to act and thereby to penetrate beyond them, to think about what experience presupposes, and to make ourselves part of a world larger than ourselves or our experiences. Lonely men stress the first of these lures, practical men the second, inquirers the third, and emotional men the fourth. Each stress, however, is tinged with the others. We go beyond experience in all these ways together; we are always to some degree alone, practical, curious and emotional.

Pragmatists are often so anxious to do justice to the richness of experience that they tend to neglect the fact that the experience testifies to realities outside it, making it possible. Peirce, to be sure, escapes from some of this criticism. Again and again he says that experience contains three distinguishable dimensions, which he characteristically called First, Second and Third – an immediate qualitative-like factor, brute compulsions, and a law-abiding nature. However, Peirce neglects to remark on the presence of beings with distinctive careers or to note the pull, on, in and through the experience exerted by realities beyond it. His Second, he should have noted, clearly testifies to the reality of something not then experienced. In the end, despite all his disclaimers, his realm of experience is, like the traditional, a First, though with facets of compulsiveness and rationality. Yet we cannot be compelled or prescribed to except by that which is at least as real as ourselves.

Both Kant and Hegel do more justice to the real, and therefore to the experienced, than their pragmatic followers do. Both know that what is experienced does not exhaust reality. In Kant there is a tendency to suppose that the experienced could be dealt with only as a component of a systematic, rationalistic, scientific, deterministic scheme. When Kant says that all knowledge should begin and end with the experience, he in effect means that we should deal with experience only so far as it had been caught and partly transformed by various alien forms and categories. This is one reason why he never could discover how to relate the experienced to a reality beyond it, which he himself rightly says was presupposed by it.

Hegel had a more muscular, a more complete, a richer experienced world than Kant had. There was not in fact any type of entity or occurrence which it did not contain. Experience for him encompassed struggles, values, purposes, freedom, art, religion, and philosophy. He saw that the experience of any man at any time was incomplete, but then went on to suppose that it was incomplete only because other experiences were lacking, and that these others pulled on what was here and now enjoyed, forcing one to move on and on until the whole range of the experienceable was covered. But what is not experienced is not necessarily identical in kind with what is experienced. Not only is it not being encountered now, but it may have a power and a unity which the encountered does not have.

Once it comes within the orbit of experience it will of course fit in with the previously experienced. But before and apart from our experience, what is not experienced may, without being entirely other than it, have a different nature, a different role and a different meaning from it. With Hegel one ought to affirm that the real is reachable from what we experience but we ought also to say that what is so reachable is not more experience, or even the experienceable, but a reality as ultimate as the being who *can* experience.

We have no warrant for saying that experience, as pointing away from the experiencer, faces continuations of itself, any more than we have a warrant for saying that it then faces what is entirely alien to it in nature or in being. The experienced is distinct from the experiencer, but it is not without relevance to him or he to it. Similarly, the experienced is distinct from the real beyond it, but it is not without relevance to that reality, nor is that reality irrelevant to it.*

The experienced stands between two ultimates: the knower in himself and a reality beyond him. It is a function of the two of them, one of a number of ways in which they can be together. It has a nature of its own, distinct from that possessed by the beings which made it possible.

Hegel and Peirce see that the experienced is not created by the experiencer and that it has a status apart from him. What they fail to see is that as apart from him it has, even as that which is to be experienced, a career distinct from what it has when involved with him. We really have no alternative but to give up all attempts to show how experience is possible, if we do not try to grasp what it presupposes. We can rightly hope to explain experience only so far as we know that we are not altogether unrelated to what lies outside experience.

He who merely experienced would lose himself in a natural or a supernatural mysticism. Each of us was a natural mystic before we became mature, sophisticated, reflective. But then we had no experiential knowledge. The supernatural mysticism

---

* Panpsychists, such as Hartshorne, see this. But they go on to suppose that the reality is a "psyche," and that the best or proper way in which the two of them can come together is by means of feelings. But it is hard to see why reality must be a psyche, and why thinking or acting are less legitimate ways than feeling to get to that reality.

in contrast must be achieved. It requires a man to penetrate the veil of knowledge, discourse, practice and local interests to lose himself in another being, unbounded and absolute. This means that he will have experiential knowledge no longer. We have experiential knowledge only when we impose categories on experienced content. The experienced common-sense familiar world of every day results when the experienced content is ordered by means of the categories — conventions, beliefs, traditions — characteristic of our society.

An experienced man is an habituated man who, after many trials and errors, has become attuned to the way familiar things behave. If he fails to supplement his accumulated wisdom with the outcome of disciplined reflection, he will act well but know little. The unconventionalized and the unfamiliar will distract, disturb, upset, surprise him more than they ought.

Initially we have limited experiences and are driven to go beyond them by our awareness of a reality outside them. In the course of the attempt to reach that reality we come to have experiences we otherwise would not have. Toward the end of his *Critique of Pure Reason* Kant became aware of this and pointed out how Reason led the Understanding on to get more and more experiences. Usually, Kant thought of himself as accounting for a scientifically respectable world. By identifying it with a Newtonian one he committed two errors. He not only supposed that the world known to science is the most substantial of known worlds, but that this was Newtonian in character. A Kantian philosophy would be impregnable if it concerned itself with accounting for the common-sense world of every day, for this is the product of a juncture of a given manifold and useful classifications. C. I. Lewis has perhaps seen this point better than any other Kantian. However, with other Kantians he fails to note that he has no way of talking about the experienced data that his classifications help convert into the stuff of daily life. To know what that experienced content is like, outside the categories which structure it for daily use, one would either have to employ other classifications, engage in other modes of apprehending the content, or understand what could be available for classification by us. Scientists are interested in the first approach, aesthetic and many religious men in the second, and speculative philosophers in the third. The Kantians make no provision for any one of these three alternative ways of dealing with the contents that we daily organize, and, therefore, cannot know what it is they presuppose.

It is characteristic of a number of Anglo-Saxon thinkers today to translate the problem of experience into a problem of language. Most of those who hold the position wobble between an Hegelian and a Kantian outlook, holding both that there is nothing outside the language which they can acknowledge, and that language is not the real but is only an indispensable structuralization of it. They are somewhat matched on the continent by various phenomenologists who seek to isolate in experience different essences, freed from an involvement in a larger world. These lose something of the experienced content by their dissection of what is given; they also lose the real world which they in the end seek to know. Both the Anglo-Saxon and the continental schools fail to make provision for the forces that sustain and pierce experience.

So long as we are alive we have experiences. If we are unconscious, their nature and import will, of course, not be known, though they will occasionally be made manifest in behavior and may eventually be recovered by us when we are conscious once again. Nor do we ever free ourselves from experience, for even when we spin out fancies we have many bodily and even emotional and cognitively tinged experiences. The outside world and an inner one echo through the most idle follies. We have experiences of those worlds even when we turn away from them. And we can get to those worlds in non-experiential ways.

We are now having experiences, and so long as we live we will continue to experience. But we need not stay with experience; indeed, we can never wholly stay with it. We not only imagine, day-dream, introduce arbitrary divisions and useful distinctions into experienced data, forge hypotheses and build systems of knowledge, but we are concerned with what lies outside the confines of experience.

Discontent, sympathy, wonder, and hope are not purely subjective states. Sometimes they provoke us to leap over the barrier of experience to get into some other region. Strictly speaking, though, they are relations which move in and through present experience to what lies outside it. They pull us through the chinks of experience, chinks which experience has, as a consequence of its being pulled away from the experiencer toward an external, independent reality.

ii

THERE ARE MANY types of experience; all have distinctive tonalities and supports. There are ethical and political experiences, aesthetic, historical and religious experiences. Much would escape the mesh of these experiences, if they were confined to what is only sensed, localized or utilized. Yet nothing is so characteristic of the classical empiricists — Locke, Berkeley, Hume, Mill, Russell — than the view that the experienced is a tissue of sensations and impressions (atomic, simple, momentary, inert, a set of passive particulars) caught inside the minds of men. They suppose the content of experience to be precisely what is in fact never available to any man. That the experienced is spread out in space, in time, in depth and in influence is a truth they overlook in good part because they take space, time, being, and influence to be our constructions, and not constitutive dimensions of what is encountered. We can abstract the nature of space, time, being and causation and hold them over against the content that fills them, but this does not imply that the content is not still spread out, sometimes spatially, always temporally, necessarily ontologically and often effectively.*

In every experience one can distinguish a *focal* region and a *peripheral*, what is *mine* and what is *not-mine*, the *private* and the *public*, the *episodic* and the *constant*. Though these stresses sometimes overlap and intersect, they are distinct. Each deserves some attention. The focal and the peripheral are the most evident; an examination of them will help us to master the others more readily.

We are here, now. There is no other place or way for us to be. We are apart from others for moments, and moment after moment, but not altogether. We are always lonely but never wholly alone. Our solitude is partly a state and partly an

---

* Kant knew that the Cartesians and the empiricists were mistaken about the nature of space and time. But he mistakenly thought that the experienced in itself was inchoate and ineffable, and that as available for knowledge it was necessarily temporal, possibly spatial, but never casual or final.

achievement. No one of us ever loses himself entirely in any limited region, or attends to one for very long. Not only does a man change his position constantly, not only does he live through time, not only is he assaulted from without, but there are no sharp borders separating the focal from the peripheral. Neither has a fixed place or range. Neither has a distinctive content. We do not fit neatly in the one, and do not stand altogether away from the other.

The focal is focal for the peripheral. It is what we separate out, what we hold over against the peripheral. Our "here" could be a pin point or a continent, our "now" a second or a year. But no matter what their magnitude, they are related to a "there" and a "then." What is here is away from there; what is now is distant from what had been or what will be. Our children across the room are here; our love affair is now. We see a chair over there; we are aware that a letter has not yet been sent.

The focal is unstable in time and place. When identified with the "now" or the "here" in discourse or by intent, it turns out to be a universal. As Hegel saw, it is then a repeatable abstraction, without concreteness, offering no certitude or ultimacy. But as experienced, despite its variable range in magnitude and localization, the focal is a particular, not a universal, not a conceptualized feature but a stress. And though all of us, because of its bearing on our interests are attentive to the focal, we are able to see that we are part of an objective world only so far as we are also aware of the peripheral. It, with the focal, makes up a single domain in which we have a place.

Though the peripheral is thin, and the focal rich, the peripheral attracts, making us willing to ignore or forego what we are now enjoying. The moon for which the child cries is already focal, and more than something experienced. It wants to hold it – not to enjoy it – to bring it in closer connection with its other toys. But when it asks, "How far is up?" "When will tomorrow be?" "Who am I?" "Why do the waves keep coming in?", the child makes evident that the peripheral, despite a difference in quality and availability, has perhaps as much significance for it as the focal.

The child turns to the peripheral in spirit if not in fact, and in imagination if not in act. Sometimes it asks its questions idly.

It surely does not understand why it asks them or what it wants to know. But its questions betray an awareness that it is not trapped inside the focal region where it now is. It is aware that the peripheral could be focal too. All of us, children and adults, look there for the answers to questions about causes and conditions that break from us again and again.

The centre of gravity of conscious beings is outside the focal regions where they mainly live. They seek to make that, which is outside the focal, part of one world with it. Were this not so, the peripheral would not be there at a distance from them. Forever encircled by the focal, they would consequently never try to move to the peripheral.

By taking account of the peripheral, men live as beings in a world, belonging in principle no less to areas within as well as to those outside their control. Interest and motion testify to the fact that the peripheral need not remain so always. They make us aware of our capacity to break through the confines of what is now focal, and have as focal what is now peripheral. The fact that the peripheral is for the focal shows that conscious beings are not confined to this or that limited space, time, expression or power.

The peripheral is at a distance for us. It now lacks features which the focal possesses. Will it retain those features when we get to it? We soon learn that this rarely is the case. The peripheral is, let us say, vague and outside our present reach. When we shift our position in act or thought, more likely than not we will face it as clear and within our grasp. We can often watch the change taking place as we gradually alter our position with respect to it, and we come to expect the change whenever the peripherally experienced is experienced focally.

The peripheral is faced as that which could be focal. The recognition of this fact is perhaps what is behind the Hegelian supposition that what is now experienced focally is homogeneous with what is not so experienced. The non-focally experienced, if real, is thought to be for the moment outside our intellectual and perhaps physical reach, that is all. It is not clear, though, whether or not Hegel thinks that this is peripheral and is now being experienced but with a different tonality than that characteristic of the focal. Nor is it clear whether or not he recognizes that the relation connecting the focal and the non-focal is not forever biased toward one end. But it does seem clear that he denies there is a reality presupposed by the non-focal, a denial which, I think, is the outcome of a mistaken idea that the experienced is the real.

The peripheral is not identifiable with the real. The one is experienced; the other makes the experience possible. If we alter our positions with respect to various experienced contents, we give new opportunities to presupposed realities to provide us with new experiences. These realities make it possible for the peripheral to be focal. Were there no such realities, we could never say that the peripheral could become focal, for on the hypothesis, having no more reality than it is then and there experienced to have, the peripheral will cease to be when it is no longer experienced in just that way. The peripheral, shorn of support by a non-experienced reality, could never become anything other than it is, and we, therefore, could not say that what we now experience is distant, remote, effete, and that it could become here, now, enjoyed, and effective.

To be sure, when the peripheral becomes focal, even if it is then qualitatively identical with what it had been before, it will have a new role. Before it was peripheral; now there is something peripheral for it. The black at close range is as dark as it was when I was at the other end of the room, but now it is environed by peripheral experiences that I did not have before.

We approach the peripheral as though it could enter into other relations with us. We give ourselves to it, as it were in advance, endowing it with the status of being focalizable; at the same time we yield ourselves up to it as that which awaits us, as that which stands over against us by virtue of some sustaining agent.

I take the peripheral not only to be continuous with the focal, and capable of becoming focal, but as capable of being focal for another peripheral content. As a consequence I find myself living in a world much larger than the here and now. I am a cosmic being. Over the course of my life I become more and more aware of my cosmic status, of the homogeneity of what is now experienced both focally and peripherally, and yet all the while I remain a being not altogether at home anywhere. I live in an experienceable world in which focal and peripheral items are equally objective and equally open to me. But all the while I remain here and now facing a distant there and then. No matter where I travel I find just as much space, time, being, and power beyond me as ever there was. No matter how ready I am to take what is not close to be like what is, and no matter how insistently I claim that the peripheral can become focal, I continue to face it as distant from me.

What has now been said semi-genetically and psychologically (and presupposing a good deal of what has been learned by attending to what no experience reveals), can be stated objectively. The peripheral is distant from and homogeneous with the focal; the whole of experience has a structure imbedded in it which stretches from here to there, now to then, surface to depth, the effective to the ineffective. Each one of us lives in only limited parts of it, but as in principle able to be anywhere else. The experienceable is a world as wide as livable space and as long as human time, perpetually coming to be and passing away.

iii

WHAT IS FOCAL, "here," is usually identified with myself, as "mine," and what is peripheral, "there," is usually taken to be part of an independent world, "not-mine." But this is not always true. "Here," where we are, may be another's house. We can be aware of our car a block away. Even where the mine and the not-mine coincide with the focal and the peripheral, we distinguish the two. The mine is the adopted, that to which I lay claim; the here is the accepted, that to which I submit. The not-mine is over against me, the there is only away from here. "Mine" and "not-mine" are contrastive terms, oppositional, challenging one another; "here," and "there" are correlative terms, interrelated, supporting one another.

The mine and the not-mine contract and expand in magnitude. Sometimes items in the one will move over into the other. Nor is it altogether clear where the mine ends and the not-mine begins. My body is mine, the eyeglasses are mine, the painting on the wall is mine; my college is City College, though I teach at Yale; United States is my country even when I am in Mexico. The mine and the not-mine are distinct, separated by an invisible barrier which, though letting this or that item slip across it in one direction or the other, will forever keep them apart.

What is mine is usually vivid, luminous, malleable, but it can be rather faint, dim, or hard to bear. Sometimes I experience the not-mine with a sickening vividness. When I am downcast the gaiety of others is painfully experienced as not-mine. And sometimes what I do not and cannot experience is luminous in a way that no experience ever is. Some things I imagine so vividly that I think I remembered them. Occasionally, I mistakenly take what I have myself vividly imagined to be something I experienced. None of these would be possible were the classical empiricists right in their belief that the content of a waking experience is always more vivid than any other. The content of a waking experience *is experienced* as mine or not-mine. What I remembered or imagined is remembered or imagined as *being* mine or not-mine, or as *having been experienced* as mine or not-mine. Both the mine and the not-mine, and this remains true whether they be experienced, remembered or imagined, can be vivid or dim.

I can identify the mine only by contrasting it with a not-mine. I am aware of that which I push aside. I experience it in fact as that which defines the experienced mine to be mine alone. The mine is now unsharable, over against what is not-mine. Without an experience of that not-mine I would be lost in pure immediacy, sunk irretrievably inside the experiencing, unable to say that any part of it was mine. Because of the not-mine, what is mine is not only something distinctive but is also both not not-mine and that which belongs to me.

Another may have an experience of the same reality that I do, and his resulting experiences may be like mine in structure and in terminus. But, since his and my experiencing are distinguishable, and since these experiencings are not altogether sunderable from their termini, he and I will terminate in different not-mines. I have my own way of experiencing what is mine and this which is mine is distinctive. I also have my own way of experiencing what is not-mine, and this not-mine is also distinctive. Each of us faces different mines and different not-mines; possessing the one over against the other.

The not-mine lacks something which the mine has. But if it lacks what the mine now has, why should I ever want it? I would like to experience as mine what I am now experiencing as not-mine, even perhaps at the price of giving up what I am now experiencing as mine. Why should I be willing to do this?

Is there something desirable, attractive about what is not-mine? Surely not as that which is not mine. Otherwise I would want to have it remain not-mine. Docs it promise to yield, once made mine, much more than what I now experience as mine? How could it make such a promise? Or is it that I am confident that I can turn the not-mine into the mine without necessarily abandoning what has already been experienced as mine, since I can hold on to this in my habits, attitudes and values as well as in my memory? But then why should I not hold on to both the mine and the not-mine? Why do I try to experience as mine what I now experience as not-mine? Is it not that there is something desirable in the mine, making me want to extend that way of experiencing over a larger area?

I experience the not-mine as a large area which is receptive to an experiencing of it as mine. I want to make the mine encompass and thereby transform this which is experienced as not-mine. When I make the not-mine mine, will I change? Will it? Will the "mine" and "not-mine" have the same weights they had before? I see quite often that this is not the case. Some things can become mine sometimes only at the price of my becoming involved with them in a way I had not been before. Were I to adopt a child, it would be mine as surely as my others, but in making it mine, I would discover that I am involved in sibling rivalries and in new financial problems. I am acutely aware at times that what another is experiencing most poignantly I am experiencing only as not-mine, and that, when I subject myself to conditions similar to those now governing him, what is mine gets an edge and a bite to it that I never imagined it could have.

Sometimes the not-mine changes in nature when it becomes mine. In acquiring the painting I find that it is both more and less precious, more and less interesting than it had been when it was in the gallery. Sometimes what is not-mine fails to live up to a promise I expected it to realize in becoming mine; it becomes less attractive, less amenable, more demanding. How good it would be, I think, to hear those cheers directed at me. Yet I find that when they are, the adulation does not touch me deeply. I discover that I am being praised as an object, as a producer, for what I had been, as a public figure, and that I get very little of the warmth I hoped would be mine.

What I experience as not-mine seems to have a life of its own. It seems to be obstinate, maintaining its own nature even when I make it mine. Because of it, I come to know that what I experience as mine is not altogether mine. Both the mine and the not-mine are evidently quickened by a power pulling the mine away from me and allowing the not-mine to belong to me. What is not-mine is *my* not-mine, what is mine is *not* entirely mine.

What I experience as mine always has over against it what is not-mine. The mine is a part of a much larger experienced world. Any part of that larger world could be made mine. But I do not ever succeed in making all of it become mine. Yet anything that is not-mine could conceivably be experienced as mine. Though any part of the experienced world could be mine, I am nevertheless unable to make it so in fact. I am omnicentral in spirit but not actually so.

I speak of "my sweetheart," though I do not really know if she really is mine, or how much of her is mine. Still, no matter whatever happens and what anyone else says, and sometimes in the teeth of my or her denials, I am aware that my experience of her is an experience of something that is distinctively mine, apart from all categorization by concept, belief, or attitude. The world of experience at every moment breaks up into two regions, one of which is warm, intimate, of a piece with myself, the other open, cool, out of gear with me. The break is objective, though not fixed at any point. I, who am largely responsible for it, can make the break occur elsewhere, but when I do, I find that it is a break which answers to an opening in fact. The experienced world at every point is able to be mine or not-mine, and when I make one part mine, I but enable other parts to stand out as not-mine.

Paradoxically, there is something not-mine which I tend to think of as being closer to myself than anything I recognize as mine. Some of what I am *not* now experiencing as mine evidently belongs more truly to me than anything experienced as mine; what I experience as mine is a veil hiding from me what I really am and own. This truth psychoanalysis has made patent to all. The not-mine too I know I ought to have; what I now possess does not altogether satisfy me. It is too personal, too limited, too contingent in structure, occasion and location to make me feel content with it. The mine too seems to have spent itself, to have no reserves; no matter how vital and penetrating it be, it is too much on the surface. What is not-mine is more insistent, and thus more objective than what is mine. I find too that the not-mine is more fundamental, more malleable, more capable of accepting me and my way of experiencing on its own terms than the mine is.

The not-mine is stratified, structured in different ways, and what is mine as a consequence subdivides into regions which contrast with these different stratifications. I try to get to one or more of these stratified not-mines from the contrastive regions which are mine. But no matter how or how far I move into the not-mine I do not lay hold of what is hidden, what ought to be, the root of insistence, what is absolutely fundamental. I find myself still in experience, still confronted with what is not-mine. It is vain to hope that I can improve this state of affairs by simply postulating the existence of a non-experienced world, a categorical imperative, an immortal soul, or a God. I must either know what is outside experience or must content myself with saying that my experiences are sustained by realities of which I have no knowledge whatsoever. But the latter is not a true alternative, since it leads to the contradiction of supposing that we know there is something of which we know nothing. That which sustains or produces what is now experienced is not itself experienced. If we know that there is such a reality we have a non-experiential knowledge, and, therefore, must already have been able to get outside of experience. This means that we are not entirely confined to the mine and the not-mine.

iv

THE MINE and the focal, we saw, are not always coincident. Nor is either always coincident with what is *private*. I have a pain; it is mine and it is private, but I rightly say of it that it is "*there* is my foot" and not "*here* in my head." I watch the child talking to the "emperor of ice cream." The child's pleasure is not mine, but I privately savor that pleasure while wanting it to continue to be not-mine. So long as I privately experience the not-mine there, my pleasure will be unalloyed. But I can also experience the excitement of the mob as here, as mine, and yet as *public*, something in which I share. The public experience encompasses me and the others. We function as subjects for it so far as we are willing to face it as that to which we are subjected.

Privacy has an indefinite reach and many locations. It does not include all my experiences. I am also conscious of what is public, though to be sure the consciousness is private. And, there is perhaps some truth in Jung's contention that I share in tribal memories, that I participate in a common unconsciousness. Nor is a private experience always an experience of something psychical in nature. I experience my own body, and this experience is rarely, if ever, confused by me with an experience of my mind or will. And when I lift something, the weight is experienced as not-mine, but a not-mine which is now being privately encountered by me.

Dewey is surely correct in recognizing that the objective situation is indeterminate for the individual who has not yet participated in it, resolved it, made himself one with it and come out at the other end. Both the individual and the situation achieve determination by their interplay. But for various purposes we can recognize, as Dewey does not always seem to allow, a kind of objective world of language or inquiry, and can speak correctly of entering it and leaving it.

There are experiences which have no public role. But an experienced "privacy" is either promissory or limitative; it expresses a capacity to enter into or to leave a public domain. This point has been brilliantly developed by Wittgenstein. He dealt with the issue as essentially having to do with language — an unnecessary and even unfortunate restriction, unless "language" be understood to include all the conventions, manners, signs and activities that are shared by a number of men, or to refer to an ur-logic to which all things are subject. In these cases references to an experienced privacy are unintelligible except as anticipating an entrance into or as an interpretation of a previous participation in the public. This is not to say that we are to deal with the experienced privacy solely in behavioristic terms, or that it is illegitimate or meaningless to speak of the private side of men, but only that an experienced privacy is inseparable from a public experience. And that means, as Wittgenstein did not recognize, that there is a sense in which public experience can be said to be a projection and complication of private experience as surely as private experience can be said to be an anticipation or interpretation of public experience.

It is tempting to identify the language of the "here" and the "mine" with that of the "private." But they are distinct. The language of "here" is one of perspectives, of positions from which starts can be made. It is the language of patriotism, of provincialism, of the familiar. References to "mine," to possessions and identifications, contrast with references to what is not possessed, to what does not belong to me. The two together make up a language of property and contracts, of claims and counterclaims. Both the language of the familiar and the language of claims, of the "here" and "there" and the "mine" and "not-mine," deal with what is public and speak of it in public ways, but each is distinct from and stands opposed to the common language in stress, rule, purpose and consequence.

The experienced private is referred to intelligibly by others only so far as they make use of a common language. All another knows of me is what I succeed in conveying to him, explicitly or implicitly, deliberately or inadvertently, in discourse or in other ways. My private experience is publicly known as what has been readied to be part of or is already withdrawn from a public experience. No matter how lost in myself I become, I never lose all readiness to enter the public world; no matter how I subjugate what I have taken from the public I never free myself from all public associations. The freshest freest poetry vibrates under the forces of everyday sounds and meanings. The most I can do is to make the public more and more vague and empty; I can never make it vanish. Yet the private is not public in any sense. Nor is private experience reducible to public experience. A private experience is unshared experience, an experience over against a public experience, and over against the private experiences of others.

Private experience becomes a shared experience only so far as it is viewed as a part which can be seamlessly merged into a larger public experience. It will then function as a singular limit of the public world. This dull pain is my own, down to its brackish roots, but I communicably say it is a dull pain and not a sharp one, not grief, not anguish, not discomfort because I look at it in a context of public causes, public remedies, public responses. I know it is my own and not another's just so far as I know that I offer the public world a limited content distinct from that provided by anyone else. The private experience is at the limit of the public, a limit which moves in some independence of the public, while perpetually pointing to that public to enable itself to have a relation to other limits reached through that public domain. I privately experience in relation to other publicly related private experiences. We are in accord with one another in public; we are in accord with ourselves in private.

Private experience is almost, not-yet public experience. The publicly experienced could become privately experienced. Neither is fixed in nature or range. The public is rule-governed, but not rule-permeated; it is not necessarily the regular, the rational or the controlled. The private is possible only to the degree to which a man is able to stand outside the rules, or can adopt them, subject to unexpressed rules of his own. It is no amorphous mass, it is no realm of sheer freedom, but it is free from public control.

The private expands and contracts. What is encompassed by it may become public, and conversely what is public may become private. The laughter we shared I now take into me as a private joy; the pleasure I privately feel breaks out as a smile in which you too can share. Private and public vary in density and intensity from moment to moment, depending on what we privately introduce into or remove from the public, or what is publicly accepted or rebuffed. And I would like to be part of that public. I often look out at it as a world which is more insistent on being itself, as somehow therefore having more right to be than I privately have. Again and again I try to discover how I stand within it. It is to it that I look to determine what viable meaning my privacy has, who I am for others. My pain is offensive when the party is gay; I try to keep my joy hidden when others are sad. I don't want to be a conformist blindly keeping abreast of others who are trying to keep abreast of one another and possibly me. But I do want to be acceptable, to be one who could be part of the public world and not be lost in an incommunicable privacy.

If I am to share in a public experience, I must open myself up to it. When I do, I find that my privacy is assessed, evaluated, and given a place within that public. I find out what that private experience amounts to by seeing what happens to it when I let it become merged into a public experience. I of course then risk losing something that I may take to be essential to my private experience. I want my private experience to be structured by public rules, but I do not know whether or not or to what degree it will thereupon be distorted or covered over. My giving myself up to public experience is an adventure in which I can lose more than I gain, and may achieve what I never did expect or prepare for.

When I separate myself from public experience, when I subjugate what I confront to my own rhythm and tonality, I make use of the public. What I then do others can know only by inferences based on the manner in which I make evident my place in a public experience, or by sympathetically penetrating beneath the surface of my being to my self, where I make private what had been public. My privatization of the public involves me in another risky adventure.

It is possible for men to speak to one another and never have a conversation. They may exchange salutations, or signals and cues, and may thereby succeed in working together. But they will not have a conversation until they have a public experience of a language, produced by each in turn assuming the role of a speaker. And unless each contributes to the public experience something that is expected or accepted by the other, they will not yet have communicated with one another. In neither the conversation nor the communication is there any need nor any claim to duplicate, imitate or even represent in privacy what had been experienced publicly. Conversations and communications presuppose private experiences, but neither demands of these private experiences anything except that they be elements capable of being merged with and detached from public experience.

A public experience has a reality; it is objective and rule-dominated. It is to be distinguished from a common and public world, as well as from what is ultimately real. A common world is the product of the accord of a number of private beings. It exists so far as any actions relating to the same objects are supplementary or at least are not in conflict. It need not be experienced and may have no reality apart from the accord which private beings are exhibiting. There are a great number of these common worlds, some large, some small, since sometimes only a few and at other times many more actions mesh together. Some of the common worlds are momentary, others are long-lasting; there is no span of time beyond which actions must cease to be in accord. None of these common worlds need have a status apart from the accordant actions.

A public world, in contrast, stands over against actions and beings. It is a conceived world, offered to account for what actually occurs, and particularly for the way in which private beings interlock with one another. A public world offers an explanation, a common world offers a summary of concurrent activities. A public experience, in contrast with both, is a single, objective realm in which private beings partake only so far as they have subjected themselves to its rule. Just as a husband and wife are affected by the very union they constitute, so each one of us is affected by the public experience we help make possible.

A public experience is participated in by individuals but only as something to which they are subject, not as that which they face as subjects. It does not exist except so far as there are individuals conditioned by it or who will enter it, and realities beyond it which sustain it.

No one wants to have only private experiences. All want to share in a public experience and thereby be with others. When we sing together, dance together, work together we share in public experiences, and then usually find ourselves enhanced, enriched, strengthened. Still none of us ever ceases to have private experiences. The public experience is something which we want to make our own, but that experience remains forever outside our full control.

I, who privately experience, am one who had and may have other public experiences. I can share in and turn away from public experience at any point. And I can be with others even while having private experiences apart from them. My experience, though private, is relevant to what is publicly experienced, and what is publicly experienced is relevant to what I privately experience. No matter how much of my life is involved in public experience, I continue to remain a privately experiencing being.

The more I publicly experience, the more I want to publicly experience. But no matter how extensive my public experience I never get to the end of it. What lures me on? If it is not an illusion, I must be lured by a reality outside the public experience. Public experience also has a compulsiveness to it; I seek constantly to adjust myself to it. Sometimes I try to master it, or to insist on myself in the face of it. No matter what I do, it is as insistent as it had been, demanding that I yield to it or share in it. I cannot lay hold of the compulsiveness in it. Where does it come from? If it is not an illusion, it must have its source in a reality outside the public experience. Public experience also seems to have an endless capacity to enrich me. I would like to plumb it, to get to the source of its power. But no matter how much I take from it, there is still more for me to take. Where does it get its incredible wealth? If this is not an illusion there must be a reality which perpetually endows it. Public experience seems also to have a finality to it. It is there, to be shared in, to be subjected to. I try to get to the bottom of it, to reach to it as it stands over against me. But I find that no matter how far I go into it, no matter how much of it I privatize, it still is beyond me, always eluding me. What enables it to keep away from me? If it is not an illusion there must be a reality beneath all public experiencing which enables it to escape me.

Stated statically: public experience allows for multiple acts of privatization; private experience can be joined to public experience anywhere. Outside the private and the public experiences there are realities which cannot be reached except so far as one is able to do something more than experience, privately or publicly.

v

EXPERIENCE is not only focal and peripheral, mine and not-mine, private and public; it is also *episodic* and *constant*. The episodic experience may, but need not, be focal. A shooting star is episodic and yet peripheral. What is mine is usually episodic, but sometimes the not-mine is episodic too — the anxiety I discern on the faces of the rushing commuters. Private experience is more or less episodic; still, the public elation of the spectators at a game is more episodic than the pain in my tooth.

My interests fluctuate, my sense of values is not steady, my attentiveness varies in degree and range. Sometimes all about is calm; usually the further away from me and my concerns an occurrence is, the more unaltered it seems to be and the less likely to vanish. The episodic is usually that on which I concentrate, the constant is that which I allow to serve as a backdrop to a passing scene.

No experience is necessarily episodic. No experience need be constant. These are matters determined by the sensitivity of the experiencer and the nature of objects and their contexts. Both the episodic and the constant occur together. They are in fact the product of a single effort on our part to keep something existentially before us, to live with and in the rhythms of others. The episodic testifies to our ability to impose ourselves on that which is other than ourselves. Hume spoke of his episodic experiences as "impressions." He intended to imply that these experiences were impressed on him, but the episodic is primarily the outcome of an effort to make an impression on what is confronted. Most thinkers, in contrast with Hume, acknowledge that the experiencer has a reality outside the experience, and as such does not share in the transitory adventures characteristic of a good deal of the experience on which he is concentrating. But experience is not wholly rooted in an experiencer; it has another end in realities outside him.

The individual who experiences does not passively await the intrusions and acts of others. Were he a truly passive being he would have comparatively few episodic experiences, much fewer than he in fact has. Experience is the product of an interplay of different realities. But other realities often have a greater power and magnitude than the experiencer. As a result they tend to make the experience exhibit more of themselves than of him. If the experience of the infant were initially a blooming, buzzing confusion, it would be a constant confusion. More likely, though, the experience of the infant is a thick silence occasionally paced by thin sounds, a warm darkness crossed by occasional flashes of cold light.

As it grows older the infant impresses more and more of itself on what it confronts, but it never succeeds in achieving full mastery. Episodic experiences point to conquests, mainly by ourselves but sometimes by others. Constant experiences reflect the stability, sometimes of ourselves but usually of others. Both are achievements, both come to be together, the product of an interplay of realities outside experience.

I try to lose myself in episodic experiences; if I do not succeed, I will lose them. But if I do not also have the episodic as a twin product with the constant, I will lose myself, not have episodic experiences. I know episodic experiences to be singular, something distinctive because I not only live through them but look at them in terms of the constant.

The episodic is experienced as outstanding, eccentric, while I experience the flat, the regular, the constant. Nevertheless, the constant has something grand about it. We admire what can withstand time, disintegration, external forces. We sense intimations of immortality, unlimited power in anything that can be detached from the hurly-burly of everyday. We feel we can count on the constant. We enjoy a kind of impersonal satisfaction when we note that fluctuations in our attention or activity do not affect what we confront. Our awareness of such a constancy would depress us; it would make us feel inconsequential or dislocated, were we not aware that it has a place for the episodic. We look at it as that in which the episodic might fit, which allows the episodic to have neighbors and consequences, and to instance the constant's structures and laws.

The episodic seems to defy our understanding. We therefore hopefully look to the constant for a clue to its nature and import. We do not know whether or not the episodic would be radically altered if it were dealt with in terms of the constant. But because we suppose that it will not become so altered, we see the constant as that which provides a context for the episodic. The constant we readily suppose will ennoble the episodic, give it a greater dignity than it now has, and this without forcing either itself or the episodic to give up whatever virtues they now possess.

Though the episodic and the constant are coordinate products, the constant has a status and a power which makes me take it as a guide. In terms of it I try to understand and deal with the episodic. On turning down a road, I come upon a beach and at once hear the waves. The noise is part of a sequence of episodic experiences, but I treat it as a constant, attributing its episodic nature to the accident of my coming to a particular place. The flash of light that suddenly breaks with a crackling sound through the darkened sky is but lightning, I say, a meteorological occurrence, exemplifying laws repeated endlessly over countless years and unmeasured regions.

If I am to understand the episodic I must allow it to be evaluated by the constant, dealt with by the constant in its own terms. I can explain the episodic only if I give it up utterly to its correlative, see it as objectively fixated by that correlative, made into a part of it. I must make no reservations, hold back nothing, put no conditions on the constant. Only thus will the episodic be able to obtain from the constant all the benefits that the constant could bestow. But I have no protection against the prospect that the constant might then annihilate the episodic. In the very provision of terms for the understanding of it, perhaps even as the very condition for ennobling the episodic, may not the constant make it vanish? This I do not want to have happen. Fortunately it could never happen. I can never get rid of the episodic no matter how much of it I allow to be ennobled or explained by the constant. The constant forever stands away from the episodic as a coordinate product of something other than the two of them.

Experience is produced through an interplay of myself with other realities. But as an experiencing being I never can do more than turn from episodic to constant experiences, from constant experiences to episodic ones, from episodic to episodic experiences, and from one constant experience to another.

I am tempted to look beneath myself as an experiencer to myself as *capable* of experiencing both episodic occurrences and constancies, but what I usually find is another set of episodic occurrences. I am tempted too to look beyond all experience to a principle of rationality in terms of which I could estimate the legitimacy and value of the transformation which the constant imposes on the episodic. But all I ever get to in experience is the kind of rationality which the constant itself has and imposes. I also try to reach the power which expresses itself in the double product of episodic and constant experiences, but all

I ever reach in experience are episodic compulsions to which I give way sooner or later in various degrees. And, finally, I try to have both the constant and the episodic together, without losing the distinctive values they so clearly possess, but all I ever reach in experience are constants which I try to make yield the episodic by combining them with one another, and then qualifying them by an experiencer. New experiences are used as surrogates for realities I would like to reach, but never can so long as I continue to be only an experiencing being.

vi

EXPERIENCE is at once focal and peripheral, mine and not-mine, private and public, episodic and constant. All of the pairs are present in every experience. Sometimes one or another of these pairs (or one of their components) stands out sharply. At other times some one or more may be hard to discern. Independent of one another, the boundaries marking off the components of one pair will not necessarily coincide with those marking off the others.

Whatever part of experience is at once focal, mine, private and episodic is a foreground for a background, at once peripheral, not-mine, public and constant. The more we concentrate on the foreground, the more we cut ourselves off from the background, thereby losing the awareness that we are facing a foreground. The background enables us to see the foreground as one of many possible foregrounds. We are thereby enabled to know that our foreground may be different at some other time. Since we can think of others as now occupying a position which we could have occupied and from which we could have a foreground differing from the one we now have, we know that it is possible for others to have foregrounds too. The background is felt to be more basic than the foreground, and we look to it as capable of accommodating what we have already accepted as foreground. We thrust our foreground against the background in the belief that it will be accepted. The awareness of an accommodating background is one with the awareness that our foreground has an objective status, a place within a larger whole.

Our lives together rest upon the correctness of our belief

that our foreground experience is inseparable from an experienced background. We could be wrong, but if we are, we are hollow men filled with vain imaginings. The background, though, is no passive receptacle. It adopts the foreground which we thrust into it, giving it a desirable objective status, but only at the price of making that foreground subject to it. The background subjugates the foreground, makes it fit inside itself in ways which may require the foreground to be considerably altered. But no matter how willing we be to allow for such an alteration, no matter how ready we are to lose ourselves in the background, we find that we always face a foreground, or some facets of one. The background constantly attracts us and constantly eludes us.

Experience is omnipresent, produced through the interplay of realities existing outside it. It has a being of its own, dependent though it is on these other beings. I never have it as a single whole, but at the very least as divided into a foreground and a background, and usually into facets of these in shifting relations to one another. Experience belongs to me and I to it. I have part of it under my control and the rest of it has me under its control. As a consequence I am tensed, in disequilibrium, forever trying to close the breach between parts of experience, in the attempt to have it both fill up my consciousness and yet stand over against me. But no part of experience has a power of its own. When I am tempted to yield to the background I am tempted not by it but by what lies beyond it. I am beckoned to by realities outside experience, but I do not know this until I have lived quite a while, and have reflected on what experience is and can do.

Experience is capable of being possessed, privatized, and fragmented anywhere. I never wish to abandon it, but I do want to go beyond it. No one saw this point more clearly and dealt with it more perceptively than Kant. He thought, though, that the attempt to reach the real behind experience was at once inescapable and futile. He did not see that the very occurrence of experience, the nature of the breaks in it, the attraction of the background enable us to move beyond experience toward the realities which it presupposes.

So long as we content ourselves with ordinary experience we will, when we peer through it, become aware of hardly anything more than a cosmic spatio-temporal dynamic reality. But if we open ourselves up to a religious experience, we will not only make contact with God, but will discern something of the nature and power He has outside the experience, making the experience possible.

3. Religious Experience

THERE ARE MANY types of experience, each with its distinctive grain. In all of them we can discern something peripheral and focal, the mine and the not-mine, the private and the public, the episodic and the constant. In all, the texture, divisions, rhythms and quality of confronted content is lived with.

Each type of experience answers to a different side of our separated and interrelated selves. *Aesthetic* experience is qualitatively toned, and encountered through the agency of emotions, partly mediated through the senses. Undergone in privacy it has a distinctive texture; sometimes it has a different one when undergone by a number of men together. In *secular* experience we confront rather conspicuous regions through the agency of organically defined reactions, appetites and needs. It is normally shared with others in fact or in prospect, and when privately undergone, continues to bear the marks of what it exhibited to men together. *Ethical* experience encompasses values sensed through the help of our attitudes and beliefs. The experience here is usually individual, but small groups of men sometimes have the experience together more or less in the way they had it privately. *Religious* experience, which has features when private that are distinct from those it has when public, brings us into relation with a felt power that assesses what we are and have attained.

No one of these experiences is ever in steady focus. No one of them is free of all alloy, change and obscurity. Since they constantly interlock, no one of them is ever completely cut off from the others. To have one is to have them all. Any dimension of experience is at once ethical and religious, aesthetic and secular in tone, though it is rare that we attend to more than one or two of these at a time.

Very soon we impose various classifications on our experiences, and make various divisions and demands on different parts of them. When we do this we break up the experienced content into a *locally adumbrated* and a *cosmically adumbrated*. Both are discerned through a veil of imposed conditions. Both are surfaces of more substantial, sustaining realities.

In every experience we are directly involved with content. But we usually have the experience mainly in an adumbrated form, and come to know what the experience is like only through the help of intervening ideas. The well-demarcated items we daily know are the product of embodied categories and adumbrateds, inseparable from both limited and cosmic realities which give the items an externality, a context and a career. Religion is concerned with one of these realities in its local and cosmic guise. When fortunate, it is rooted in a religious experience. A religious experience helps us to identify the reality as God; the reality in turn makes an experience be a religious experience.

ii

THERE IS NO surer way of blurring the distinctive qualities and values of religious experience than by taking a part of it for the whole. Most frequently, religious experience is identified with a peculiar kind of private feeling, usually exciting, sometimes tumultuous. But then the religious experience which takes place only in a dedicated community is ignored. Religious men, when they interplay with one another and a reality beyond them all, produce a public religious experience not reducible to a private feeling. More serious is the fact that those who fail to insist on the presence of God in religious experience can have no way of distinguishing a supposed religious experience from similarly toned but quite different occurrences.

William James' *Varieties of Religious Experience* presents us with the testimony of men who are supposed to have had religious experiences, but what they often report is somewhat like that which had been found by others in a non-religious experience. Leuba and other psychologists have noted the similarity in the reports of insane people and those of supposedly religious men regarding what they had undergone. A follower of James might insist that all of them are having religious experiences, but a follower of Leuba would be equally justified in taking all the experiences to be non-religious. Having cut off their accounts from a reference to an encounter with God's being, acts or effects (which are, as we shall see, not to be treated as separated from His being), neither has a way of determining whether his experience is religious or not. The distinctive character of a religious experience can neither be had nor described by one who ignores the presence of God in it.

Others restrict religion in a different way. They deny religion a concern with a transcendent being. Since they then can provide no terminus to, or the possibility for, an unqualified faith, they offer us not a genuine form of religion but only a secular or ethical, public or private experience which might have had an origin in religion. By reducing a religious experience in this way, what was originally discerned in faith becomes only a portion of a foreground and background, gratuitously believed to be sustained by something unknown and unknowable. We effectively cut ourselves off from religion when we take it to be empirical or experiential in this sense. An opposite error is characteristic of those who suppose that every acknowledgment of God yields a religious experience. God can be merely conceived or treated aesthetically. Not every acknowledgment of God has religious significance.

In a religious experience the subject may be aware of God in a number of places — within himself, in the adumbrated content which lies outside all demarcated and categorized objects, and in the relation connecting God and himself. That experience has all the divisions characteristic of the secular and other types. Still, it is distinct from them. It alone has a nature which reflects, because it is a consequence of, an involvement of a conscious subject with a present divine assessing being.

The mystic sees himself over against men who, like him, profess to have a primary interest in God. Taking them on their own evaluation the mystic goes on to affirm that there is still another, a more penetrating way of dealing with God. But if the non-mystical thinker is as the mystic describes him to be, he is not a religious man at all, but one occupied with rituals, formulae and creeds, and then in an impersonal way. In fact, though, a mystical moment is to be found in all religious experience.

The mystic claims to have an unmediated religious experience. He thinks he can successfully cut beneath the categories he daily uses, break away from the habits, ideas and feelings these categories entrain, to lose himself in an enjoyment of God. But if he does not keep any hold of himself, he does not have a religious experience but only feelings in the presence of God.

The mystic always has a being beyond him. If he manages to achieve a relationship with God which is denied to the merely religious member of the community, or even the merely religious individual, it is because he has broken away from the conventionalities of daily life and of the religion, not by cancelling them but by transcending them, by finding a position within himself in which he is able to deal with God in ways which other men, because they have been caught within conventional bounds, cannot. Mystical experience in the end is a submission to a being, and must therefore always affirm that God transcends the experience as well as the conventionalized forms in which the religions encompass him. For the mystic too some mystery always remains.

The mystic, so far as he is concerned with making direct contact with God apart from and outside all proofs, reflections or abstractions is faced with a practical problem, not an intellectual one. His task is to get himself in a state where he can be in immediate contact with God. But he must allow himself to be guided by some idea, or he will fail to have an adequate assurance that he is not dealing with fancies rather than facts. And then he must recognize that there are many ways in which a man can make immediate contact with God, ranging from the extreme where he is entirely lost in Him, to the extreme where, though merged with God, he continues to maintain his own integrity. In any case the rest of men must be content with a religious experience which is infected with other types, or is at least mediated by concepts and beliefs, and known only with hindsight through the help of various guides, such as creeds, beliefs and speculations. But because so conditioned, a religious experience is readily confused with any one of eleven somewhat related but still different accompaniments of various acts having something to do with religion.

1.   There is no religion or religious experience which does not require some detachment from the daily world and its affairs. Even those who are most concerned with service or who think that the major task of the religious man is to work on behalf of his fellow-man, must first turn away from the world in order to achieve a proper perspective on it. But one can turn away without being religious. Mathematicians, scientists and philosophers detach themselves as surely as religious men do. Both religion and religious experience require detachment; neither is identical with it.

2.   There is no religion or religious experience which does not require some attachment to God, some acceptance of Him. Definitions of God vary, and what one man terms a God is thought by others to be not worthy of the designation. Granted though that someone's definition is acceptable, it still does not follow that the attachment of oneself to that God makes one religious. A man can attach himself to God unknowingly. And he can attach himself to God for selfish reasons, thereby cancelling the effect that God would have had on the interplay of the two of them. A religion and a religious experience require an acceptance, a giving of ourselves to God and a giving of Himself to us.

3.   A man can have a private or publicly shared belief in the existence, the power, the demands or the activities of God. He can give himself to God, the loving being who will protect and heal, forgive and save. He still would not have a genuine religious experience, though he would then be in a religious *state*. A religious experience, like experiences of every other type, is more than a process of moving from oneself to, or believing in another reality. It has a content all its own, which can be lived with and reflected upon.

4.   A religion may be reduced to a matter of practice or attitude. It may be caught within the confines of some creed or doctrine, some institution or commitment. Such a religion

could be supplemented by a religious experience. The religion will then have its value altered by the role and place accorded it by the experience. The experience in turn will be affected by the religion's stresses and divisions, to become what might appropriately be termed a "liturgical" experience. It has great value for one who, without giving up his particular faith, wants to keep himself occupied with whatever is given a role inside experience. Such an experience will not interest one who wants his religion or his religious experience pure. It will not be possible to one who has no faith or to one who keeps his faith entirely separated from his engagement with the world. It will not be possible to one who wants merely to experience or who wants his religious experience to be characterized by some idea of God or other cosmic reality, rather than by what a particular religion might provide.

5.   Consuming loves or fears may have no rational ground. One might plunge into them without knowing anything about the realities at which they are to terminate. Sometimes Kierkegaard speaks as if this is what the true Knight of Faith should do. Such a knight acts blindly, leaps he knows not where. But love or fear has religious value only when it is at least guided by some knowledge of God. When this occurs the passions make vital acts of religious *affirmation* possible. These are acts of faith at once intellectual and dynamic, undergone by the individual and the community, and directed toward and terminating in God. The result is not a religious experience. But it may be the occasion for the presence of one.

Religious affirmations presuppose religious experiences. The feeling of being accepted by God or of receiving benefits from Him, the awareness of being "called" are concretionalized facets of such a presupposed religious experience. The awareness of oneself as being attracted by God, or of being pulled into Him more and more, are precipitations from a religious experience, occasioned by a living faith.

6.   Faith itself can serve as a category, a way of organizing, dividing and utilizing a religious experience. When this occurs we have a feeling of being religiously *justified*, of having our experience rectified and our faith basically grounded. But we

will have moved away from the experience to an experientially grounded faith. That faith is caught within the context of an experience in which God is present, at the same time that the religious experience is skewed toward us, the beings engaged in the adventure of faith. But a genuine religious experience is no more biased toward ourselves than it is toward God.

7.   A faith, treated as a category, can make a secular experience religiously relevant. Here one looks at the world and one's own experiences in the light of faith. This is perhaps inevitable, for faith affects the inward parts and thereby determines how one will thereafter look upon the world. But the result is quite different from a religious experience, for the double reason that the experience is still secular (though given religious import through the faith) and is no longer a mere experience since it is transformed by the faith.

8.   Normally we attend only to local adumbrateds and ignore the cosmic. What we then know are distinct particulars externally related to one another, each being sustained by a limited reality of which the local adumbrated is the surface. But occasionally we relate the demarcated objects and events directly to the cosmically adumbrated, overlooking or dismissing the local adumbrated entirely. When we do this we make the familiar objects and events into representatives or signs of the cosmically adumbrated, and this in turn clarifies or rectifies those objects and events. By offering ourselves to an adumbrated God in an act of worship or sacrifice we sanctify ourselves or our objects. But we will then have moved away from the religious experience, for this stands neutrally between ourselves and God.

9.   Sacramental experience is an experience of foreground and background charged with religious values. Special places and moments, defined by a religion, here achieve primary positions as the poles about which an experience is undergone. Experience is then at once restricted and enhanced, for it is both kept within the confines of a religion and made to function as a moment in a religious life. Each religion has its own ways of restricting and enhancing the experience of its members; and every individual can get some of his experience in the

context of his act of faith. The result is religious experience, but narrowed, specialized and presupposing a purer form.

10.   One effect of a religious experience is the alerting of us to an experience of our own being and meaning, of our status and value. This latter experience is a consequence of, but is itself not a religious experience. It may in fact be a purely aesthetic or secular or ethical experience, though made possible by the quite different religious experience. It is an error to confuse an effect with its cause.

11.   God himself can be adumbrated behind the objects we daily encounter; He can be felt as a lure, inviting us, or as a repellent, pushing us away. What we confront will then bear evidences of Him. Sometimes He will be seen to be the most intimate but localized interior of an object, the deepest layer in it: sometimes He will be seen to be a cosmic being in which our acknowledged objects have a limited place or role. At neither time would there be a religious experience. In a religious experience God is constitutive, not a being felt or referred to. Taken as adumbrated He is at once closer and more remote than He is in a mere religious experience, since He is then approached through the veil of other entities and yet remains outside the adumbrated presence of Himself. Supplemented by further concepts, judgment and speculation, the result will yield a knowledge of the God encountered in faith. Shared by several, it will become the knowledge of the God experienced by a religious community. Encountered as a lure or a repellent He will not be experienced the way He is when He and we together constitute a neutral domain in which we both are parts, and outside of which we both remain. In a religious experience God neither attracts nor repels; He is not conceptualized nor does He provide a category for conceptualization. Instead He, together with ourselves, constitutes a distinctively toned immediacy.

iii

WE DO NOT come to know what religious experience is like until we have exercised a faith, participated in a community, categorized the experience, or used it to order some other experience. We know about our religious experience only from a non-experiential perspective. That is why it is possible to avoid confounding it with other experiences. Knowing something about God, about ourselves, about the nature of experience we are able to know what it means to have an experience qualified by God.

Religious experience is a type of experience, having religious interest because it involves God. It is a divinely qualified experience through which God can be discerned. The outcome of a divine qualification has been called "Numen" by the Romans. Occasionally it has been referred to by that name by Christian writers. Thus Jeremy Taylor: "The divine presence hath made all places holy, and every place hath a Numen in it." It was Rudolph Otto, however, who made the term, and particularly his invented cognate of it, "numinous," part of the vocabulary of modern religious thinkers. He perceptively spoke of it as giving an irreducible meaning to "holy" beyond that of mere goodness and beauty. And though he explicitly said that it is something objective and outside the self, he also spoke of it as a state of mind and a category of value. But when he dealt with it as objective, he treated it as essentially peripheral and not at all focal, and then as a tremendous, ineffable, receding Other. Taylor's way of putting the matter does more justice to the fact that God can be experienced not merely at a distance but here as well, and that the distant places where He is are not beyond all reaching.

To obtain an adequate grasp of the nature of religious experience it is necessary to note the basic divisions into which our secular experience divides, and then to note the way in which God impinges on them.

In the religious experience we are constrained by a power not acknowledged as we go about our ordinary affairs. To control that power we must exert more effort and attention than must be used when we make secular things function in a controlled or steady way. Men in all societies acknowledge the constraint as that which is to be controlled by means of magic, incantations, rituals, prayer, service, good will, good behavior and similar agencies.

Secular constraints are brutal and socially grounded. Men react to them, soon learning how to mark out special places where they seem able to control or qualify those constraints. The religious experience, even where constant and universal, is distinguished from an ordinary secular one by virtue of the additional pull it exerts. This additional pull demands an additional response by man. Since it affects a man deeply, correcting him and directing him, he must confine it, redirect it or risk becoming ecstatic, "carried away."

In religious experience men stop at various points under a pressure exerted from without, understood as having relevance to what men can finally become. Some parts of the experience may be kept apart from others. Men will then come to speak of them as being the province of distinctive Gods, or as places sacred to some single God. If one did not have a religious faith or some knowledge of God, these places would not be noted; nor would the pull which characterizes the religious experience be distinguished from that present in the experience, say, of a cosmic space-time.

A religiously experienced peripheral region is one that has been qualified by God. It is primarily awesome. A religiously experienced focal region, in contrast, is primarily insistent. Since the peripheral and focal regions affect one another, the focal region is also awesome and the peripheral insistent. The two are equally holy, but the focal is more potent and the peripheral more overwhelming. A religious experience is, in the beginning, usually frightening, fortunately it is often quickly overlaid with peace and joy.

Neither the focal nor the peripheral has a fixed place or range, or encompasses a distinct type of content. When we move from the focal to the peripheral, what was focal becomes peripheral; consequently a religiously experienced potent region can become more awesome, and an awesome region more potent. Everything we can see or with which we identify ourselves can be seen as potent. And since we can narrow the range of the "here" even to a point, everything we can see or with which we identify ourselves can be seen as awesome. As a rule what we make focal is rich, more overpowering, so holy sometimes as to be inviolate. Poor Uzzah is an illustration. He was struck dead by God when, as the holy ark was about to topple, he put out his hand to steady it.

The distance between the potent and the awesome is not a

matter of miles or geography. Religiously viewed, to be potent is to be focal, to be awesome is to be distant. And because the focal and peripheral, the potent and awesome are linked in one single experienced whole, God is encountered as an all-pervasive being, having different degrees of intensity at different places and times. But because attention to any part makes it focal and potent, the awesome always appears to be somewhat remote and sometimes even hostile.

The potent which I here acknowledge, overwhelming though it may be at times, I take to be but a faint effect of what the divine truly is. My experience is charged with divine force where focal, and points to even greater force where peripheral. And when I approach myself from the outside I see myself bereft, denied, separate from the all-powerful divine.

My experience is at once a road and a barrier. I am at once experientially related to and separated from the all-powerful divine. I keep on the surface of the focal, but I penetrate the peripheral. The more intimately I experience God focally, the more acutely I become aware that peripherally He has not yet manifested Himself fully. In religious experience I remain remote from God, the being who is more than He reveals Himself to be, either focally or peripherally.

Religiously viewed, the mine is the friendly, the warm, the intimate presence of God, and the not-mine is the strange, cold and distant spirit of God. Since the regions of the mine and the not-mine constantly contract and expand, and have no sharp borders between them, what I take to be friendly merges imperceptibly into what I had taken to be alien, and what I find friendly now I sometimes find strange later. But now I submit to the one, usually as here and focal, and I look toward the other, usually as there and peripheral. Even when the focal is so potent as to endanger my life, it is most germane to me — even friendly, if only I knew how to address it. Even when the peripheral is alluring though awesome, and even when I give myself up to it to do with me as it wills, it still is somewhat remote, turned away from me.

The religiously mine is the intimate. I hold on to it by pushing aside what is not mine. By keeping to the rules, by eating and fasting as I have been taught, I continue to have as mine what was initially given me by teacher, by God or by some unknown means. Consequently, I come to feel that God's friendly presence pervades whatever truly belongs to me. Yet He is just as surely not possessed by me. Not that another has Him entirely, for what is possessed by anyone has a dimension not his. This which is not possessed differs from individual to individual, contrasting with the distinctive "mine" of each. But there is a sense in which it is the same for all, since it is precisely that which no man can possess. It has a reality forever escaping all our encompassments.

Despite all the risks it holds for me I want the religiously not-mine to become mine; the status of being mine is one I would like to impose on all that is not-mine. If in order to achieve this I sacrificed myself without reserve, I would make the mine indistinguishable from what is not-mine, because there would then no longer be anyone to whom the mine could be referred. But I never can succeed in so losing myself and what is mine. And the not-mine, because it is experienced, is something which cannot really be said to be completely over against me.

The polarization of experience into the mine and not-mine is largely due to me. The religious not-mine, the remoteness of God, is more my doing than His. He exhibits Himself in my experience in different ways, in part because the objects in which He is resident have different degrees of relevance and intimacy to Him and for me, and in part because of the way in which I open myself up to what I confront.

What I find potent, warm, intimate is so. What I find awesome, cool, alien is so. This is because these are both ways in which God, as mediated through various items having pertinence to myself, is experienced.

That religious experience is private is agreed on by all. Those who take religion most seriously are here one with those who have no use for it. Both agree that a genuine religious experience must touch the depths of a man's being, that it is vital and secret. Those who take it seriously insist that such an experience actually occurs; their opponents deny that it is even possible. Both I think, overstate themselves, partly because they do not take sufficient account of the fact that religious experience is public as well as private. Private religious experience is marked with a feeling of dependence, creatureliness, finitude, inadequacy, incompleteness. So is the public. The fact is not often noted, particularly in the last centuries, because most writers are deeply affected by a "low church" Protestant outlook, and little attention is given to the spirit of Judaism. It is there that religious experience is at once public and private. If there is genuine private religious experience, there is genuine public religious experience. If there is no genuine private religious experience, there is no genuine public religious experience. The two are inseparably linked.

Private experience is often anticipatorily public where it is not residually so. It has its own tonality and is rooted in a distant individual subject, but the subject is in good part a subject for a public world. The religious experience of each is often a private experience of a common public treasury which each approaches from a distinct position. Were this never so, a religious man would be more radically alone than any other kind. Though he does and must detach himself from the world about, that detachment does not require him to lose all contact with everything but God. The moment of faith is one which involves a secret contact of the individual with God, but this moment need not to be completely divorced from a reference to God as mediated by other things, and thus as constituting a public experience in which all can participate.

God is publicly experienced as the *Tremendum*, to use another term brought into the fore by Otto. Only those who participate in it have a religious experience. They constitute a religious people, an invisible church, a spiritual community. Each has a private experience of that *Tremendum* so far as he is oriented toward it, and is a subject for it. What he experiences of it is a subdivision of it, a part of a public territory which he for the moment occupies. The publicly experienced is compulsive, rule-determined, and imposing. If we start there we reach the private as a limit, as that part of the public which is least involved with the rest. If we start with the private we reach the public as the arena where we are met by others. In both cases the content of the experience is the same; it is always an experience of a single *Tremendum* into which we enter and from which we can depart in the sense of sharing or not sharing it with others. This is not to say that there are no unique, unshared individual experiences. Pain, pleasure, memory, dreams, hope, are unique, private experiences. But if we wish to speak of these in common terms, it is desirable to translate them into the incipiently or residually public.

The *Tremendum* is not God. When we enter into it, we do not have a mystical experience any more than we do when we sing together. The *Tremendum* is as public as a concert, but does not exist except for those who can discern the qualifying presence of God. Such discernment it was the intent of the old agapistic feasts to promote. It is also one of the consequences we expect common worship to produce.

Religious experience is not public for non-religious men. But if it is not public for religious ones, it will sink into the singular, the non-viable. Were defenders of religion more alert to the fact that a religious experience, whether it be treated as entirely private or not, is not an exercise in faith, not a way of occupying oneself with God, but is instead a type of experience which allows one to see the difference that God makes to experience, there would perhaps not have been so much attention given to religious experience, to the neglect of that apprehension of God which is provided by community, faith and idea.

My experience is no mere creature of mine; it has an objective pole which I do not constitute. In religious experience this is an unbounded constant affected by God. It is the everlasting on which I try to act and which I hope will forever keep hold of me. The episodic, religiously speaking, is the evidence that I momentarily and feebly make a difference to that constant. There is hardly a moment when I do not make such a difference, and hardly a moment when that difference is not swallowed up almost without remainder. I dart out at the constant all the time, making momentary tiny passes at it here and there. I would like to make a greater impression. I would like to have all I have done be a permanent part of what is always, but I never succeed. The episodic is the point at which I enter the constant, the place where time gets lost in the forever abiding.

Religious experience is not an experience of eternity. It is an experience of everlastingness — quite a different matter. Eternity has a reality outside experience. Everlastingness is a quality of the religious experience itself. Though no man has a completely steady religious experience nor has it for long, the experience nevertheless is everlasting in the sense that it has a pole unaffected by him. That objective pole makes experience be an experience of something objective; it conditions and assesses the episodic experience to be inadequate and incomplete.

In religious experience we face a constant condition for what is episodic. We share in the religious experience only so far as we direct ourselves to a constant facet of it, as that which alone makes worthwhile what we are momentarily undergoing. It is an experience in which we submit our episodic efforts and results to an everlasting evaluation and perhaps rectification. All the while we are dimly aware of ourselves, as outside the experience, and of a reality lying outside the everlasting. Or more accurately, we catch faint glimpses occasionally of ourselves and God as outside an everlasting religious experience episodically shared.

To know a religious experience we must reach a distinctive immediacy and to be aware that this has a nature different from other immediacies. We must at once be in the experience and look at it from a distance. While we merely live through the experience we can never therefore know that we have it, and when we reflect on it we can never be quite certain that our ideas have not distorted it. Nor are we ever sure of the nature of the being we can occasionally discern through the fissures of the religious experience. We have vague intimations of endless power, of terrible immensity, of final judgment, perhaps even of abiding concern and steady companionship. Everything is on the edge of a sustaining dark silence, at once attractive and dismaying.

To know what it is we are experiencing and what we discern beneath it, to know even what it is we achieve by participating in a religious community or through an act of faith, we must have recourse to ideas and to evidence, internal and external to ourselves. If the ideas are good and the evidence reliable we will be able to know what the experience presupposes — and that surely is at least as good as having a religious experience or knowing what the experience is like.

2. The Sacred

4. Religious Concepts
and Sacred Objects

EACH ONE of us is a distinct individual, a world to himself.
Each of us has his own private life. No one's appetites, feelings,
or beliefs are interchangeable with mine. Still, no one of us
is entirely self-enclosed. We are all part of larger worlds. Each
of us is a member of groups, some transitory, some more or less
permanent. We live in families, belong to clubs, associate with
one another for various tasks and in various places. Each of us
too is a member of a particular society; unmistakably distinct
from others. Ours has a language, an organization, customs and
traditions that others do not have. Most of us also share in a
culture, a world encompassing more than one society, thereby
making it possible for us occasionally to look at our own society with a critical eye. And though we are not often aware
of it or of what it involves, we are all members of one mankind, sharing features and looking out at the world in terms
similar to those employed by the rest of men. That is why
communication is possible, at least on an elementary level, with
men of the most diverse interests, history, manners, beliefs and
vocabulary. And we are also part of a universe which encompasses whatever there be, a fact which is made evident in our
use of such highly general distinctions as that between what

is and is not, what is and ought to be, what is, can be, had been and must be, between part and whole, time and eternity, good and evil.

There are thinkers who stress some one of these roles to the neglect of the others. Overwhelmed by a belated discovery that each man is unique, some existentialists insist that every one of us peers out at the world in incommunicable, unduplicable ways. But were this the case no one would be able to convey anything to another, not even the thesis that all men have radically distinct outlooks. It is more common for contemporary philosophers to claim instead that the world we face expresses the interests and therefore the distinctions of some limited group. Were they right, though, engineers, business men, workers, capitalists, and law-abiding citizens might be able to form distinct communities of like-minded and like-speaking men, but there would be no possibility of the members of one group communicating with those in the others. But they do so communicate in their daily discourse, in crises and in politics.

There is more point to the claim made by Sapir and Whorf that the distinctions and connections we think we discern in the world are reflections of the language of our society. Since this thesis depends on the ability of Sapir and Whorf to stand outside their own society and language in order either to know how the structures of these carve out areas from a presumed undifferentiated mass, or to be able to compare the structures imposed by their own societal language with those imposed by others, it is evident that they cannot deny that there are distinctions which transcend the limitations characteristic of some one social group. Cassirer seems to have successfully avoided this difficulty in his view that the world is organized by a plurality of symbolic forms which reflect the interests and requirements of a trans-social culture rather than those of a particular society. His symbolic forms seem to answer to the distinctions forged by a number of basic disciplines pursued in the western world. However, we not only make less sophisticated cultural distinctions but, as Jung has seen, some of these are trans-cultural, reflecting the common experiences of all men. And as Kant has insisted, some of the distinctions reflect the structure of any understanding of an experienceable world. But we must go one step further and, with Aristotle and Hegel, attend to ways of conceptionalizing which reflect the fact that men are cosmic beings, realities who are not only over against, but who are also together with all other realities.

No one of us makes use of any of these ways exclusively. All of them are employed all the time, unreflectingly intermixed. We slip quite easily from distinctions which answer to our individual interests or natures to social and cosmic concepts, and back again. We combine concepts of different magnitudes and origins in rather haphazard ways, for we are ourselves not fully integrated and cannot therefore distinguish the different types clearly, nor interrelate them properly. We blur and distort. Our individual, social, cultural, human and cosmic concerns merge into one another. At unexpected times one or the other may come to the forefront as a consequence of insistent urges arising from within, deliberate positions assumed, and pressures and standards imposed on us from without. Sometimes we attend to one and push the others aside, but we never succeed in using any one in complete separation from the rest.

Whether attended to separately or used in some combination, the various distinctions imposed on experience bear the marks of their user, of compulsions, attractions and repulsions, and of the outcome of critical appraisals. We always reveal something of these when we observe, think and speak.

It is helpful, I think, to divide the types of distinctions which are imposed on experienced content by men as individuals and as representatives into four basic types — those, answering to the nature and stresses of the body, that make use of "material" concepts relating to contingent opportunities and answers; those, answering to the nature and stresses of the will, that make use of "deontic" concepts relating to commands, commitments, obligations; those, answering to the nature and stresses of the emotions, that make use of "intensional" concepts relating to the way beings and meanings are involved with one another; and those, answering to the nature and stresses of the mind, that make use of "formal" concepts relating to implications, structures, meanings. There is no amorphous mass on which these distinctions are imposed. Experience, as we have already seen, is internally differentiated; it qualifies any categorizations which are imposed on it by us, no matter by what agency or with how much power.

Our individual bodies have distinctive nerves and sense organs; through them course expressions of our sensitivities and appetites. We can think of these, we can act them out, and we can speak of them. If we are to communicate to one another what it is that we are individually insisting on we will have to express ourselves and our reports in common terms, and treat the distinctions we individually make as qualifications of some common set. We will then function as representative bodies. Since we may represent limited groups, as well as all mankind and classes in between these two, we must evidently express our bodily natures and stresses by means of multiple categorial ideas which differ from one another not only in range of application but also in the way they are exhibited.

If I wish to refer to my hunger in terms appropriate to other members of my group or society, I make use of our common vocabulary. But if I, as a representative of a culture or of mankind, wish to refer to the hunger, I will have to resort to translations of my societal language, will have to make pantomime serve as my means of expression, or will have to use an artificial neutral language. Similar observations are to be made with respect to my evaluations. Many of my standards are imposed on my body by the wholes which I constitute with other men. I am thereby enabled to live in terms of both local and cultural attitudes and of the appetites and repugnances characteristic of mankind. Most Americans turn with disgust from beetles, grasshoppers and old eggs as unfit to eat; incest taboos qualify the driving force of the sexual urge in all.

Through the agency of their bodies religious men categorize the world in a distinctive manner. They approach the world about in ways which are not in perfect accord with the way others do; men who hold to one creed diverge from those who hold to another. Sometimes, without encouragement, they spontaneously burst into song or whirl about, roll on the floor or dance. There is perhaps no deep rooted human impulse which has not been redirected, repressed or urged in response to the supposed presence or command of God. Jews and Muslims have bodies which withdraw at pork, a nutritious food; other religious people have other food taboos. Fortunately, there are many things all do and see in common. All seem to put some limits on sexual practices and on food consumption, though some do encourage indulgence in these on special occasions.

Our individual wills have distinctive motivations and objectives. They can help us decide amongst various attractive alternatives, help us determine the nature of our obligations, or help us become oriented toward and to bring about an ideal excellence. They can be expressed by us freshly on different occasions; they can be habituated and institutionalized. If we insist on expressing our own wills regardless of what others are, need, or can do, we will think, act and speak as willful beings, perverse and irrational. An intelligent will is directed toward the production of common ends. It instances an ideal will, a will all other men can also instance. This is distinct from a holy will. That is guided by the commands or presence of God. The holy will is not a second will added to the will we normally exercise. It is our normal will, but now operating under the governance of God.

A holy will is freely exercised, but only because our will is free to begin with. But could a holy will really be free? If it is a will, it must be free. Is not God irresistible? Yes. Is it possible for Him to command and men not to obey, for Him to be present and men to avoid responding to Him? No. Our "Yes" here refers to men as having turned away from the world and having thereupon related themselves to God. Our "No" refers to the men as having already exercised a holy will. But the holy will is freely exercised. God, as the object of a holy will, is freely faced and freely responded to. We turn freely to or from a secular context, and from or to a religious one.

A man may accidentally, or even habitually, pursue or avoid the very things another with a holy will might pursue or avoid. He will then act responsibly but not willingly. If he willed to avoid or pursue those things but had no awareness of the bearing of God on them, he would still not have a holy will. He would live according to the letter, not the spirit. His behavior would be beyond reproach but *he* would not be. The mere use of a holy will would not, though, suffice to make him *be* religious, for a man is religious only when he has a justified will, i.e., a holy will whose free decision is divinely endorsed. To have this he must will to be faithful, will a hope greater than that which he achieves by turning away from the world and looking elsewhere for completion, and greater than that which he has when he merely allows himself to be guided or commanded by God.

Our emotions are distinctively our own. They are inseparable from our unduplicable beings. Issuing from the very centre of ourselves, they are our persons made vivid and effective. But if we insist on expressing them without taking them to be representative of what others do or ought to feel in a given situation, we will not express them, but will only discharge them. Emotions are intelligible so far as they answer to representative aspirations or prescriptions. We are supported and repelled, encouraged and dismayed together with others who are members of our group or society, and we look out at the world in terms of distinctions which are pertinent to us all: facts which we express by making appropriate differentiations in our discourse and in our actions.

We are swept with fear at the sight of almost any snake slithering toward us, but the fear in hunters who know their snakes is incited only occasionally. And it then has a sharper bite and a different context from our own. The hunters in our society will speak of snakes in a vocabulary and with a grammar which differ from those available to hunters elsewhere, though most hunters in any society will act out their feelings similarly. Any logic, which would try to do justice to the way the fears of both hunters and non-hunters interlock with hopes, anxieties and loves today, will relate an acknowledgment of snakes and an acknowledgment of apples in a way that the theologians of the Middle Ages did not.

Religious emotions are directed toward objects that are affected by God. They are ways of classifying the objects we daily confront, in accord with divinely determined distinctions. We should distinguish them from the awe and reverence elicited when we directly attend to God, and from the purged daily emotions which are expressed in the course of the production of art. Religious emotions are primarily emotions of fear and joy, for God is at once awesome and fascinating, alien and friendly, crushing and inviting. The fear and joy, however, are elicited not by God but by objects. One who does not acknowledge anything stemming from God in those objects will find the fear and joy of those who do make such acknowledgments to be without cause or warrant. He would not know how others feel in the presence of sacred objects, nor would he share in the agapistic love which comes from the acknowledgement of one's fellow as a being loved by God. He could, of course, know about these emotions and even speak of them sympathetically, but then he must grant that these other men take the objects to be qualified by God.

Every object can be approached as sacred, which is to say as having been qualified by God. The religious emotions, however, divide off some of these objects from others. It takes something distinctive, striking, more than normally effective to elicit those emotions. Only such objects are faced as beings divinely modified.

Each of us, finally, has a mind of his own, through which thoughts move without regard for the way others think, or for the way we are supposed to think. If we are able to anticipate what might follow from what is now accepted, we are intelligent. We would not, however, be sane men unless we were able to see what our acceptances are like from the perspective of others, and what the consequences of our conjoint acceptances might be. Sane men think representatively, making their thoughts follow the routes which their group or society take to be reasonable. Even when they think by themselves, they think in consonance with others. But unless they think in terms which answer to the possible outcome of a unified intellectual whole, they are not disciplined men. If they are to achieve a final truth in the course of time they must, as Peirce observed, be concerned with the settled outcome of inquiry for the largest possible community of men. This, in the end, must include all mankind.

Men are not rational until they make their thoughts conform to the prescriptive conditions which a formal logic exposes, and thus think as representatives of those who submit their thoughts to the same ideal of what is forever valid. The distinctions which such a logic requires have guided a number of great philosophers — Aristotle, Kant, Hegel — in their formulation of the categories governing the divisions and connections of our experienced world. Since these philosophers did not want to limit the application of those categories to what is pertinent only to a segment of mankind, they ignored the demands of particular groups and societies. They also ignored some of the distinctive requirements of the different disciplines, as well as those which reflect distinctions demanded by our bodies, wills and emotions. Nor did they take account of the fact that the various categories are unreflectingly intermixed by us, to yield the basic concepts we daily use, somewhat distilled in the shape of grammar, with its conventional classifications, evaluations, definitions, and methodological conditions. Nor was sufficient attention paid to the fact that the application of these categories produces alterations in them as well as in the content to which they are applied – though the Kantian schematism does take some cognizance of this fact.

The purest and most fundamental of formal concepts are categories. Specialized instances of these are ideas. It does not seem to be the case that there is a single fixed set of categories; the mind is no finished whole with well-defined demarcations in it. In any case, whatever the number and types of categories that, for various purposes, one might take to be behind the ideas we have, all of them instance a single basic category. This is an intelligible form instanced by all our classifications and ideas, and in the objects at which they are directed and which they enable us to know. It conforms to the demands of logic, and does in fact embody logical distinctions, as Aristotle, Kant and Hegel all affirmed. This does not make logic a super-category, for a category is inseparable from content.

The ultimate category is the category of "reality," polarized into a unity and a fluid content, intersected by a polarity of plurality and universality. Each of these poles can be taken as a starting point, having reference to its opposite, the two being articulated through the agency of the remaining poles. The ultimate religious concept is the basic category as pertinent to things which are qualified by God. It is the concept of a sacred object.

ii

DESCARTES HELD that a knower who was sustained by God saw what was the case by means of an infallible "natural light." Spinoza put more emphasis on the object of knowledge. This, as qualified by God, was part of one single rational totality. According to him, whatever was real was so qualified. Consequently for him religious knowledge was adequate and true, whereas for Descartes secular knowledge could be adequate and true, but only so far as it was had by a mind illuminated by God. Since we do have a pure secular knowledge and apparently have it without supernatural help, we ought not to keep ourselves confined either to a Cartesian or a Spinozistic outlook.

With Descartes we ought to say that one could be divinely empowered to know with a clarity and a surety what otherwise would not be possible. But with the humanists we ought also to say that sometimes a divinely empowered man is dislocated, confused, and therefore misses what others can see. With Spinoza we ought to acknowledge the fact that one could know divinely qualified beings. But with the Franciscans we ought also to say that God dislocates the beings He qualifies, with the consequence that an acknowledgment of His effects will distort the truths of common sense. And with the rest of the world we ought to say that we have an unaided genuine knowledge of secular matters.

Berkeley held that God affects common-sense objects to give them a kind of status they otherwise would not have. In supposing though that all objects are equally affected by God he denied a distinctive place for either a secular or a religious knowledge. To allow for a religious knowledge in addition to a secular, it is necessary to take account of God's differentiating acts, His making some objects into distinctive loci, specializations or epitomizations of Himself. It is because God differentially qualifies objects that they have an order amongst themselves which they do not intrinsically have.

In the ordinary course of knowledge we make individual judgments of the things we daily confront. We then at least implicitly claim that what we affirm would also be affirmed by others in that society, and (with refinements) by all mankind. The objects we know acquire a representative character because we act as representative judges of what is the case. When God qualifies the objects which we know, those objects are made representative of others, not because we have come to know them, but because they have been selected by God. If we take it to be our task to discover just which ones have been selected, and to select them as it were after the recommendation of God, we will look to myths to tell us how to classify what we confront, and for marks in the things to tell us that they are special, and perhaps superior to other objects.

The question, how I know which objects have been qualified by God is analogous to the question how I am to behave in order to conform to God's commands. The only guides most men use are provided by the particular religions. But these make different objects function in distinctive ways; they accept different occurrences, portents, revelations, testimonies and practices as evidences that certain objects are representative of what has been qualified by a discriminating God. We need a better answer.

There is nothing in any object which requires that it be accepted or be acceptable to, or had been elected by God. Anything could in principle be divinely commanded, anything could in principle be divinely endorsed as an accepted representative. There are some things though that one would usually not take as a proper locus of Him — whatever is repugnant in a given community. And there are some things which offer signally appropriate indications of some special attribute or power of God. Water, which cleanses, quenches thirst, has its own relentless rhythm, threatens drowning, and can destroy, which promotes growth and expresses fluidity and the capacity to enter into the tiniest crevice, is admirably suited to express the nature of a divine cleansing, and derivatively to represent the qualifications God imposes on things. We find somewhat analogous roles played by sand, wine, mud, the dance. But the fact that water or these others can be used in religious context or in religious ways does not mark them off as alone able to be appropriate objects for religious knowledge or as the best vehicles for making evident God's action or presence.

Everything contains some evidence of God's nature and existence. The point has been best put perhaps by Bonaventura. He takes all things in the universe to be either shadows, traces or images of God. A shadow for him is a thing most removed from God and least distinct in nature, a result of an undetermined cause, exhibited only in what is common to all things. The term is not altogether appropriate nor is its application beyond question. Though a shadow reflects only the outline of its object and is the result of a cause not manifest in it, it is yet the result of the fact that the shadowed object is impervious to some distant light. Were the things in this world shadows of God, there would have to be a light outside Him, and He would not be transparent. A better term is "impression." The things in the world might be said to exhibit an impression of God according to their capacities, and thus to point obscurely to Him as in some sense responsible for their being and nature.

When we take a thing, not as a source of an idea, but as itself a sign of something on which it and all other things depend, we understand God as a cause who has impressed Himself on the world. But why should things be viewed as impressions of God? We gain nothing by such a device but the opportunity to infer that there is a being which in some sense is a cause of, and perhaps is greater than, those things. It tells us nothing of His nature. To get an adequate grasp of God through the use of things, we cannot treat those things solely as impressions of Him.

A trace, for Bonaventura, is a thing which points to God as its formal, final, and efficient cause. The term is singularly appropriate. A trace is an effect which indicates the meaning, purpose, and mode of functioning of its cause. A good detective story is built up by adding trace to trace, while a poor one is little more than a tissue of impressions. From the traces we are able to deduce what the unknown individual is like, what his intent is, and how he attempted to realize it; from impressions we know only that there is a being who produced them. To view the things in the world as traces is thus to use them as satisfactory bases for inferring the nature of God, His providence and power. Yet without some further supposition things cannot be used as traces of God. Their formal causes are discoverable within the natural world, and their defects and limitations usually lead one to infer, not to some divine power or purpose, but to some finite and frustrated agent. If we are to move readily to God, we ought not view the things in the world either as impressions or as traces of Him.

Bonaventura thinks that men's souls are "images" of God, and then only if they are at once distinct and appropriate representations of Him. Since images are notoriously obscure and since God's nature cannot even be obscurely imaged, it would be better, however, to give up the term "image" in favor of some such term as "concrete meaning." A concrete meaning is a thing so far as it makes God's nature public, observable, and communicable. We can now extend Bonaventura's insight and note that *any* object whatsoever is treated as a concrete meaning, so far as we attend to it as valuable, self-identical and unified. It is then seen to necessarily point to a being who is absolutely perfect, self-contained and one.

Because each thing is ineluctably private it necessarily excludes other things; internally it is the other of the rest of the world. But unless it is to be described as merely other than the rest, themselves in turn being merely other than it, it and the others must each have a meaning of its own. Inside each thing are the natures of other things, not as they exist on their own but as pertinent to and controlled by the meaning of the given thing. It is this fact which enables a being to persist as self-identical despite changes in its body and the adventures it undergoes, for it always contains within itself the meaning, though not the being of anything it might encounter. If it contained the being of the others in the way it contains their meaning, the thing would be perfect, for to be perfect is nothing other than to contain within one's self whatever there is that is real. Since it contains only the meaning of other things without their being, a thing can be only abstractly perfect, something which, throughout its career, expresses what it would be were it to remain of the same nature and yet incorporate within itself all the actual entities that now exist outside its confines. If it has a mind it will separate out some of these meanings and interrelate them, and represent their objects in judgments and assertions.

Each being at once excludes the being of other things and controls their meaning. In the former guise it is imperfect, separate from all the others; in the latter it is an abstract perfect being which contains within itself the meaning of all the others. Each is a unity of abstract perfection and concrete finitude, interrelated and interdependent. As abstractly perfect it contains within itself the meaning of every other reality, as other than, yet essential to it. These contained meanings represent the natures of real objects lying outside its boundaries. The abstract perfection of a thing thus expresses the nature of that thing only so far as it also expresses the fact that the meanings which it contains are equally basic and objective, that there is, in short, an objective world in which they are all concretely embodied. The finitude of a thing, on the other hand, expresses the fact that outside things are objects which the thing limits, just as they limit it. The finitude of a thing is thus at once essential to the thing as well as a mark of the limitations of other things.

Since a thing is a unity of abstract perfection and finitude, as concrete it embodies two concrete meanings, the one expressing the nature of a totality of independent realities, the other expressing the fact that what is other than the being is limited by it. The two meanings, interrelated and unified, constitute the concrete actual being as portraying the nature of a unified, limited totality of all actualities. Each, since it portrays the unified totality, expresses the nature of something relatively perfect. At the same time each expresses the fact that it limits and is outside the very perfection it portrays. Only as the two together is it divinely qualified.

Only those divinely qualified items that are religiously conspicuous are of religious interest. They are taken not only to be affected and sustained by God, but to be freed from the environment and daily values, and to be known only when made the object of a distinctive attitude. They are treated, consequently, as being more heavily laden with the divine secret than other objects are. Analogous to what some moderns call a phenomenological object, and to what Merleau-Ponty calls an object of perception, they are objective, desocialized, but infused with the observer's interests. However, as these moderns and Merleau-Ponty do not seem to allow, they are also unitary substances.

The character of being "sacred" has a role similar to that characteristic of the features of aesthetic objects. The acknowledgment of those features is one with the acknowledgment of a real qualification of them by a being which exists outside them as their ground. If we look at a cave with an architectural vision, we see not something in neutral nature (since this is irrelevant to us) or a work of art (something architecturally *made*) but the contoured space of an external aesthetic object. If we look at that very cave in a religious spirit, we see it instead as sacred, with a unitary nature at once divinely qualified and grounded in God.

We know fellowmen, "other minds," similarly, so far as we attend to their acts as exhibiting a distinctive style. The acknowledgment of such acts is one with the acknowledgment of a consciousness embodied in those acts and as outside them, making them possible. We are unable to know subhuman beings in the way we sometimes know one another because they have no style, but only habits, reactions, and law-abiding moves.

Their acts neither embody nor refer to a consciousness, but instead exhibit and are sustained only by a life or energy.

A smile, a glint in the eye, a movement of the wrist could be treated as aesthetic or sacred objects, no less than as mere reactions of a body. But not until they are looked at as consciously qualified are they seen to be expressions of a man. And we do this quite simply, without being taught, and without preparation, by noting the response our gaze and acts awakens in him. We know one another because we see one another's acts to be distinctive, by virtue of what they embody and in what they are grounded. We have such knowledge from infancy. It becomes the norm in terms of which all things are dealt with. The child "anthropomorphizes" everything it confronts until it learns to distinguish things and animals as precisely those realities which do not accommodate those readings. The classical rationalists and empiricists take this residual outcome to be the primary fact of knowledge. They are bachelors in spirit if not in fact, and quite forget that they were once children.

In the history of culture a beginning does not seem to have been made with an anthropological outlook. The primitive's norm, it is often said, is the sacred object. This outcome may overlay or interlace with the anthropological tendency he has as an individual. In any case the primitive tries to treat everything as sacred until he learns that some men, animals and things do not readily allow for this evaluation.

It would be more correct to say, however, that the primitive begins with an acknowledgment of ultra-natural objects. He sees everything not as simply sacred, but as also vibrating with the force of all nature, (i.e., as *substantial* aesthetic objects) and as purposive, contoured by final values. Only much later are these different stresses separated out. But long before this occurs he finds that there are many repetitive and mechanical occurrences, frustrating his attempt to deal with them as charged with vitality, and many useless and trivial things, leading him to resist the tendency to deal with them as instances of some primary excellence. The world of common sense in which we live, contains both the ultra-natural objects (but not the ultra-natural realities which made them possible) and the residual items which have been denied an ultra-natural status. The positivists and naturalists take the residual outcome to be a primary one. They are members of no known society, in spirit if not in fact, and quite forget that they had ever looked at anything with wonder.

Things and animals and men have their own designs, and are to be approached in distinctive ways. When any of them is treated as ultra-natural, and of course when it is treated as sacred, it is faced in a new spirit.

All these approaches — the aesthetic, the anthropomorphic, the valuable, the sacred — can be and should be taken directly, though one can only gradually win the position at which they can be sharply distinguished and used in independence of one another. If we do distinguish them, we will approach the beings about us as humans, animals and things, some of which are treated as aesthetic, valuable or sacred, and the rest of which are dealt with anthropomorphically or conventionally.

Because nothing is entirely recalcitrant to a "primitive" approach, there is a sense in which every object is sacred. But it is also true that every one is also qualified in other ways. Traditional theology is inclined to assume that the divine qualification is or should be dominant always. But then it is forced to ignore the other qualifications, even when most insistent, or to suppose that they are to be assigned to different areas or functions of God — His mind, "body," etc. But one is then still left with the question of the unity of that God and the fact that these other qualifications are equally present. We must instead assume that everything has a sacred side referring to God but that this is sometimes subordinate to other dimensions, requiring a reference to other beings as ultimate as He.

Sacred objects are precious objects, worth attending to. They offer us evidences of God and some intimation of His sustaining role, in whom they and others are reproduced. God from this perspective is the great conserver, the preserver of all values, the lover of all good, the harmonizer of all conflicts, the being in whom all things find their place and are perfectly adapted to one another. But no one is satisfied to remain with sacred objects for long, since they can exhibit this nature of His only within the limits of a dense finitude. Reflective men sooner or later move away from sacred objects in the attempt to get a better understanding of God than those objects can exhibit or promote. Most are content to participate in a dedicated community which, as providing an occasion for the production of sacred objects, does more justice to God's nature and purpose than any objects can. But only if we have an adequate idea of God can we understand what takes place in the dedicated community, and what it is to which we turn when the community and the rest of the world are put aside. Since only an adequate idea of God will tell us what is encountered in an act of religious faith, it is eminently desirable to turn from sacred objects and try to get such an adequate idea.

5. The Idea of God

BY THEMSELVES men could perhaps manage to become good or bad, but without the idea of God to force them up or down, they could never reach the limits where ultimate virtue or vice, wisdom or folly, are to be found. The idea of God has weakened and strengthened, crippled and ennobled as no other has. To become really brutal or to achieve the sublime, men need the help of the idea of the divine. It has drained men of their energies and crushed them beyond the possibility of recovery, converting them into fanatics, painful to meet and look upon. It has raised sinners to the level of saints and made possible the achievement of works otherwise beyond man's reach. It inspired a literature and built a church, provoked an inquisition, and sent children out to be slaughtered by the Turk. It has forced men to their knees, lifted them above their time and place, ruined their lives and immeasurably enriched the meaning and value of the things to which they were most concerned. No other idea has proved so dangerous or has done so much good.

But an idea, whether of God or anything else, cannot work for good or evil unless it be impure. A perfectly pure idea would be the barest of possibilities, devoid of all structure and substance, an emptiness fruitlessly intending to express the meaning of "unity" as divorced from anything that could be one or unified. Such a pure idea could not possibly be conceived; it hasn't body enough to exist or to sustain a thought. The closest we can come to it is in the shape of an ultimate law of logic, for this contains nothing more than is necessary to distinguish the parts of it from one another. If a law of logic had less foreign content within it than it has, it would lose all definiteness and meaning; if it contained more, it would lose that transparent clarity which makes it so intelligible, and that flexibility which enables it to apply to everything in fact or thought. Nothing is so thoroughly lucid as the idea that each thing is what it is and not some other thing – and nothing is so bare. No other idea has such wide application, but then no other has so little to convey. The price a law of logic pays for its stark clarity and inexhaustible flexibility is the inability to express the specific nature of anything concrete or real. Some impurity must get inside the meaning of sheer unity if there is to be an idea at all; even more is required if the idea is to stand for some particular thing or things.

The idea of God is the idea of one who is the perfect unity of all meaning and value. It obviously cannot be as pure as a bare law of logic. Otherwise it could not express the distinctive nature of "meaning" and "value," or reveal how they could come together as a single unity. To be most adequate it must be less than perfectly pure.

Every idea is either *directly derived* by abstracting it from the being whose nature it portrays; *indirectly deprived*, by working over other ideas; or *engendered*, as a consequence of the effort to reach some end.

An abstracted idea is an idea directly derived. It is the nature of a thing, torn from its substance, rooted in our minds and used as a substitute and representative of the thing itself. It is by bringing into our minds what Aristotle termed a form of a thing that we become "informed" regarding that thing. To become "informed" in short, is to abstract an idea, to isolate an aspect of an object and use it as a surrogate of the being in which it was originally resident. Such an act enables us to retain a hold on the nature of the object while the object itself goes its own way. As a consequence, we are able to recall the object when it is no longer present and can recognize it when it comes again.

Abstraction is a precondition for memory and recognition. Yet an occasional thinker can be found who denies that there is such a thing as an abstracted idea. But since he is unable to affirm that his ideas have any necessary relevance to what actually goes on in a world which exists apart from him and is the source of what he knows, he cannot claim to know that the world is as he describes it to be – a world from which presumably no ideas could be derived by abstraction.

Most men, however, are not so easily trapped. They see that some of their ideas must be directly derived from and must accurately represent the things we daily perceive. Unfortunately, many of them think we never really perceive such concrete objects as tables and chairs, men and women, birds, bees and flowers, but only portions of them, and that, as a consequence, the only abstracted ideas we could have are ideas, not of things, but of fragments of these. Some of them, for example, affirm that the only abstracted ideas we could have are ideas of shape, size or motion. Others make the same claim for colors; a few defend the claims of beauty, virtue, goodness or truth. Each neglects the features the others emphasize, and all of them fail to acknowledge the concrete things without which these fragments could not be obtained at all. In different ways these men have jumped to the conclusion that, because true ideas accurately report the nature of things, those things must have less in them, must be less rich than men normally suppose them to be. But though the idea is an isolated aspect of a thing, it is that aspect as standing for something more concrete and complete.

It is not harder – perhaps it is easier, to judge from the testimony of artists – to perceive, and to obtain an idea of a man than of a color. We certainly seem to know the former before we know the latter. A sheer color, neatly cut off from an actual object, without any taint of shape, life, or substance, is something no child certainly, and no man usually, can obtain. To know a bare color taxes all one's powers of concentration and restraint. In any case, whatever reason one could offer for denying that we perceive and have abstract ideas of men and tables would be equally effective in destroying the supposition that we have abstract ideas of colors or sounds. If we deny that we directly perceive the concrete things of common sense because our ideas of them have less in them than those things are supposed to have, we would have to deny that we directly perceive colors and sounds, for the ideas of these are less rich than and lead a life different from that characteristic of their objective counterparts.

Again, if we deny that we can abstract an idea of a man and have it accurately portray the man as something more than what the idea of him contains, we would have to say that we have no abstract ideas of anything. We would then be confined solely within the circle of our thoughts and would know nothing of a world more substantial, and therefore more vital and dynamic, to which ideas might be referred and from which they were in fact obtained. But we are able to know things and yet use ideas which are not as rich as those things because we do not know by means of ideas alone.

To know anything in the field of perception, for example, we not only must have an idea of a thing but must integrate that idea with an acknowledgment of the location of the object, and refer the result to a world beyond, directly and intuitively apprehended. To perceive a dog we must have an idea of a dog as judged to be here rather than there in fact. Unless, however, we are also adumbratively aware of the dog as a being in which what we indicate is one with what we contemplate, we would have nothing to which we could refer, nothing to give our judgment body and truth. We must have abstract ideas in order to know, remember, and recognize, only because we use these ideas as components in judgments which purport to express the concrete source of those ideas and of the other components in the judgment.

One of the things that set the philosophic controversy going was perhaps the fact that ideas were confused, by the different proponents, with images. It is difficult, to be sure, to distinguish between the idea of an experienced color and the image we have of it. But that we sometimes distinguish them is evident, since we occasionally note that the image we have is irrelevant to what we understand. Moreover, there are men who seem to think without images, and they, as well as the rest of us, seem perfectly able at times to grasp the nature of things.

Images have an excess of impurity. We need not use them at all, since we can get ideas directly from the things we confront. But we can and do use them to serve as handy marks for the shape things normally have in the rough commerce of daily life. They are closer to the concrete being of things than ideas are. Consequently, we feel sometimes that we are getting closer to the heart of things by refusing to acknowledge any other abstraction but that of the image. Yet we could not abstract an image and know it as an abstraction (and thus as an image) unless we also had some knowledge not provided by that image. We could not know the *nature* of a thing as something intelligible, unless we turned from the image to the idea as less impure and more impartial and abstract. Nor could we reach the knowledge we have of the virtue or vice, or the promise or tragedy of men, unless we left images far behind. The image is carried on the crest of the moment and changes as the conditions of observation do. We need ideas if we are to reach outside the present to beings which remain self-same while their features and our observations vary.

We know there are beings which exist beyond the range of our ideas and images. That is why we know that what we understand or imagine is an understanding or imagination *of* something. To acknowledge that there are abstracted ideas is thus but another way of affirming that we do contemplate meanings, values, and natures which pertain to beings that are more than and other than what the ideas portray of them.

We must, if we are to obtain an abstract idea of a plant, animal or man, go far beyond the reach of the senses. To obtain an abstract idea of a living being, we must penetrate beyond the body in which it appears, for otherwise we would not know that it was alive and sensitive and perhaps responsible. And we have an abstract idea of a man only so far as we have caught something of his spirit and have thus an idea of him which reveals the dependence of his body on a consciousness beyond it.

An immersion in the being of a living thing, an identification of one's self with it, is a precondition for an adequate abstract idea of it. But to abstract the idea we must break up the union of ourselves and the object. To have the idea is to hold ourselves apart from the object of the idea. For an idea to stand for its object, there must be a distance between the being who has it and the object to which it refers.

To obtain an abstract idea of God, we must first make contact with Him and then abstract the idea in the course of a return to one's self. In one sense such an idea would be the most satisfactory of all the ideas of God we could get, for it would be an idea of a being whom one does not merely understand but whom one encounters and enjoys. In another sense,

however, it would be the most alien of all the ideas we could
have of God, for not only would it be almost without intelligible content, but it could be obtained only after a number
of very difficult conditions had been fulfilled. Since an abstract
idea of God is the idea of Him as existing in Himself, it demands
that one first arrive at Him. Also, it could be obtained only
after, on the one hand, we had lost our individuality and
neglected God's conceptualized nature for the sake of being
in Him, and on the other, only after we had lost our contact
with God and obtained a distillate of Him which could serve
as His representative. An abstract idea of God thus would
presuppose first a loss of ourselves and then a loss of the very
reality which that loss was to make available. The abstract ideas
we have of other things have similar virtues and limitations.
That is why we are not content to know through the agency of
abstract ideas alone, and instead have recourse to the experiments
of science, the constructions of mathematics, the productions of
art, and the speculations of philosophy in order to understand
what things really are. Just as we have to abandon perception in
order to know the world adequately, so in order to obtain a
clearer idea of God than that which could be provided by an
abstract idea, it is necessary to turn from abstract ideas to ideas
obtained in other ways.

ii

MANY OF OUR ideas are the result of a reflection on, a
working-over, a distillation of other ideas. The idea of what an
idea is, and the ideas we have of the laws of logic and higher
mathematics must obviously have some such source, for these
are concerned with objects much more formal than those
portrayed in ordinary abstract ideas.

The idea of God cannot be obtained by reflecting on the
abstract ideas we have of perceived things. Such a distilled idea,
is more tenuous and relates to objects less concrete than does
the abstract idea from which it was obtained. But God is not
a being less concrete than the things we daily meet. An adequate
idea of Him does not take Him to be less rich than the objects
of ordinary abstract ideas. If an idea of God is to be obtained by
distilling the ideas we normally abstract from things, it must
be an idea which, though highly general, nevertheless expresses

the nature of something most concrete and individual. This result can be attained if the distilled idea adequately expressed not only a nature, but the being in which that nature resides, for only then will it express more than any other idea possibly could. If we are to obtain an idea of God by some process other than abstraction from His being, it must be by deriving it not from ideas but from other beings.

A long-intrenched traditional answer to the question of how we can obtain an idea of God is that it is forever present within us, placed at birth by God Himself inside each man's soul. That answer unfortunately will not do. God is always in us but we do not always have an idea of Him. To suppose that we do is not only arbitrarily and somewhat circularly to hold that we have a knowledge of God only because He first bestowed His idea on us, but it is hard to reconcile with the existence of villains and atheists. If God had really put the idea of Himself in them, nothing they could do could dim its radiance even for a moment. If there is something divine in us, it cannot be a conscious idea of God, but only material out of which such an idea could be obtained in the course of the mind's activities. But unless we alone have some relation to God, similar material ought to be present within the recesses of every being, whether God put it there or not. No being can be cut off completely from God without God's dominion being seriously diminished. The most modest of Gods must, to be a God, be exhibited in everything. If we can find one thing removed from His province, we have proof sufficient that, no matter how dignified and eternal His nature, He is not worthy of the designation "divine."

We do not get an idea of God by distilling the ideas we have of other things, though as we have already seen, fear and terror, religious experience and sacred objects do make us aware of the awesome presence of God. If we wish to know God we must get an idea of Him through some other means than distillation. We must engender it.

iii

IDEAS CAN be engendered in two ways. We can work over and combine the ideas we already have or we can produce them within ourselves spontaneously. By the former method we obtain our ideas of fictitious creatures and mythical beings.

It is this fact which tempts many philosophical atheists and skeptics to maintain that the idea of God is obtained by exaggerating power into an unlimited force and combining it with a similarly exaggerated knowledge, love and life. They seem to think that if they can successfully hold this view of the origin of the idea of God, they have shown that He cannot exist. The contention has apparently alarmed some theologians to the extent that they have gone to the extreme of denying that the idea of God could possibly be obtained in some such way. Their contention is that the idea of God is a simple idea just as God is a simple being, and that any complex idea, resulting from a combination of other ideas, must falsify His nature.

It does not follow from the fact that an idea is engendered by combining others that it is therefore an idea of that which does not exist, or even that it is an idea of something complex. We have ideas of many existent things which are the result of combining other ideas. We build up our knowledge of regions far beyond our present reach on the basis of what we know goes on here and now; it would be tedious and intellectually stultifying if we were to affirm the existence only of those things which we have already encountered. We do not always wait for the objects of the world to present themselves before we frame ideas of them; we anticipate, predict, and deduce them and their traits on the basis of other things that we know. Much of what we truly know of the world is a result of reorganizing and combining what we previously knew. If, then, the idea of God were obtained by uniting other ideas, that fact would not in any way exclude the possibility that it was an idea of a real existent — though, of course, it also would not provide evidence for it.

Nor is there weight in the contention that the idea of God is the idea of a simple unity and that this simple unity could not possibly be obtained by bringing together a multiplicity, for the point is, not that the unitary being of God is achieved by adding together lesser beings, but that the idea of Him as a unitary being is the result of uniting other ideas. And it is not harder to unite ideas to form a single idea of God than it is to unite the idea of a horse and the idea of a man to form the idea of a centaur, or the idea of roots, trunk, and branches to form the idea of a tree. Just as there are no seams in the ideas of centaur or tree formed in this way, so there is no undesirable division in the idea of God obtained by bringing together lesser ideas. The ideas of centaur and tree are the ideas of unitary beings, and what is true of them is true as well of the idea of God.

But where do we obtain the idea of unity, so essential to differentiate the collection of a man's head and a horse's body from the unity which is the centaur, or the collection of roots, trunk, and branch from the unity which is the tree? The obvious answer is that any one of these parts will yield the idea of a unity more general than itself — an idea wide enough to encompass the part from which it was derived, as well as other things. That answer would be satisfactory were it not for the fact that it does not explain why it is that the idea of unity, instead of being the most abstract of intellectual concepts, is deep and rich, involved with our emotions and feelings. We have a different attitude when we think of a horse than when we think of its aggregate parts as merely alongside one another, and that fact cannot be accounted for by indicating how the idea of unity can be derived by abstraction from some idea which it is subsequently made to include.

The emotional element in the concept of unity is derived from ourselves. It is because, in trying to bring together a multiplicity of ideas, we are forced to retreat within our unitary selves, that our idea of unity is drenched with the feelings which permeate those selves. The more things we have to unify, and the harder it is to bring them in harmony, the more fully do we acknowledge them with feeling and concern. We are forced further back in the attempt to grasp the unity of animals, and still further back to grasp the unity of man. A man without emotions, one who is unable to recover his own solitude, can hardly be expected to see beyond the surface appearance of another. It takes one who thinks of others from the vantage point of his own most inward being to know what another man is like. There is a profound psychology contained in the Golden Rule that we should treat others as we would have them treat us, for in recalling ourselves to ourselves it enables us to see a little better just what the unity of another is like.

To get the idea of God, we must have a unity within which every possible idea could fall. This means that we must retreat far within our solitude to have a perspective in terms of which everything can be seen to belong with every other. In this way we obtain a standpoint from which all ideas can be solidified into a single unity. Thus, if we begin by framing the idea of sheer rationality and the idea of sheer power, we can obtain a single idea of a being, complementary to ourselves, at once completely reasonable and all powerful. Since the unity of that idea is provided by our most inward selves, it will be a unity which is permeated by spirit, and will itself express the fact that its object is a being something like us. But unless this object is recognized as an object of longing it is not to be identified with God. To obtain an idea of God as the object of a root desire, we must depend, not on our power to unify other ideas, but on our free capacity to bring forth a new idea.

That there are ideas which have no other origin but the spontaneous activity of the individual is a heresy in philosophy and a platitude in psychoanalysis. Psychoanalysts have rightly observed that ideas can be generated by men out of the stuff of their frustrations and inhibitions. Such origination does not, of course, disqualify them from being accurate reports of the things they portray. Both reliable and unreliable ideas are produced by the transmutation of one's unsatisfied desires into ideas. Sometimes the very nature of things is discoverable only through the agency of ideas which owe their origin to unsatisfied desires. If we were never hungry, nothing would be identified as food. It is hunger which converts the seed into an edible nut, a carcass into meat, a flame into a fire. Its value is not diminished but obscured when it leads us to mistake the toadstool for a mushroom, drives us to overlook the needs of others, and distorts the taste and smell of things. On the other hand, we are often aware of things in the world as inadequately expressed by the ideas we now have of them. We find it difficult, for example, to formulate an adequate idea of one whom we love. Only by forcing the mind to conform to the demands of our feelings do we achieve an idea appropriate to that which we confront. It is by following the lead of our feelings that we reach ideas appropriate to the things we have deeply experienced and thus in a sense already vaguely but surely know.

We can forge an idea of a being other than ourselves, existing over against us, uncaused and underived, necessarily existing in reality as well as in our minds. When we think that it exists outside our minds we do not of course make it exist there; what we do is frame to ourselves the idea of "something existing outside us." We forge the idea to answer to a fact, though we do not know the fact of course until we forge the idea. Having forged our idea, we may later discover that it answers to something in reality.

Our needs reach outward toward the world about us. When prevented from finding expression or satisfaction there, they are often repressed within us. They then seek egress through the avenue of the mind, coming to expression in the form of an emotionally tinged idea of what we actually need. Pictures of heaven, paradise and true bliss are largely ways of expressing the requirements for the perfect satisfaction of our repressed desires.

The idea most of us seem to have of God is one of our own unconscious making, forced out of the matrix of our bodily and mental frustration. It is an idea which goes far beyond the nature and meaning of the material out of which it is engendered. The idea is incidentally produced in the attempt to reach a goal not now within actual reach, offering a conceived satisfaction which is the other side of an actual disappointment. It is an idea of a God who is the counterpoise of our needs, and who expresses not only the meaning of unsatisfied desires, but the nature of that which we deeply feel regarding the things about us. The idea of God which we engender is the idea of a being to possess whom is to be satisfied, and who unites in Himself the felt values of the things we experience within and without us. It is an idea of a being one and self-identical, for it is an idea expressed in the unity which is ourselves. By means of it we refer to a being passionate and compassionate who satisfies our otherwise unanswered desires.

We obtain the most adequate idea of God as a being concrete, self-identical, omnipotent, and concerned, by retreating deep within ourselves in the effort to discover what it is we need, already know, and in some sense already possess. It is an idea which represents God as a being who is spiritual and one, concerned with finite beings beyond Himself. Unlike any other idea, it expresses not only something of God's nature as an object of the intellect, but something of His being as the object of need. It is the idea of the satisfying unity of all our wants.

Unlike any other idea, it reveals something of God's being as well as of His nature. Impure, being flavored by ourselves and our emotions as no other is, it is nevertheless an idea of God and not of ourselves. The unity of our desires as ideally satisfied, it requires neither revelation nor great intellect. We all have it to the degree that we are aware that we are not completely satisfied with anything less than that which is the answer to every basic need we may have.

We forge an idea of God for ourselves. This is true even if it be the case that God revealed Himself or even if we also had an a priori idea of God which He inserted in us. The idea which issues from our depths exists alongside our other ideas. We manipulate it as we manipulate them; from it we can draw implications. We can analyze it and synthesize it. And we can know through it that God exists.

iv

EXISTENCE is a predicate, an intelligible idea in terms of which we understand something. It makes sense to say "Griffins do not exist but giraffes do." But "existence" is not a predicate like "long-necked," "spotted" and "winged." It does not name some one feature in a thing alongside others. It does not tell us about some consequence which we can derive from the features which the thing has. Given an idea of something we do not add to that idea some extra character when we say or think that the thing exists. But then when we say "giraffes exist" do we say no more than "giraffe?" This seems absurd.

The fact that "existence" doesn't add another feature to an idea we have of a thing does not mean it contributes nothing at all. "Existence" locates the idea, places it outside the mind. Even those who follow Kant and deny that "existence" is a predicate, assume this. Kant himself tells us that something exists when it is part of the realm of experience, when it is connected with what is being experienced here and now. To know that something exists is, for him, too, to know more than what is contained in the idea of that thing. It is to locate it outside the idea, in a field where something occurs, not envisaged from the perspective of the idea. To exist is to bring about something which cannot be deduced. It is to be present and effective, having more consequences than the idea of the thing allows.

To predicate existence of something is not necessarily to confine oneself to the natural world. Platonic ideas do not exist there; nature itself does not exist there; God does not exist there. No account of existence is adequate, if it does not allow us to note the different ways and domains in which beings can be outside our minds and ideas.

Substances exist. By virtue of the existence in them, each is present, dynamic, possessed of power. If they can lose the existence which is in them, they are transient beings; if they never lose it in fact, they are permanent beings; if they cannot possibly lose it, they are necessary beings. We are transient beings; God is a necessary and therefore a permanent being.

Any idea or fancy we may forge is produced by us here and now. It is an existent idea or fancy. What it purports to speak about does not of course exist, but the purport, the intent, the idea of this non-existent thing exists, by virtue of being part of an existent being. When God knows anything through one of His ideas, those ideas exist because they are aspects of Him. Since the existence in Him is qualified by Him, the existence of His ideas will be different from the existence of our ideas, even when those ideas have the same reference or meaning. God's true idea of me has a different existence from my true idea of myself. It has different affiliations, different neighbors, different powers. It comes about through different efforts and has a relation to me which is different from the relation which my existent idea of myself has to myself. Similarly, my idea of God has an existence in me different from the kind of existence it has in Him. This idea of God which I have and which also exists in Him — as it must, if He is to know what I know of Him — is of course distinct from the idea of Himself which He has, regardless of what I think. My idea of God is, at best, an idea of an ultimate reality into whose depth I hardly go. His idea of Himself, which He has always had, is an idea that expresses what He is within Himself.

The most complete and satisfactory, the most neutral and systematic idea I have of God is existent in me in a way in which it is not existent in Him; its existence is also distinct from the existence possessed by the idea which God always has of

Himself. If God says "I exist" He says something different from what I say when I use the same expression. He also says something different from what I say when I assert "God exists." He says something different too, from what He would were He to say "You truly know that I exist."

It is possible to affirm that God exists and yet to deny that an omnipotent God exists. But though the two expressions are distinct, they say the same thing. One is merely more explicit than the other. All that is true of God is contained in the expression "God exists." To say this is to affirm the existence of an omnipotent, omniscient being. When we speak of His omnipotence and omniscience, or of His self-causation, person, forgiveness, etc., we speak of Him as related to something outside Himself. When we speak of His existence we speak of Him as having a career and being, standing over against those realities, exercising a power in independence of them. In and of Himself God necessarily exists. In relation to space He is omnipresent. In relation to time He is omniscient. In relation to the contingent, He is self-caused. In relation to things, He is a person. In relation to man's virtues, activities, promise, He is just, wise, loving, forgiving, merciful, wrathful — in short, a judge.

To know God's attributes is to know God's existence, but only so far as this is relevant to the existence in other existents. Such knowledge presupposes knowledge of those other existents and of the existence in them. And this is perhaps what the demythologizing theologians have in mind today when they speak of God's response to existential questions posed by men. If we know what man's existence requires, we know how to express what God means for him. However, it is to be noted that man is not the only existent being; God's nature answers to the "questions" posed by other existents as well. Also, God has a nature in and of Himself which does not depend on man's or any other being's questions. And since there are other realities besides God, each with its own existence, there must be questions which God asks that are answered by them. "What is extension," "what is vice," "what is emotion?" are questions which God may ask but which other realities alone can answer.

References to questions and answers are bound to be misleading, if they tempt one to suppose that first the questions are given and then the answers are provided. It will not improve matters to suppose that answers are first given and then that questions for these are found. Nor will it help to suppose that the questions come from one place and the answers from another. Questions and answers are coordinate, since they are constituted by whatever beings there are, in interrelationship with one another. Made verbal, given conscious form, question and answer both reach clarity together. We know what questions are asked by seeing what answers are forthcoming, and we see what the answers are by seeing what questions they answer. Progress in refining question or answer promotes progress in refining answer or question.

Were it not for the fact that God has a relation to other realities we would never have any basis for supposing that He exists. And since He, as related to, and ingredient in other realities, is a relativized version of what He is and of Himself, it would be wrong to suppose that in and of Himself He has the very properties that He reveals Himself to possess when involved with other beings. There are then two errors to be avoided: the denial that God is involved with other beings, thereby making Him into an ineffable, ultimate ground, and the supposition that by Himself He has the very properties He shows Himself to have when involved with other beings. The first of these errors is tempting to those who believe that God is the creator of all else, for then He is one who, before creation, is not involved with others, and thus is not necessarily involved and could conceivably not now be involved with that which He was supposed to create. The second of these errors is often made by those who defend the teleological and cosmological arguments for God, since they suppose that if God makes things work for an end, He too has as that end in view.

If we are aware of the presence of God in ourselves or others, we know Him as in the form of effects or in some other relativized and not necessarily separated consequence of Him. Because God exists in us and in others, we are able to have the true idea that He exists apart from us.

v

THE IDEA of God is distinct from any other. But it is one thing to have the idea, and another to know God by its means.

The fact that we have an idea of that Other which unifies all meaning and value does not mean that there is anything corresponding to it, or that if there is, that we have any acquaintance with it. Only because the idea we have is also ingredient in something else are we able to know that there is something answering to the idea, and only because we already in the idea have made some contact with that being that we can have an acquaintance with what answers to the idea.

It is possible to have an idea, and possible for that very idea to be possessed by some reality, and we not know that reality. We may fail to make the idea which we possess coincide with itself as elsewhere. A man can refer a sound idea of God to stones, statues, images and men. When he does he gives it a place in a finite reality. He then distorts its nature by taking it to be a part of that which is not able to fill out the idea. The idea can enable us to know truly only that being which allows the idea to be unaltered when it serves as a beginning of a more intimate contact with Him. To have a true idea of God our idea of Him must be unaltered when faced as exterior to itself in a context not provided by us. This does not mean it may not acquire new determinations, relations, affiliations. Indeed, this is inevitable. The idea is initially vague, without many details; it acquires determinations, becomes adequate only so far as we reach out beyond it for content which it does not now possess. Such additional content we usually get by participating in a religious community or by engaging in an act of faith.

6. The Dedicated Community

THE WORLD intrudes and God remains remote. Yet the religious man feels closer to God than he does to the world. To sustain himself in his venture, so perplexingly brightened and darkened in sudden ways and at unexpected times, he needs support. Only if he belongs to a dedicated community can he keep from slipping too soon or too swiftly from peace and joy to despair and anguish, from a confidence that he is justified and purified, to a feeling of loneliness, neglect and rejection.

A community of religious men arises in part because men need to have their individual follies curtailed, their lapses reduced in number and degree, and themselves strengthened and redirected. They are rarely conscious of these needs; the result in any case is soon overlaid with the pleasures which accrue from fellowship, the benefits derived from the corrections of others, the steadying habits of repetition and regularity, the lift given by celebrations, commemorations, dramatic events and holy days, and the power gained by joining in a common venture, particularly in the face of grave opposition by others.

It would be misleading to allow these observations to remain without a supplement. By themselves they might wrongly suggest that a dedicated community arises when a number of solitary religious men come together for mutual support and guidance. Such a view is freighted with all the difficulties that have hounded the theory of "social contract" from its inception — particularly, questionable history and untenable supposition. There is no warrant for the view that there ever was a time when men lived all alone for a while and then came together with others for mutual protection and help. They could not do so without somehow already being in agreement, for without such agreement they could not communicate, make a "contract," and keep to it. Men are societal beings as surely as they are individuals.

We are born into societies, and we mature in societies. These societies have traditions, powers and standards so imperious and stable that they are thought to be sustained and perhaps directed by a divine being existing outside the societies. Some men go so far as to suppose that the religious man's private life is but a delimited version of what is inescapably secular and public. But then what could be meant by "legalism" as a term of abuse? What could be meant by the distinction between the "letter" and the "spirit?" How could one account for prophets, heretics, ascetics, mystics, or the clash between the claims of society and a religion?

A man must change his attitude if he is to become a part of a dedicated community. The change has two stages. He must first replace his tendency to accept secular values and activities by a readiness to accept religious ones. And then he must replace a willingness to live in or in consonance with a dedicated community by a readiness to live as a contributive, constitutive member of it. A convert from the world to religion goes through the first stage; a monk goes through the second many times every day, reinstating himself, rather than converting himself. Both activities should be marked by some signal act. Circumcision, tattooing, sacrifice usually accompany the former. They are ways of cutting oneself off from the secular world. Even when the acts are easy and minor — sprinklings with water, statements of belief, the change in a garment, the swearing of an oath — their import is often tremendous both for the individual and the community. Though the monk has already taken this first step, he must constantly repeat it in the attempt to intensify and even change the direction of his thought and acts. This he can more readily do by reading sacred books, saying his prayers, or using his rosary. In all these cases a change in spirit is required. The change is thought by some to be produced by the signal act. But the act merely signalizes it. With time its edges can be worn and it may pass for something familiar and commonplace. It will then more likely than not preclude a change in spirit.

The men who come into dedicated communities often have some religious faith. When they retreat from those communities they purify and enjoy in privacy what they had obtained through participation. Religion is at once a public and a private matter. Were it only private there would never be a Judaism, a Catholicism, an Islam, a Buddhism. Each man would go his own way; the religion of each would be ineluctably closed off from that of every other man. The most that one could then expect is that the men might publicly act and speak in some accord, somewhat as lovers do. But not even Quakers, to whom the Holy Ghost is thought to speak in private, would go this far. If they did, their meetings would not be religious meetings, but just a concourse of bodies waiting for some soul to be quickened and forced to express rather than communicate the divine assault to which it was being subjected. Were the religion only public, it would be just a cult, a state religion, a common life having a quality and a reference marking it off from other common lives, but nothing more. There is nevertheless a point in distinguishing the private and the public side of religion as a way of getting clearer the nature of the problems each raises and the kind of contribution each makes to the other.

A dedicated community, even one that is world-wide, is distinct from all other types. It (and its members) are governed by distinctive aims, stresses and values. No man can belong only to a dedicated community, and some never enter any. There are always secular things to do, if only in order to be able to be well enough to be a member of a dedicated community. And those who give themselves to the religious life must distinguish daily commonplace acts from those in which there is a concentration on religious values. This is true even when one affirms that God is omnipresent, and that the most inclusive life is a religious one.

Religious men form a dedicated community only so far as the unity they constitute has something divine in it and refers to a divine being beyond it. Even if the community takes itself to exhibit only some effect of God in the form of a divinely established tradition, practice, mode of discourse, some revelation or message, it will encompass something of the very being of God. God's effects are not separable from Himself. He is present in what He does.

The acknowledgment of divinely qualified items in a community involves an at least implicit acknowledgment of God as the source of the qualification. That there is anything so divinely qualified or that there is a God beyond it is of course not known to anyone outside the circle of the dedicated community — though the fact that there is a God and that He is involved with other beings can be known through proofs and dialectic without entering into or ever participating in a dedicated community.

A dedicated community occupies a sacred place. This results from the conversion of a place outside the community into one where religious objects or practices occur. The conversion involves somewhat the same problems as those which confront the architect who must take account of the engineering, three-dimensional commonsensical space in the new space which he architecturally creates. Though the sacramental place has no being outside the dedicated community's identification, acceptance and prospective use, it is not entirely divorced from the space of every day. Every day space environs it; the sacramental space is a bounded, impervious region within it.

The space of a dedicated community provides a distinctive area within which individuals interplay. The connection between these individuals in that space is measured not by inches and feet, but by their affiliation to one another. It is a sculptured, divinized space of a multiplicity of men having a relation to a divine being existing outside that space.

Ideally, the dedicated community has a plurality of functions. It edifies, disciplines, supports and protects its members. It therefore insists on calling their attention to the primary facts on which it is grounded. In addition it inculcates fasts, stresses taboos, demands support, rejects blasphemies and heresies; it helps the children, the wayward and the lax, empowers the strong and cuts off those who are disloyal. Historic occasions are commemorated in its holidays, ceremonials and references, to make it the locus of an accumulation of traditions and funded knowledge. It is the ground for a determinate expectation with respect to the future of the group, and a defining base for an ideal end. A training ground, a laboratory, an educational centre, the dedicated community enables men to find their proper place in relation to God. Sacred itself, it is the occasion and may be the source and support of various sacred objects. It also provides a set of supposedly divinely sanctioned activities, and offers a sanctuary set off over against the rest of the world in which men can find some indication as to how they ought to direct their energies and use their time.

ii

MEN ACHIEVE many kinds of relations to one another in any society, religious or otherwise. Three are fairly common — the effective, the affective and the formal. If they have an effective relationship with others, they act in terms and in places which the rest help to define. If they have an affective relationship, they are prepared to unite with others in more or less intimate ways, thereby acquiring new qualities and careers. If they have a formal relationship, they are subject to rules and structures over which they do not have full control.

In the dedicated community all these relationships reflect the immanence and transcendence of God. The effective relationship there is between men who have an absolute status because they are taken to be loved by God for the eternal values they embody. No man is merely to be helped or dealt with considerately; each is to be seen as already partly and eventually fully a member of God's kingdom. He is to be attended to for his own sake. If use is made of him, it is not to achieve or maintain a superiority, even momentarily, but in order that he be benefitted.

In a secular society one sometimes puts oneself at the disposal of the other. The subordination is usually a means to make possible an eventual superiority. In the religious community a man makes himself the servant of another for that other's sake. He sets himself to do things which neither society nor ethics requires of him. The act is a self-sacrifice in the sense that the individual could have remained free from or on a footing with the other. Since he is a servant, not secularly but religiously, he may exercise this role even to his slave. The slave is then taken to be of eternal worth. It is no relief of course to the slave to be dealt with by his master in this way. The religiously sustained affective relation operates on a different plane from the secular. It brings about goods in one place while allowing evils to flourish elsewhere. This shows that though there is value in a religious context, there are also independently instituted values in other places.

One can enter into a formal relationship with another by making oneself and the other subject to some rule or law. Whatever is then done occurs inside a structure linking them all. In a religious community men are subject to a structure in which they are to participate in diverse but related ways, as a consequence of which they possess traits and have responsibilities they otherwise would not have. The acceptance of a responsibility greater even than that which others accept may, however, still leave one deficient in deed and virtue.

The priest, monk, or prophet is not necessarily superior to others anywhere but in the religious context, and then only as carrying out a role. The formal relation he has to others stops short of their personalities. It connects them all as having a generality of nature because linked by a general relation. Conversely, a man might take himself to be subordinate to others, and this not because of any intrinsic virtue or power they may have or he may lack, but because this alignment has been formally prescribed.

One can also enter into a formal relation with others so as to constitute a sensitively tuned set of elements. The structure here makes the items coordinate, without however precluding one of them from being an initiator and the others respondents, or from their taking turns as initiators and respondents. A religious formal relation of this sort relates men to one another in ways which neither they themselves, nor any secular device can provide. They are delicately attuned to one another so that they answer to one another's promise and intent; they penetrate beyond one another's surface because the relation starts and ends further within them than a secular relation does. God as it were intrudes the relation deeper within them than any mere movement into a public domain could promote.

Men effectively come together to constitute cooperative groups. They form communities, societies and states for mutual benefit. Religious men instead bring about a communion. They make a single body with one another. Each so unites himself with others that the interest of each is one with the interests of the rest, thereby constituting what Rousseau called a general will. Like Rousseau the religious man has faith in the ultimate integrity of each being, believing that he and others, through love, can constitute a realm where all are truly free.

It is often said, in the West particularly, that we ought to love our neighbor as ourselves because he is loved by God. So far as this is understood to mean that were it not for God's love of him he would not be lovable, the doctrine shows a singular insensitivity to the nature of man and the worth he has. But the formula hides a searching truth. The kind of love we owe a neighbor because of our love of God and because of God's love of him is distinct from the love we owe him in a purely secular or human situation. We are asked to love him in situations where hate is dominant and when we are unable to find a lovable trait. The love we are to give him for religious reasons is a love which has to do not with what he is in himself, or what he may prove himself to be in relation to other men, but what he and we are in the eyes of God. We are to love him for the love of God, and as a being who is loved by God.

When it is said that one is to love one's neighbor because he is loved by God we should intend to affirm not that the neighbor is not lovable in himself, that he has no worth, but that the kind of love which we extend to him is not possible except so far as we enter into a religiously affective bond with him — or more accurately, that to enter into a religious bond with him is one with loving him religiously. To love another religiously is to make an effort to deal with him as a being who is somehow like God, because loved by Him. No involvement with him as an individual is here implied, but only a giving up of one's own perspective and interests for the love of God, in order to enter into the perspective of another as already loved by that God. It is to be compassionate.*

No matter how closely linked men may be with one an-

---

* Compassion has often been understood as a kind of pity for the unfortunate; taken in this sense it is distinguishable from true religious love or charity. Complete compassion involves a mutuality of sensitivity. Each is aware of the defects and failures and sufferings of the other. Each orients himself in that other and does this because that other is grasped as one whose proper destiny lies outside the area where the suffering occurs. The solidification of mutually compassionate beings is the production of a unity which is oriented toward God because each of the beings approaches the other as one who is to be translated, lifted out of the situation where the suffering occurs, and dealt with as one whose true nature and career is to be understood in new terms.

other, no matter how much they may be affected by one another, in the end each must evaluate in his own terms what he obtains. Each man is as surely outside the community as he is inside it. He is able to enter into it with a nature and power of his own, and what affects him there is given a private assessment by him. But before he can attain this stage he must learn to stand apart as one who had been and will be in the community. Whatever is then said of him will relate to an individual whose meaning, values and career are given by the social system. Sociologically-minded thinkers suppose that it is such a withdrawn individual who enters into relations with others. If they think that he does not have a private life of his own, they are surely mistaken. Yet for the most part, our language, our beliefs, our attitudes and even our moral principles are rooted in the social world over against which we for the moment stand. The reformer, the revolutionary, the rebel, and the criminal are all social men, even though they stand over against and even oppose the established order.

Additional powers, virtues and rights are achieved in religious communities. If those communities are accepted by men, the men acquire new powers, virtues and status. It is this fact which Socrates apparently had in mind when he awkwardly said that men have no right to commit suicide because, like cattle, they are the possessions of the Gods. Yet whatever status they achieve in a social context they can withdraw from because they have a being over against that context; there they can continue to enjoy what they had previously acquired. But they cannot escape from a religious community without giving up what they had thus gained. Religious men withdraw from religious situations as beings who had subjected others, been subjected by others, or been co-ordinated with them, effectively, affectively or formally. The virtues and values accreted there require continued participation, if only indirectly.

A community is an aeon, a unity of time and eternity, a "moving image" in the sense that the eternity is reinstated at every moment in a dynamic way. Each dedicated community recapitulates or restates in finite terms the nature of the divine being who is a constituent of it. Each provides a plurality of occasions, all of which are to be united and ordered inside a single meaning or truth. Since the individual not only always is but insists on being private to some extent, there is always a component of "sin" within him which requires him to resist or reject God, even when submitting to Him. Even the religious community rejects God. If it did not, it would cease to be over against Him. Even while it embodies Him it holds itself over against Him so as to have a life of its own.

A dedicated community embodies God and refers to Him as outside that embodiment. The embodiment is constitutive of the community and has no being or meaning outside it. It can be said to be a miraculous occurrence producing the difference which separates off a dedicated from a secular community. Inside the dedicated community there may be outstanding occurrences which we prefer to term miraculous, but these all presuppose the first miracle, the embodiment of God in the community. Such a miracle does not involve a violation or suspension of the laws of nature. Those laws still characterize the beings and occurrences in the community, but they fail to encompass all the meaning and value that is present there. Though it is traditional to speak of the miracle as simply produced by God, from the perspective of the community it is an occurrence which is inseparable from the way in which its members interplay. If that interplay be thought to force the entrance of God into the community, we have magic; but if it is only the occasion for such entrance, the miracle can occur even without deliberate action on God's part. The effect of the miracle is to alter the men, to transform and to save them by virtue of their acceptance of and participation in the great event.

Miracles are always occurring, or there is no such thing as religion, for a religion is nothing more or less than a locus of unions of God and men. Every miracle reflects the fact that God is entering into a domain in which He attends to something outside Himself, at the same time that men attend to Him.

All revelation, and thus all miracles and sacraments, dissolve a mystery, divulge its secret, and yet at the same time testify to the fact that the mystery still remains. This paradox arises because the mystery and its dissolution exist only for a participant and only so far as it points to a reality outside itself. For one who does not accept or share in a revelation, the mystery of the religious man is twice-removed. He fails to grasp what is divulged and he fails to grasp the fact that there is a deeper secret still to be learned.

A mystery in religion is always both dissolved and un-touched. Were it not dissolved at all one would not only be faced with something unproved, but would not know that there was something there which was of religious significance. Were the mystery entirely dissolved, the divine would have been captured in an alien setting and thereby precluded from con-tinuing to be and act as an independent reality. It is conceivable, however, that one mystery could be completely revealed, there-by making another evident. A religious book or a set of laws, though divinely instituted, might be transparent for a true believer; but he will then find, in the very act of grasping the import of the book or laws, that there are still other mysteries facing him. These others could be said to be forms of the first, or all of them together could be taken to be expressions of a still unproved divine truth. Either way, no matter what mysteries are resolved, there will always be others still unresolved. But a religion is only one of a number of ways in which contact is made with God. What is mysterious for it may be quite under-standable from another position.

A mystery does not necessarily lie beyond the power of the finite mind to dissolve unaided. It is not necessarily that which defies the intellect. A speculative philosophy might conceivably explain it. Though the intellect is not as effective as emo-tions, faith and worship are in achieving an intensive intimate union with others, it does have a greater range and reach, en-abling one to grasp what God is not only for the religious com-munity, but in relation to other communities as well as to other realities not of concern to the religious spirit. But no philosophy of itself will enable the individual and God to interpenetrate.

There are many ways of dealing with ultimate realities. Each way achieves results not open to the others; none is wholly adequate. Each therefore faces mysteries it cannot master. None can justly claim that what is mysterious for it cannot be mastered from other positions. No one can, therefore, justly claim that there are mysteries which never can be resolved, for such a claim would require him to have somehow understood the nature of the mystery and have fully grasped the nature, strength and weakness of every possible mode of dealing with it.

Every approach to reality is streaked with dubiety. Each leads to an understanding not open to others. The philosophic is no exception. A complete philosophic study has as its aim the examination of what is, from all basic positions. It seeks to distinguish the essential dimensions of reality, and to clarify the way in which beings are together. The exhaustion of all possible approaches and their unification in the philosophic system takes place over against the actual use by artists, religious men, historians etc. of one or more of these approaches and the neglect of others. For philosophy, too, then there is a mystery. This is dissolved by dealing with it concretely and directly through the various particular, limited approaches. Conversely, what is mysterious to any and all specific approaches is not mysterious for it.

Each specific approach faces a mystery which some other specific approach may dissolve, but all the specific approaches face a mystery that is to be resolved only in philosophy. A given specific approach has its mystery dissolved thus from two perspectives — a specific and a general. Both are necessary. If some specific approach did nothing to clarify what was left mysterious by others, it would not impinge on the same reality from a distinctive and effective angle; if all specific approaches exhausted reality, the fact that they did would not be known. Nor would one know that there was any thing which they diversely specified. The object of all approaches is not to be found in any one of them.

The religious approach to God is but one of a number. Ethics, history and art supplement the work of religion. Each approach throws some light where the others face mystery. The God on which they all converge is a God who can be known apart from them, in theology and in philosophy for example. These in turn do not confront God in a particular community. The God to which the philosopher attends is, however, not religiously available to the theologian. In turn the religiously available God is mysterious to the philosopher. But the philosopher can know the nature of God and understand what it is for Him to be both immanent and transcendent. He can know what is faced in other approaches though he does not himself take these other approaches.

God exists outside all dedicated communities. He also exists inside all dedicated communities. He is at once transcendent of and immanent in them. If those communities cease to exist He ceases to be immanent in them. But nothing they can do, nothing that happens to them, can make Him lose His transcendence.

A member of a dedicated community is aware that God is outside the religious community while he participates in that divinely affected community. The mystic instead starts with the revealed God and goes beyond this to the being of God as outside the revelation for he is primarily concerned with what the community defines to be a mystery. The community for him is thus but an occasion enabling him to encounter God. If successful he experiences God in himself and experiences himself in God. God still has a being of His own not encompassed by the mystic, and which can be known by the philosopher and acknowledged in faith or worship. These are desirable ways of facing God which are distinct from the mystic's, though the mystic sometimes speaks as if they had none or little value.

The mystic gives himself to the God which the community acknowledges to be outside it. In the giving of himself, he does not affect the God as in the community. While uniting himself with the God pointed to by the community he leaves untouched and mysterious the very dimension of revelation which the religion in fact enjoys.

God has a number of dimensions, each of which has its aura of mystery. He is embodied in a community and is pointed at by it as still outside. He is an integral element in non-religious contexts, such as ethics and politics, history and art, and is sometimes referred to in non-religious ways. He can be mystically encountered outside these specific contexts, while continuing to be in them. In addition He is an object of knowledge, a knowledge which recognizes the mystery that confronts all the other approaches in their severalty.

From the perspective of a dedicated community, God has a status of His own, relevant to that community and its members. It knows Him in its own terms and points to Him as one who can become available to others. It tries to come closer to Him, but it also at times moves away from Him — or more accurately, individuals in it sometimes move closer and sometimes withdraw from Him. The withdrawal is no idle movement. Withdrawal is an act by which a man moves away from the context with what he acquired there, somewhat modified. He who withdraws from a religious community is rewarded or punished. He gains or loses meaning or power. The religious man's withdrawal is evaluated by God. If there is a gain it has the form of a reward or a forgiveness, depending on whether a good is divinely added or an evil is divinely taken away. If there is a loss it has the form of a punishment or a deprivation, depending on whether some evil is divinely added or a good is divinely subtracted. God adds to or subtracts from what the man acquired. Though he is withdrawn he is therefore still related to God, and some of the items acquired before the withdrawal are made part of the individual's private being. The result is of course not known to others. Often it is not known to the individual himself. But did it never occur, public adventures would not have repercussions on a man in his privacy.

Participation in a situation, whether effectively, affectively or formally, involves some risk. A man can conceivably be subjugated to his detriment; he may be overwhelmed even when he starts off as agent. But in participating in the larger situation some good is done — if it is good that that larger situation be in existence. When a man withdraws from such a good situation he can be accredited by God with some of the value he helped bring about. He will then in effect be rewarded for what he did inside the religious context. The recognition that men are elected through no act of their own or that they are incapable of purchasing a divine reward, does not conflict with the fact that they can be rewarded for what they have done, for the rewarding here is but a redefinition of them, the enhancing of them by what had been accreted in the situation.

Since time cannot run backwards, what has been done cannot be undone. To speak of forgiveness is not to speak of undoing anything. The forgiveness is oriented toward the situation; it enhances what before had been involved with others. It is not then the impossible act of changing the past, making what had been not be, but the redefining of beings and their effects so that they have a higher value, when withdrawn, than they had before when part of a particular situation. God forgives by the wiping out of regrettable states, by removing a stain which a being has in relation to others. This is done by giving him a new boundary and import as he stands away from others. There is a divine forgiveness so far as a man is enabled to hold himself apart from a situation and be free of some of the stain he there acquired.

Divine punishment is no act of violence, no expression of anger or vengeance, but the redefinition of a man in the light of what he had or had not done. When he stands apart from others, he who is punished will lack those powers and virtues which he would have had were he religiously together with them. The sloth that marks a man in a social context is divinely shaped into a vice when he stands apart from that context.

There are some goods which can be accredited to a man only so long as he participates in a situation. Some such idea as this Milton seems to have in mind when he speaks of the loss which the highest of the angels, Satan, suffered on withdrawing himself from the beatific vision. On his withdrawal from the relation he had to God, Satan lost what he had achieved before.

The religious man's relation to the dedicated community is similar to the relation which a secular man has to society. Both men can be viewed as truncated, anticipatory or residual forms of what they are in the public context. Since on withdrawing both can give a private meaning and role to what they publicly accreted, both must also be recognized to have a private side which is quite distinct from a truncated, anticipatory or residual form of the public.

Faith is a private religious act as surely as participation in a dedicated community is a public religious one. It is as wrong to take the former to be a variant of the latter as it is to make the latter into a variant of the former. One might conceivably enter into the community from a secular one, or from a privacy which had no religious import. The first of these moves contains the second as a part. A member of a secular community, in order to become a part of a dedicated community, must first withdraw into a non-religious privacy. To become part of the dedicated community he will then have to undergo something like a conversion. But unlike one who, on privately acquiring a religious faith, turns from the world to God, the turn here will be toward a public religious world, itself oriented toward God.

iii

IN A DEDICATED community the activities of a number of men are regulated in relation to one another and to other beings.

The dedicated community may have its own rules and property. It can exist without a creed — as it did when it was little more than a series of agapistic feasts, and as it does for the most part now in contemporary Judaism. The members of the community have features it does not have, and it has features they do not have. Not alive, without passion, it gives them a new status, powers and promises. Usually it outlasts any one of them. But to all it adds determinations, to all it provides affiliations. It habituates them all, and continues to do so as long as its members act harmoniously. It gives fellows to each at the same time that it cuts him off from other men and makes him part of its mystery. Yet no one ever succeeds in being only a part of it, not only because all also belong to other groups but because each man is an individual with a distinctive life and career.

A dedicated community has an esoteric and an exoteric side. Some of its members devote their lives to it, while others seem only to share in its benefits. Both of these classes subdivide. There are professionals who turn away from and professionals who attend to other men and claims. Some laymen support the activities of the community, others are supported by it.

A dedicated community may be but need not be organized. The Jewish community has no organization; nor does the Hindu. If there is an organization, it has rules or laws, an authority to back them up, and individuals to whom they apply. Unlike a secular society, it is usually not built up out of families. Nor does it usually support itself. It is not final or self-sufficient. Its members or others must function outside it at times in order to enable it to exist. It could be built along Hobbsean lines and deny intrinsic rights to its members, but it would be better for it to follow Aristotle's lead and make it a universe where men can have rich careers, with the religious purpose governing the ethical, educational and perhaps even the political, historical and aesthetic lives of its members.

A secular society has as its end the promotion of peace and prosperity. A dedicated community has as its end the effective enhancement of its members through the glorification of God, and the glorification of God through the effective enhancement of its members. The society and the community ought to support one another. Men have a right to belong to and to participate in a dedicated community. The ideal secular society will make it possible for them to have a richer existence in some dedicated community, and the ideal community will make it possible for them to participate more fully in society as well as in other domains.

iv

EVERY GROUP imposes sanctions; otherwise it would have to content itself with futile admonitions, gratuitous pieces of advice and the episodic good will of its members. The dedicated community demands obedience or cuts one off from itself. This means there must be power behind it, particularly the power to punish by exile, separation, the denial of a right to share in the fellowship.

A compelled obedience, it is sometimes thought, is of no worth. But men must be made to behave in certain ways even in the face of their refusal to heed, both in secular society and in a dedicated community. They ought to be habituated in their responses, particularly if in this way they will do what they ought. It is one thing of course to compel men to adhere to a certain mode of activity because they are thereby brought to do the things they ought, and another merely to claim that is the case.

The dedicated community not only sets conditions which must be met if one is to continue to be part of it; it sets conditions which must be met before one can be admitted into it. The one set of conditions defines the loyalty of the members, the other defines their religious status. It is possible for one to have a religious status and not be loyal; it is also possible to live in conformity with a community without having taken the requisite steps to be a member of it.

A dedicated community categorizes a public experience and thereby enables its members to relate themselves to God, outside the community and the experience. It offers a place and provides the occasion for the glorification of God, the acknowledgment of Him in appropriate terms. But it need not make use of a particular building or locality. It may be content to have the men come together, at various times, and then and there constitute a vital religious body. But it should provide protection for sacred objects, and offer the norm for their use. Usually it tells about or exhibits an excellent being which its members are urged to imitate or submit to.

A dedicated community can be viewed as something final, the very being of God Himself as interrelated with man. This will not preclude it from still remaining outside God, or for being dependent on other realities and interacting with them. It always has determinations of its own, and always lacks determinations which God and man have apart from it.

It is one of the functions of the dedicated community to show men how to act with reverence toward sacred objects, and thus toward an immanent God. God is of course also transcendent; He exists outside those objects and the community. He is in fact symbolized by the former and referred to by the latter. The members of the community come to know God as immanent so far as they sense extra powers in sacred objects; they know Him to be transcendent so far as they worship.

From the standpoint of the dedicated community, God is a final reality to which it and its members should submit. If a community were to view God merely as its unity, it would have Him too close. If it were to view Him as completely outside itself, it would set Him too far away. A genuine dedicated community brings Him close but not too close, precisely because it faces Him as outside it. It also faces Him as distant but not too distant, precisely because it embodies Him in the form of its unity.

To ask whether the God of some community exists is to ask whether the community is a dedicated religious community. The existence of such a community is inseparable from God as at once immanent and transcendent. Might not the community be mistaken? Not in what it experiences and not in pointing beyond itself, but only in what it affirms, only in what it asserts to other groups. Might not the immanent God be an invention or a mere product of the community? He surely could be, were God not faced as transcendent too. The community points beyond itself, presumably to a God outside it. But perhaps there is no being at which it points? This certainly could be the case. But if it were, the community would be deluded, not truly dedicated. However, no one can rightly say that it is in this state unless he can show that there is no God to which its members in fact point, or that the members of the community do not act together as religious men should. Since apart from the community, the existence of God can be demonstrated, and since He can be encountered in private prayer, there is evidently a God outside the community who could conceivably be embodied in and pointed at by the community.

The dedicated community is a union of men only because and so far as those men are at the same time united with God. God is present in the community as its distinctive unity, transforming the men into a plurality of avenues and agencies for Him. In it God becomes present and men achieve a distinctive dignity. A divinely determined unity with divinely constituted agents, the community is thus a one and a many together. Since the unity which God provides is inseparable from Himself as outside the community, men by participating in the community are inevitably related to God as outside it. Since each man has a being, nature and career outside the community, God, to make use of them, must also take account of the way in which they exist apart from the community.

The dedicated community has relations to other groups, larger and smaller, such as the family, village, society, school and state. And in the end it must be related to all the people in a community, to mankind, and to the basic types which define the culture — hero, ethical man, prophet, worker, soldier and the like. It is also to be treated as part of a political, historical or instrumental world and should then be evaluated in terms of the way it contributes to or hinders the achievements of the particular outcomes of those worlds.

The dedicated community provides distinctive affiliations for its members, and makes distinctive claims. It has its own codes and eventually its own laws, which may conflict with the positive laws of the state or be out of gear with the laws which govern other groups. In relation to the people which make up a larger community and eventually mankind, it is at its best when it functions as an epitomization, guide, teacher or reservoir. To evaluate it, account should be taken of the contribution it makes not only to its own set purposes, but to the larger or at least different purposes which men have as beings who exist not only in dedicated communities but in other ways as well.

When the members of a community look at the world outside in terms provided by the community, they, in effect, treat that world as a continuation of the community. The world for them then has a divinely constituted unity and a transcendent referent. It is seen to be a more attenuated but larger community than that in which they participate. In constituting a dedicated community men then evidently provide God with a new opportunity to be encountered, here and now by anyone. But since the members of the larger community are unaware of the unity which the religious man takes them to constitute, they can be said to be members of a genuine dedicated community only as intermediated by the religious man and the dedicated community to which he belongs.

v

A STATE sometimes makes place for a dedicated community. Why should it? Why not deny it all rights?

One can think of religion as a kind of device for keeping people quiet or for teaching them to obey the sovereign; societies and states have again and again taken over religions as agencies for the promotion of social and political ends. But no matter what they do, they leave over the private individual and his private relation to God. The acknowledgment of this fact has led some to make political provision for the freer exercise of this right. But the best reason why men should be allowed and even encouraged to be religious is that it is commanded by a natural law which has a supranatural sanction.

No consideration of the nature of the state demands that all knowledge be encouraged or supported. Yet a state ought to encourage the pursuit of knowledge. Its customs and laws should make provision for the adventure and risk of inquiry. To justify a concern for knowledge on the part of society or state one must have recourse to God, the being who qualifies the Ideal Good to justify a concern for values outside the scope of political interests.

The care of the sick and the aged, the toleration and even the feeding of animals, the rejection of various foods and resources, and the utilization of others are incorporated in many customs and positive laws. Such acts are politically gratuitous. They evidently cannot be defended on the grounds that they benefit society or state or most of their members. The gratuitous acts might, as a matter of fact, increase the risk of failure in man's perpetual combat with nature and other groups. It is true, of course, that there are societies and states where the ill, the aged and the alien are treated well, even though they benefit no one. This fact does not undermine, but instead supports the view that when societies and states take the opposite tack they are to be opposed, not on political but on religious grounds. Men in a state help the useless because this is what is required of them by their God; apart from divine prescription, there is no reason why any one of them should help. God, too, makes provision within the very heart of politics, for various ethical matters. Politics and ethics are after all quite different in intent and objective. Ethics is absolutistic, universal, comprehensive, applicable to all men and eventually to all that is. Unchanging in content, it is an object of intent and will, affecting one's character as well as one's world. The political world, in contrast, is a world of public beings engaged in public acts. It is relative, particular, changing, limited, never encompassing man's privacy or his character except so far as public acts have their repercussions on what a man privately is. But customs are modified and laws are forged in order to take account of what is ethically discerned. In order that what is politically viable have ethical import it is necessary to deal with the political in terms which are broader than any it can provide, and which in fact take account of what men privately are, ought to decide, and individually do, sometimes without having any public consequences. The bringing to bear of the ethical common good on the political good to constitute a general good is the work of God. Without Him we would be forced to say that the introduction of ethical considerations into politics is at least impertinent and at most dangerous and misleading.

There is a distinctive natural law for every society. To account for its presence and particular nature recourse has to be made to God. When this is done the law becomes supranatural in nature. If we acknowledge it we can recognize our own society and state as being part of a larger whole when and while we remain within it. We will have a distinctive destiny and distinctive duties, but will be able to see them as analogous to the destiny and duties of others. If we did not recognize that the supranatural law was pertinent to our own society, we would be able to go no further than to recognize that our society is different from others. Our specializations would have no genuine relation to one another, but would be only diverse instances of the common good.

A supranatural law is grounded in God while pertinent to us; when it is dealt with as the latter it is also recognized to be the former. If we follow a supranatural law we are at once subject to a natural law and to God. While we live up to its demands we will belong to a particular society or state. We will also attend to a rationale, a power, divisions and values introduced by God. We may act as does one who conforms only to a natural law, but we will, unlike him, be able to turn away from the world governed by that law. We will be chained in a cave in such a way that we could, should we wish, drop off the chains and go elsewhere. We will stand in between cave-dwellers and those outside, but be capable of immersing ourselves in the affairs of either. The supranatural law enables us to act inside a context and yet remain outside it. It enables us to do our duty in our situation and yet cut ourselves off from the fruits of our acts and thus make ourselves able to identify ourselves with any and all fruits. We become citizens of the world not by immersing ourselves in a limited situation or by turning away from the world altogether, but, while functioning inside a limited situation, recognizing that we belong to a larger one. Such recognition is ours when we see in a natural law, which is open to the secularly minded man, the marks of God's concern, the source of supranatural law.

Men have rights in themselves. These come to expression in the form of civil rights. But one cannot determine from the perspective of a state whether or not this translation is correct and adequate, particularly since the state as such does not recognize native rights except so far as they have been translated into civil ones. The translations, and the evaluations of the translations, depend upon a perspective outside the natural law. This God provides. Supranatural law is a natural law which takes account of the fact that men have rights apart from the state, and that a state is to be judged as good or bad in terms of the way it satisfies those native rights.

To see anything in subhuman beings deserving of respect, consideration or compassion is to become alert to the fact

that they too possess values which owe their presence to
God. In and of itself there is value in a snake or a fish; but that
it has rights outside the social context and beyond the ethical
claim that unnecessary suffering is to be avoided, is not knowable
without making a reference to the religious dimension. The
rights of subhumans are supranaturally possessed.

No matter how pertinent an ethical common good might
be, and no matter how beneficial it might prove for men to
follow the natural law which that good prescribes, men may
not find it appealing. It must be made persuasive. Natural law
to be sure makes an appeal to man's conscience. It awakens
the reformer's zeal, and guides the reflective judge's decisions.
It has an insistence to it which it does not derive either from the
end men together constitute or from the structure which it
itself has. It is what ought to be followed if we are to bring
about the social and political good. But though we aim at that
common good, it does not follow that we will in fact conform
to the natural law it sanctions. Nor does it follow that the common good at which we aim is one which we really adopt. We
may point to it, accept it as a goal and a lure but not in fact
use it, identify ourselves with it, adopt it as an end which is
felt to be that which we ought to adopt. By acknowledging
God to be the power behind the natural law and the common
good which endorses it, we come to feel that a violation will not
only make us do what we ought not, but that God in fact will
take our act to be wrong. There is considerable desire in most
men to follow some natural laws, and this not merely because
they do not like the feel of guilt but because they do not like
the divine judgment behind this, and thus the sin which underlies the guilt.

It is tempting to take natural law to absorb supranatural
law, or conversely. But were there no natural law, all groups
would be governed by conventions and positive law for which
there was no evaluation except by divine decree. Were there
no supranatural law there would still be a plurality of natural
laws. Some of these though would lead men to realize their
apparent, not their actual common good. It is supranatural law
that tells us, as we have seen, that men should be encouraged
by their states to pursue goals, to achieve values, to engage in
activities which have no political value.

Men who live in the light of a divinely sanctioned general good, and the supranatural law this entails, live in a religious state. But not until all conventions and positive laws are in consonance with the laws which the general good demands for a secular state, will that state, without losing its political integrity, be a religious state, exhibiting some of the values of a dedicated community. That state, like a dedicated community, will then embody and make reference to God, but unlike a dedicated community will do this only through the mediation of the general good.

Men would live in a just but purely secular state were they governed solely by natural law. If the state ignored the natural law, or lived in opposition to it, the state would be unjust. Most states today are partly religious and partly secular, and so far as they are secular are only partly just. Only some of their conventions and positive laws are in consonance with what a divinely qualified good, i.e., with what the general good demands; only some of the remaining conventions and laws are in consonance with what their common (secular) good demands.

A religious state is not to be identified with a church-state. A church-state is a dedicated community which is constrained and subjugated by being brought inside the confines of a political system. A religious state is a political system which has been ennobled by becoming attentive to divinely determined values. Nor does the religious state depend on the presence of pious men or religious institutions. A religious state requires no more acquaintance or concern with God than that which is open to a deist or a philosopher. All one need know is God's effect on the common good, and thus on the natural law pertinent to a state. This knowledge can be achieved through speculation. But a dedicated community requires participation by a number of men in the adventure of a direct embodiment and reference to God. A religious state offers a political substitute for such a community; it does not replace it.

From the standpoint of politics, the dedicated community is to be tolerated only so far as it is in consonance with the structure and demands of the religious state. When that state encourages religion, it does so only so far as the religion is seen to make for a full life of a public man who is primarily political in interest and activity. The subjection of the church to the state does not preclude the encouragement of the church or of private worship. The state demands merely that the church not go counter to what law requires. The state need not stand in the way of parochial schools, tax-free religious buildings; it may grant privileges to the clergy and encourage religious education on the grounds that these contribute to the full life of a politically governed man involved in multiple activities which are all subordinated to the political life. But it cannot support any of them as independent enterprises, any more than it can support art or sports or speculation or any other activity so far as these are taken to have precedence over the political, or to have the right to ignore or oppose the laws of the state. When then in the United States, the Roman Catholic Church demands tax-supported services for the children taught in its schools, it must so far be willing to submit to supervision to see that its teachings do not lead pupils to suppose that religious values have precedence over political ones. Religious values do have such precedence, but only from the perspective of a dedicated community, and not from the perspective of a state, religious or otherwise.

When the demands of the dedicated community and the religious state conflict, the answer must be war, or the adjudication of the claims of both in terms which neither dictates. They must be dealt with from the perspective of a possible full life in which each man accretes all the values obtained by the devoted pursuit by different men of the goods of the various basic enterprises. Short of that, the religious state, though more powerful than the dedicated community, from a religious standpoint, is to be viewed not only as an inadequate substitute but as a dangerous competitor. It offers even more of a threat to the community than a purely secular state does, since it does find room — though only in its own terms — for values and activities which the secular state ignores or even precludes.

7. Religious History

A SECULAR HISTORY has its own time, space and dynamics. It is an autonomous, self-contained domain with distinctive items and pace. It cannot, I have elsewhere tried to show, be properly understood unless account be taken of God's role in keeping the past in being (and the Ideal's role in keeping that past relevant to the ongoing present). God preserves the secular past outside the present without altering its nature or import. This action has nothing to do with religion.

The time of secular history is distinct from the time of nature, as well as from dancing time, musical time and theatrical time. Its qualities, contents, rhythms are not reducible to those of physical nature or of isolated man. Its present is not only constituted by the coming together of men and nature, but it covers a distinctive historic space, and through it there surges a distinctive process of becoming. The past is effective in that present, and through that present it has some effect on the nature of the future that is to be. Its future, by operating through the present, dictates that every occurrence which had been is to be related as cause or obstacle to what is taking place in the present. Only the present is vital and ongoing, but without the past and the future, it would not be a moment in historic time.

A religious history acknowledges occurrences, powers and meanings beyond the reach of a secular historian. No one, inside a secular history, can know if a miracle occurred, for the miracle does not take place in the time of that history nor need it make a difference to any of its occurrences. An orthodox Christian theologian affirms that Jesus Christ is involved in activities which are unintelligible unless one understands Him to be a God, who is kind and wise beyond the capacity of any man, who understands what the world imports for us, and who has the power to do what no man could. In other religions somewhat similar virtues are to be accredited to other beings, places, times and activities. In all these cases God is taken to transform and perhaps enhance nature. His is an act of incarnation. The interplay of the result with men yields an entirely new fact which takes place in a religious history.

The temporal present of history is an extended span in which something occurs. All its subdivisions are also present. They are before and after one another, not earlier and later; were they earlier and later they would break up the present into a series of smaller presents occurring in a sequence. The magnitude of the present is determined by the nature of the act which occurs within it. Different presents will consequently have different magnitudes.

Viewed from the perspective of a secular present a religious present may be too short, i.e., a number of religious presents might occur sequentially in the span of that secular present, or it may be too long, i.e., a religious present may span more than one secular moment. Conversely, from the perspective of a religious present, a secular present may be either too short or too long to have the status of a genuine present. Occurrences which are secularly past or future may thus in a religious history be copresent, and conversely. It is improper, however, to measure one present in one domain by the present in another. Each present is a unit to be subsequently replaced by another similar unit.

As ongoing, each present has a terminus in the future, and is so far part of a larger present. A secular future offers a boundary at a distance, which defines certain past occurrences as relevant and others as irrelevant to what is now taking place; it makes the present determinate by giving to every past item a determinate role in relation to it. But in religious history it is a *final* future, the end of time, that makes the present determinate.

Eschatology is the study of last things. It tells us that whatever occurs in a religious history is relevant to and partly determined by what will be at the end of time. This end of time is a purely religious end. It in no way warrants the supposition that there will be an end to secular history or to nature itself, any more than the beginning of religious history requires that secular history also begin at that time, or that nature exist only inside a religious historic context.

As providing a boundary for whatever occurs, the last day makes whatever precedes it to be present. Despite the fact then that the items in a religious history are in a relation of earlier to later they are also defined by the eschatological end to be all present in a relation of before and after. The city of God is governed eschatologically. But it does have its own vitality and its own boundary — and its moments do pass away.

As merely present a moment is indeterminate; as past it is in a determinate relation to relevant predecessors and successors; as qualified by the future, it is made fully determinate with respect to the remaining irrelevant items which otherwise would have an unspecified role for it. Apart from a determination by the future, many items in the past would be unrelated to what was happening in the present. The present offers a medium through which the future dictates to the past what items have the role of being causally productive or of being obstacles to the coming to be of that present. The action of the future on the past through the agency of the present thereby re-aligns what had been, relating all of it to what is now taking place. If the future did not operate on the past through the agency of the present in this way, it would not be truly future for them.

We arrive at whatever future we do through time, but the time is teleologically determined. When the future is eschatological some items achieve a religious role. Because of that future, events in the past to which a religion may look for inspiration or grounding achieve a new import. The eschatological future dictates that whatever occurred in the past is a religious occurrence, no matter how secular it may seem. This does not mean that the eschatological future is irresistibly realized. Such a supposition would put it outside all time.

Time occurs only so far as there are genuine presents succeeding one another. The eschatological future makes past occurrences part of one single determinate temporal whole, ending in that future, but it does not prevent those presents from also occurring sequentially as single units. History ends at every moment with a distinct present terminating the whole past.

The fullness of time is a religious present defined by an incarnational act. That act and present are dictated by the eschatological end, not conversely. The present determines only what and how past items are to be made relevant to that end. Since the present changes constantly and since each present has a different past from every other, the eschatological end changes too, not because the present makes it do this, but because that end makes itself relevant to whatever occurs. By making itself relevant to a present, the end defines an appropriate time for an incarnation. That time is a present as qualified by the end, not necessarily deliberately or with intent, but surely in fact.

The present of religious history is an opportune or appropriate present, a "kairotic" present, which turns a secular past and future into its own religious substance. That present is an incarnational moment, a time in which God is present. This alone is a truly religious present. The idea of such a present is not peculiar to Christianity. The Hindus rightly speak of an endless number of incarnations, which need never involve the divine assumption of human flesh. It would in fact be proper to take every divine qualification, and thus every prophetic message, every miracle and divine message to be a kind of incarnation. They are part of religious history; all alter the secular significantly.

In some recent accounts there is a tendency to speak as though the religious present occurred by virtue of what men did. But this is to make God's presence a function of man's activities; it is to re-introduce the idea of magic into religion in a sophisticated form. Even classical authors make this error, speaking as though certain acts on the part of men would make for the coming to be of a Messiah, or of a day of last judgment. To be sure the beings who live in a religious time also live in a secular one, and even in a non-historic one, but what occurs in that religious time is not occasioned by or grounded in these others.

Moments of crisis, turning points in the dynamism of the religious community occur in the "fullness of time." Only when the world is ready, only when it has arrived at a certain stage, does some special divinely determined occurrence take place. God is of course not beholden to the nature of the world; men do not dictate when their Messiah is to appear. Yet the time is not arbitrarily set by God. If it were it would have nothing necessarily to do with the course of events. The "fullness of time" would then be a tautological expression of the fact that some crucial event had been divinely brought to pass. The fullness of time is a point in the interior development of the dedicated community, where a change in direction or emphasis occurs; it is to be understood in terms of what had developed before and what will develop afterwards. That point, so long as it is not replaced by a more signal crisis, continues to measure all the occurrences before and after. In most religions it takes place at the beginning of religious time or close to it. It is a climax in terms of which subsequent developments are to be understood, even when it is the case that some equal or greater climax is expected at a later time.

A kairotic moment is an intensified present in a dedicated community. It is this moment which is expressed in the liturgy, the established form of the religious service. Here an attempt is made to commemorate a great event, supposed to express and refer to a divine being. One can extend this idea so as to relate to basic conversions, for these too occur in the fullness of a time — not in a time which pertains to the being who is entering into or in a time outside the dedicated community, but in the time of the community. Conversions are usually marked by the performance of some ritualized solemn action, signalizing the entrance into a new world. Circumcision, tattooing, great sacrifices mark the radical change in attitude which is to characterize the convert. The activities are usually said to be done on behalf of God or given to Him, but they are in fact ways of cutting one off from another community, and are given to God only in the sense that the new community acts as an intermediary between the convert and God.

Both secular history and religious history have calendars. In both the calendar is the outcome of the selection of some occurrence whose repetitions define the temporal units to be used. There is no way by which one can see if these units are all of equal length, for anything which would be coincident with one of the occurrences would pass away with that occurrence. We must rely on such suppositions that what appears to be regular in motion or act is in fact so, and occupies as much time as another similar motion or act. The calendar in any case is an abstract measure; nothing passes away in or for a calendar. The future and the past are for it on a footing.

The occurrences in a religious history are made important, given prominence, achieve a value they can not have in a secular history. He who does not acknowledge the intrusion of God, the operation of the eschatological end and the autonomy of religious history can not know of this change. The situation is something like that which we confront when we enter a theatre to watch a performance. The theatre offers an occasion for the performance; it does not provide a place in which the performance occurs. The performance has its own distinctive space — and its own distinctive time and dynamics. In a similar way the calendar of a religious history is produced by transforming and transcending the calendar of secular history. Though the very dates and divisions which the secular history provides may be apparently duplicated, all will be changed in meaning, value and role.

Under the influence of the physical scientists, some philosophers and occasionally an historian make an attempt to deal with history as a predictive science. They look for laws which the particular occurrences might instance. Since all inquiry in root has the same pattern and requires the same virtues, they are tempted to look at history as a variant form of science, differing from it only in content. But it is not reasonable to try to deal with a domain which is the outcome of the interplay of various realities in the very terms appropriate to those realities so far as these are independent of one another. Nature has its law-abiding character, and so do men, but it does not follow that when the two come together, there will be any laws governing what takes place. And even if it were the case that there were historic laws and we could know them, our predictions would pertain only to things in general, and not to the specific, the concrete. Yet whatever takes place in history is concrete, produced in a fresh and free way even when under the aegis of fixed laws. What has been, grounds no sure predictions regarding the historic future.

Though the occurrences in nature are also novel, they are for science all instances of general laws, and nothing more. The scientist is interested in occurrences only so far as he can understand them in their law-abiding roles; what he cannot so understand he dismisses as the product of some eventually understood conjunction of laws. But the historian's interest is in the particular, the concrete, the self-determining and the self-centered, the items as outside all law, even when related to a past and a future, and made intelligible by being brought inside the context of a causal scheme.

Even if there were laws in secular history, there would not necessarily be laws in religious history. If there were, the laws would not necessarily be identical with those which prevail in secular history. The closest we can come to a law in religious history is when we turn from causes and effects to reasons and rewards, both expressing God.

To say that such and such an occurrence will be followed by a cataclysm is to speak inside nature. To say that such and such an historic occurrence will be followed by an historic cataclysm is to speak inside secular history. The first can be predicted, the second anticipated. But there are neither predictions nor anticipations in religious history — only prophesy, the moral evaluation of occurrences with a report as to what this entails religiously.

To say that, because of such and such an historic occurrence, man will be punished by God, is to prophesy. The punishment, if it takes place, will occur inside a religious context. A cataclysm cannot therefore be classed as a punishment except for one who places that cataclysm inside a religious context where it is related to preceding and succeeding religious occurrences. Karma and justice, forgiveness and mercy, the spirit of the Holy Ghost, the wisdom of the councils, the fulfillment of prophesy and the like are so many ways of indicating how it is that the present, though a distinct reality with its own internal nature, nevertheless acts in ways which require a reference to a religious past and future.

The historic past is preserved in the historic present. Were it not present in any sense, we could only point toward it and never be able to check our reference by an encounter. Since we encounter only what is in the present, an inference to the past can be certified only if it is filtered through a present. The past is there however, only effectively, not in its being, not as the present which it had once been. In religious history, too, there is a kind of retention of what had been. Having made a difference to some past moment in religious history, God makes a difference to all subsequent moments by virtue of the ingredience of that moment in them. Since He also directly qualifies those moments when they become present, the effect of God on the religious present is evidently highly complex. He makes a difference to what is now taking place not only in the light of what is to be, but in the light of the effect of the past inside the present.

The past helps determine the nature of the present. History does not repeat itself either secularly or religiously, precisely because the past, by being preserved in the present, precludes any subsequent event from starting where some predecessor did. In a religious history the past gives a new moral weight to the present. As a consequence the history has a direction. A religious people now acts in this or that way, burdened down with wickedness, disdain or rejection, or lifted up by the approval and power which its past deeds, through the action of God, give to it.

ii

SUBSTANCES, such as the cat, you and I, are not necessarily and can never wholly be historic, for we are not public and interrelated enough. We are present realities making selections from a private recent past and making a private use of a possibly common future. Nor are events historic occurrences. They are happenings in the present which have neither an external relevant past nor an external relevant future. Whatever past and future the events are acknowledged to have are but derivatives which we have carved out of them. But historic occurrences are inseparable from and utilize real, remote, public, uniquely relevant pasts and futures.

An historic occurrence stretches backwards into the past and forwards into the future as surely as it unites that past and future in a vital ongoing present. Something like an event can be isolated in it in the shape of a series of radiations. These radiations do not remain within the present; they move out of it to terminate in and thereby define the occurrence's relevant past and future. The past of the occurrence is its determinate content stretched backwards to end at some resistant past item; its future is its vitality projected forwards toward an end. Something like a substance also can be isolated in the historic occurrence in the shape of an interlocked unity of past and future. That substance is produced out of a return movement from the past and future at which the radiations terminated. The spread of the occurrence into a distant past and future has its reciprocal in the solidification of that past and future in the occurrence. When and as it exfoliates as a past and a future, the occurrence reconstitutes itself as a solidified unity of that past and future. The occurrence is consequently both eventful and substantial.

The radiation backwards and forwards of the historic occurrence is in effect a temporalized articulation of that occurrence, leaving nothing over but unextended present points of reference. The historic occurrence is nevertheless extended because the past and future are substantialized within it. The occurrence is, as it were, a pyramid whose apex functions as a final point of radiation forwards and backwards, and whose base serves as the present locus of the past and future, interlocked and mutually supportive. Between apex and base the occurrence can be said to be in a process of dissolution, constituting thereby a continuum of pyramids each with its distinctive apex, but all with the same base. Equally, it can be said to be in a process of integration, constituting a continuum of pyramids all with the same apex but with different bases. If we acknowledge a single base for all the pyramids we stress the process by which the substantial occurrence is articulated temporally; if we acknowledge a single apex for all the pyramids we stress the interior organization to which the occurrence is subjecting past and future.

Secular history has secular occurrences which radiate toward and solidify secular pasts and futures. Religious history has religious occurrences which radiate toward and solidify religious pasts and presents. A dedicated community is a religious occurrence publicly structuring a number of men in a distinctive extended religious history. In that history what is now occurring terminates in and utilizes a distinct past and future. The items in it, whether past, present or future, are never rightly located in a secular history any more than the items in a secular history are as such ever rightly located in a religious history.

Are the histories independent, and equally ultimate, irreducible and real? There are three ways in which one might try to answer this question. Religious history may be treated as an inclusive domain within which the occurrences of a secular history form a limited and special subdivision. This position can be reversed to make the secular history the more inclusive domain within which a religious history can be located. Or, thirdly, one can take both these histories to be independent realities, with occurrences having distinctive meanings, relations, values and affiliations.

The first two ways adopt a similar approach, though with opposite stresses. For both there is only one real history, within which there is an abstractable part that is derivately called a "history." Both views avoid cluttering up the universe with a plurality of histories, governed in different ways and moving at different rates over different items; they avoid too the difficult task of trying to find a place from where and a method by which these various histories are to be interrelated and ultimately unified. Few men today, however, would take seriously the claim that a secular history is only a subdivision of a religious one. Not only are there many religions, each with its own calendar and distinctive items, but the documentation, the research, and the dating employed by the various religions are secular in origin and secular in reference.

Only some occurrences in a secular history have religious significance. These take place at various distances in secular time. We hear of Jesus' birth and associated events and hardly anything more until we come near the end of his life. His birth, his baptism, his great acts and his death are interrelated as relevant antecedents and consequences within a religious history. What he did in between is not mentioned because presumably irrelevant to these occurrences. But they are irrelevant only because they have been so defined by the religious occurrences.

On this view, each religious occurrence defines all secular occurrences that occur in the stretch from itself to a relevant antecedent as irrelevant to it. These irrelevant occurrences do not vanish; they remain part of a larger secular history, and in addition are used by religious history to determine the tempo at which its occurrences succeed one another. The more items that are defined to be irrelevant to some religious occurrence, the more sluggish the pace at which the religious history moves from some relevant antecedent to the later occurrence. The religious history, in taking account of the existence of a secular historic world, thus does not allow the secular items to have any other role for it than that of determining with what rapidity a religious occurrence will follow on its predecessor.

The difficulty with this plausible view of the relation which a real religious history has to a more inclusive secular one is not only that the occurrences in a secular history have a relevance to one another, no matter what role they have for a religious history, but that the occurrences of a religious history offer limits within which secular history occurs. There is a sense in which secular history is subordinate to religious history.

Secular history utilizes the items in a larger religious history to give itself a direction, as surely as a religious history utilizes secular items to give itself a tempo. The birth and death of Jesus are, from a secular position, the termini of a period of thirty years. That birth and death have a distinctive reality in a religious history, and are related to one another in a single span. A secular history converts the religious span into an abstract direction governing the relatively less momentous items which make up that secular history.

The third of our alternatives acknowledges the reality of both histories, each with its own occurrences, time, space, values and causality. Their reconciliation can be understood only by one who stands outside both histories, and knows occurrences which are capable of entering into either or both of them. And this is possible so far as one has knowledge of such ultimate realities as God and the Ideal.

iii

MEN INDIVIDUALLY and together struggle constantly with nature. Because of their success in keeping it somewhat under control, and in making its force one of the binding factors of human groups, the struggle, once direct and violent, is today partly hidden by what has already been achieved. The very existence of a human realm shows that men have been successful to some degree in their struggle with nature. The world of man, consequently, stands out over against the world of nature as an achievement.

A dedicated community is an intensified form of the human

realm, bearing the marks of the presence of God. So far as that God qualifies the nature which still remains outside, the community can become part of a religious history, having a dynamism of its own, with its own rhythm and meaning.

A dedicated community has a distinctive time (and space and dynamics). This is emotionally sustained, constituted by the interplay of the members of the community, and punctuated by its specific dramatic activities. In that time men are related not only to one another but to a God at once inside and outside the community. This time is distinct from and is held over against the times of society, state and nature. The community ignores these except so far as they mark moments when men are to be recalled to the community. They are for it nothing more than secular times for determining when one is to move away from the secular world. A holiday therefore for it is only a signal secular occasion when men can participate in a holy day.

Dedicated communities as well as religious states come to be and pass away. They can be studied by secular historians in the very same way as are wars, discoveries, the rise and fall of nations, and the like. The substance of a religion, the legitimacy of its claims, the very nature of its time will not however be encompassed thereby. Secular history relates to religion only as a public occurrence. It makes no reference to any providential, beneficial or injurious power of God. The only God secular history presupposes is one who ontologically sustains its past.

Secular occurrences can radiate to religious past and future termini. When those termini are substantialized in the occurrence they are secularized. Such secularization sometimes awakens the ire of religious reformers and prophets since it involves a radical change in the values of what is religiously important. But it has the value of giving religious events a role in another world, without necessarily compromising their place within the religious.

A secular history of a dedicated community attends to those radiations from it which terminate in a secular past but which are in fact made into the present religious substance of the community. This history is of interest to those who search in the secular past for events having a prophetic importance. A similar approach is made when providence or the day of last judgment is treated as having a present inspirational value.

A religious history of a dedicated community terminates in a religious past and future. That past and future may have items approachable in secular ways. The religious history of the community does not deal with such secular objects; what it terminates in are religious items, having a religious role because they are reached from a religious position. The dedicated community's origin and future are one with its being.

A dedicated community exhausts a distinctive type of causality; this not only moves forward to bring about effects but also reaches toward the men to bring them into closer union with the community. Men and God thereby become involved in the rhythms of the community, and are to be represented by occurrences or portrayals which follow those rhythms.

In the community, past items are made relevant to future ones. It reaches into the past and is affected here by it. Activities which are commemorative of what had happened are for it not merely repetitions or memoranda. They are ways in which the past is revitalized so as to function here and now. In a dedicated community the vitalization occurs in reference to some crucial event.

A religion need not be inescapably oriented towards the past. It can be freshly reinstituted at every moment. Whether reconstituted at every moment or continuing as before, each will however vitally understand God differently from the way others do. All of them will embody Him, and all of them will point to Him, but some will do this better than others.

Which one does it best? This question cannot be answered except by first going outside all dedicated communities and getting to know God speculatively; second, by isolating the common indispensable nucleal components and referent of all religions; third, by noting which religion distorts or obscures this the least; and fourth, by seeing which contributes to the fullest possible life for man. The first has been attempted in *Modes of Being*. The second is one of the main tasks of this work. The third and fourth are consequences to be drawn by those who have not only mastered the first two but have come to know the nature and effects of the various religions.

8. The Competing Claims
of the Various Religions

THERE ARE "Christian" theologians who say that Christianity is not *a* religion. They intend thereby to give it a special dignity over against all other religions. In fact, though, they but show most clearly that Christianity is precisely one religion among many, for it is characteristic of a particular religion to urge itself as being superior to all others.

It is possible that what is meant is that Christianity at its best is a dedicated community, to be taken on its own terms. It should be. But Judaism, Islam, Buddhism and others at their best are also dedicated communities, to be dealt with sympathetically and intelligently. Taken by themselves each is unique, incomparable, final. But they can be contrasted with one another. When they are, each is bounded off from the rest. Only then is each properly termed a "religion." A religion in this sense is a dedicated community viewed from the outside, one among other dedicated communities, each making distinct and often opposing claims.

Each religion claims — and by its very nature must claim — that it alone is right and the others wrong. A religion, now and then, speaks of itself as tolerant, as being willing to recognize that other religions also have value and truth. In practice and theory, though, this means little more than that it views these others as parts, fragments, anticipations, or precipitates of itself, as fitting somewhere within its own spacious scheme. It thinks of them as being wrong if and so far as they take themselves to be absolute and independent, as making an all-inclusive claim. It is ready to view them as tolerable and even as partly right, if only they, contrary to their intent and claims, will subordinate their claims to its.

Christianity is often spoken of as preserving and completing Judaism; Islam says that it preserves and completes them both. The religion of the Sikhs is designed to reconcile the truths of the Muslims and the Hindus; the Hindus quite often speak of finding room for every variety of religious belief and practice, every prophet, saint and God, that others might endorse. In all these cases the others are accepted not as on an equal footing but as subordinate. Understandably, the tolerance exhibited toward them is accepted with poor grace. These others never asked only for elbow room, or for a recognition of a right to be subordinate to some other, or even just to be alongside all the religions there are. Each insists that it is absolutely right, and that the others, therefore, are radically wrong. It may grant that it has no more right than any other religion to exist, to teach, to proselytize, to propagate, to expand and to practice in a given society or state. But this political equalitarianism does not compromise the belief of each that it alone is unqualifiedly, finally, and irreducibly right, as is evidenced by some revelation, document, book, prophet, history, or circumstance. None grants that it is but part of some more inclusive religion, none accepts the irenic proposal that it is only one of many equal claimants to the truth. In its own eyes it is unique and paramount. It asks its followers to accept some things which other religions find abhorrent, and to ignore what other religions think is precious and essential. It sees the others as wrong, particularly so when they claim to be on a par with it. Truth, value, justification and finality, it supposes, are maximally only in it. Each, in silence or in violence, insists that it is a one for the many, a one apart from the many, a one which includes the values or truths of the many other religions which mankind has unfortunately allowed to flourish.

Interfaith conferences are attended by representatives of but a few religions. While together the men seem to work in harmony. But it is a question whether the harmony achieved is not in good part due to the fact that they all quietly pass over the sad and inexpungable truth that no one of the religions sees itself as one among many. The competing claims to absolutivity, and the opposing beliefs and practices of the different religions, create little difficulty for one who keeps inside the frame of one of them. His religion he takes to be on a different plane from the others. He sees its claim to absolutivity, its beliefs and its practices to be justifiable; the competition and opposition of other religions are for him little more than a competition and opposition among errors, some better than others, but errors nevertheless.

ii

A JEW, for example, sees his religion in quite different terms from those which the Christian and the Muslim assign to him. His is the faith of a man for whom there are no synods, no edicts, no authorities to whom he can turn for final answers to his questions regarding the specific nature of things, mundane or divine. Even his Bible fails to give the Jew clear answers to the simplest questions; his God speaks in a language for which no man seems to have a key. In order to know all he should, the Jew is forced to think for himself, to follow the trail of truth wherever it may lead, under the guidance of the wise who have gone part of the way before.

The theology of the Jew is theology at a minimum. It affirms nothing more than that God is One, leaving open even the question of what His nature is, what it means for Him to be, and what His unity implies. The Jew's cosmology, too, is at a minimum. It affirms little more than that the world has a history, man a dignity, and each thing some degree of value. Beyond these bare affirmations, whatever the Jew asserts he asserts precariously. The religion of the Jew is the religion of one who passionately desires and wholeheartedly tries to understand what is demanded of men in this world. He can be true to his religion only to the extent that he faithfully pursues the truth under the guidance of the Hebraic past.

The Jew seeks to know what is, and to bring about what ought to be. He is one who is constantly aware that he fails to know or to do all he should. If this be an essential characterization of the Jew, many who are Jews by birth and church, in habit and in ritual, must of course be said not to be Jews in fact. No one can inherit the status of being a Jew. Birth and ritual may make it possible to merit the designation more readily; they do not and cannot guarantee it. The fact that there are many Jews by census who are not Jews in spirit reveals not that the census should be the guide, but that there is much work for rabbis to do.

The true and the good transcend all creeds. But for the religious Jew they have special significance. For him they are ideals he endeavors to embody, because he believes that they support what he once affirmed and now affirms, and the acts in which he once engaged and in which he now engages, and because it is these that he discerns to be the meaning behind or over against the apparently absurd and wrong things he hears that others are divinely urged to think and do. His ethics is universal, absolute, and onerous. Its minimum demand is that one should not do to others what one would not have them do to oneself. To subscribe to this Golden Rule is to grant that what is evil for oneself is evil for others. The ethics of the Jew, therefore, is the ethics of one who acknowledges a common human nature, in terms of which the strong and the weak, the wise and the foolish, are absolutely equal. For him there is no such thing as a religion that asks him to do only what he can, no such thing as a world in which men are not responsible, no such thing as a good that exists only in thought. He ought to do what he cannot, is free to do what he ought not, and loves what he has not. An optimistic theology, a deterministic cosmology, and a relativistic ethics — these are the indelible marks of the gentiled Jew. A true Jew lives in the light of the fact that in this world there is no good without evil, nor evil without good, that man is free to make himself better or worse, and that all that happens is to be judged in terms of divinely sustained universal principles applicable to all beings everywhere. In addition, he pledges himself to commemorate by word or deed some unique past event, such as a covenant, marking off his group from all others. He thus consciously and openly shares in the history of the Jews, and thereby becomes a Jew in spirit, one who consciously and publicly identifies himself with historical Judaism.

What makes him a Jew is not so much *how* he commemorates but *what* and *why*. He denies himself a future when he becomes so orthodox that he attempts to commemorate everything that happened once before. He reforms himself into a mere historic

figure when he commemorates solely to remind himself that
he has a past. The Jew need commemorate no more than a
single event, but then he must commemorate it as a peak in
an historic attempt to know the truth and do the good. His
commemoration may take the form of a well-entrenched ritual,
but there is no reason why it may not have a different form at
different times and for different individuals. What is important
is that it be his way of making a public avowal that he is a
Jew, that it make manifest in word and deed that he deliberately
accepts and tries to fulfill the convenants his ancestors made
long ago.

One thing more is necessary before a man can become a full
Jew. He must be picked out from the multitude. Men are born,
but Jews are chosen. The method of choosing Jews, however,
seems to vary with the ages. Once it took God to choose a
Jew; now it needs only a Gentile. There is no true choice, however, unless a designation from without is met with a pledge from
within to live a life that God would approve. To be a Jew in
fact, one must so manifest oneself through word or deed, pledge
oneself to be kin in spirit and act, as well as in birth, with ancestors who promised to love the truth and pursue the good.

Chosen men are men apart. They are a minority, aliens. They
have the unique privilege of standing outside the confining
boundaries that hold the rest together. Since they are free from
the restrictive and transitive dogmas that hem in even the boldest
thinkers of their age, it is to them that one can turn in the
hope of discovering what lies hidden to those immersed in the
civilization of the day. The Jew, because he is a chosen, minority
figure who has renewed the pledge of his ancestors, is obliged
to think boldly and freely, and to do good everywhere. His
is an acknowledged infinite obligation. Since he has only a
finite power, he is a necessarily guilty and tragic being who
does not and cannot do all he should. He might try to escape
from this Hebraic conclusion by echoing the question of Cain.
But to this one must answer: to detract from one's responsibility
is to detract from one's humanity, to stand apart from human
kind. A man has infinite value because he is infinitely obligated.
It is his duty to care for whatever is nourished by the nature
that mothered him.

No man can fulfill his obligations fully. All are tainted with this original, native "sin." Theologians have sometimes confused this sin, which is a sin of omission, a sin that follows from the fact that man is a finite being with an infinite reach, with the sin of commission, the sin of freely choosing to do what is wrong. Since men are and must always be finite, they cannot as individuals avoid committing a sin of omission. None can rightly look to a Messiah to wipe away such a sin. The function of a Messiah is to make it possible for men to act together so as to circumvent it. The true Messiah introduces men to a way of life in which they together can do what is beyond the power of each. Men must work together as a unity if they are to do all they ought. The sin of omission is avoidable only in that ideal Messianic state where all men do what all men should.

The sin of omission accounts for the Jews' need of a Messiah. Its acknowledgment stands in the way of that easy optimism which supposes that man is somehow already redeemed — an optimism that demeans man by demanding that he see himself as an adjective of another, even one who is divine in intent, origin, or function. That optimism, thinks the Jew, defines each of us as at best but half a man, dependent for his hope, his meaning and his being on the substance or acts of another.

The dignity of man, for the Jew, is the dignity of one who suffers, not vicariously and partially, but in himself and unrelieved. It is the dignity of one for whom the tragedy of existence cannot be solved or negated by the death of another, no matter how pure and good, and to whom the fundamental flaw in man is not his arrogance or his ambition, his willfulness or his ignorance, but his inability to do all a man should. If men are already redeemed in principle or in fact, the world in principle or in fact has already come to an end for the Jew.

There are exultant shouts of joy in the Bible: a heavy cloud of sadness hangs over the Gospels. But the story of the Bible is that of a broken covenant, of what men should but cannot and do not do, whereas the point of the Gospels is that the covenant is at an end and men therefore already renewed. Judaism is one long drawn-out lament; for the Christian this is but the necessary birth-cry of a joyous miracle. The two positions cannot be one, for it is of the essence of Judaism to deny and of Christianity to affirm that there was a day some two thousand years ago in which darkness suddenly and forever gave way to blinding light. Judaism is Moses in the wilderness straining to reach a land he knows he never can. For the Christian this truth is but the necessary first act in a Divine Comedy. The history of the universe for the Christian is in principle already told. It is a delightful tale with but a spicing of momentary woe. For the Jew history is in the making. It has peaks and valleys, goods and bads, inseparably together and forever.

Every reduction in value must be justified as an unavoidable wrong that will be compensated for by the production of at least an equal good. An eye for an eye is a sound and modest demand once it is freed from the misconception that justice is done when losses are multiplied. "An eye for an eye" means that for an eye that is taken at least an eye ought to be given. It is a good ethical maxim that science today is showing us how to fulfill. It would be folly to say that an eye ought to be taken so as to wipe out the wrong that the loss of an eye involves.

A man inevitably obligates himself to make good whatever losses in value he brings about. If he cannot fulfill his obligation, he reveals himself as one who acted without possible justification. We do unjustifiable wrong when we act so as to destroy a value for which no compensation is possible and promised. We are doubly guilty because we do not fulfill a cosmic obligation to benefit all things, and because we do not fulfill an ethical obligation to make good the losses we voluntarily bring about. We are always guilty because we are beings too weak to do all we ought; sometimes we are guilty as well because we voluntarily do wrongs we cannot possibly make good.

The pain that should accompany a suffering for wrongs voluntarily done ought not to be confused with the suffering that sometimes comes to men because they are limited, faulty instruments of the good. The pathos of the tale of Job lies in part in his inability to see this. He thought that if he did no wrongs voluntarily he ought not to be made to suffer. But acts of omission deserve punishment too. Job was punished not because he was unethical or because he did wrong voluntarily, but because he was a man. Nor was he punished for the sake of others, to redeem them or to improve them. He was punished as Job, and the punishment was deserved. He was punished severely but not unjustly. And it is hard to find any warrant for the death of his children and his servants, except on the ground that all men deserve punishment. Rightly understood, the story of Job makes evident that everything, short of suffering, profound and continuous, is an undeserved gift calling for thanksgiving. It should be a matter for rejoicing that there are so few who are punished much.

It is unfair to Job to suppose that punishment is deserved only if it is invoked against the deliberate perpetrators of ethical wrongs. Job was an ethical man. His innocence as an ethical being but pointed up the truth that ethics and religion are quite distinct. An ethics requires no religious sanction, explanation, or support, as is evident from the fact that a rule of ethics, such as the Categorical Imperative, can be known and followed by men who are not religious. A religion, on the other hand, may demand such unethical acts as the sacrifice of an Isaac. The commands of ethics and religion may be, but are not necessarily always, compatible, and so far as they are compatible, the one must be subordinated to the other. It is desirable that religious men endorse and encourage the ethical life, but they have lost their religion when they forget that for them ethics must play a subordinate role. Ethics should, from the perspective of religion, stand to religion as the lower to the higher, the easier to the harder, the negative to the positive, commands to avoid to commands to do.

The crucial problem for the Jew is whether he will hold to a natural or to a revealed religion, a religion rooted in a cosmology and submissive to ethics, or to a religion rooted in divine commands. A natural religion demands that men do what they know to be good. A revealed religion makes equally positive, but from an ethical position, quite arbitrary demands. It sometimes requires what, for ethics, is often wrong or indifferent. If a Jew takes his religion to be revealed he must therefore be prepared to believe and do what may appear to be wrong or absurd to others. The faith he has is Abraham's — that what is revealed is more right and reasonable than anything else could possibly be. But if he accepts only a natural religion, he can still be a full Jew, and in addition will have the virtue of not defying what men know to be ethically wrong.

Every religion is justified so far as it reflects the nature of man and the enhancing acceptance of him by God. Still, it can be criticized. The Jews have been rightly criticized for excessive legalism and disputation, for being narrow, self-righteous and stiff-necked. There are analogous faults in the competing religions. Buddhism, particularly Hinayana Buddhism, has been rightly criticized for its lack of sympathy for the plight of men. The Hindus have been criticized for allowing men to take themselves to belong to distinct castes with quite definite tasks and limitations in rights and privileges. The Christians have been rightly criticized for encouraging womanly virtues, slave mentality and a hypocritical affirmation that one will or can love one's enemies. The Muslims have been criticized for being sensuous, belligerent, cruel. The truth in all these charges is but the counterweight of the devotion, the compassion, the renunciation, the humility, and the submissiveness which are the primary characteristics of those who best represent these religions. All of them can evidently be defended in equally laudatory terms. But though some might hold to every truth that interests the others, they specify those truths in act, creed and outcome in distinctive ways. All, in the end, diverge in belief and practice, in virtue and in vice.

iii

THOSE WHO STAND outside a man's religion can accord his religion no special status. They see a problem and not an answer in his claim that his religion is paramount and final. Everyone in fact has this problem with respect to other religions. There seem to be but three solutions to it: 1] all religions are false, wrong, illegitimate; 2] all are true, right, legitimate; or 3] all are partly true, right, legitimate, and partly false, wrong, illegitimate.

For most contemporaries there is an alternative — the only correct one they think — that is here being ignored. For them, religion, like poetry and metaphysics, says nothing meaningful and therefore cannot be either true or false. It was precisely because I had this alternative in mind that I have had recourse to such additional expressions as "right and wrong," "legitimate and illegitimate," to characterize the various religions. Even for those who see no cognitive content in any religion it is a fact that the religions compete, and that each, rightly or wrongly, legitimately or illegitimately, makes claims contrary to those made by the rest.

To say only this much, though, is to grant far too much. Religions are not only right and wrong, legitimate or illegitimate; they are true and false, and this in two ways. They are true and false in the way men, clocks, and scales are true and false – as supporting and betraying justifiable expectations. They are also true and false in the way in which science and engineering are true and false, by virtue of what they say and do. In creed, ritual and act, different religions make claims that such and such values, beings and modes of life are better than others, and that he who thinks otherwise is mistaken. To refuse to attend to those claims is to make no attempt to see why religions must not only oppose one another, but must oppose as well some of the claims of moralists, philosophers, historians, semanticists, and scientists.

1.   One of the most brilliant chapters of Hegel's magnificent *Phenomenology of Mind* is on the Enlightenment. Among other things Hegel there shows how the Enlightenment presupposes the reality and strength of its opponent, how it can function only so far as religion continues to act as a counterpoise, and why it is that the Enlightenment is at once naïve and dogmatic. It needs religion but takes it to be undesirable. It talks much about religion and yet leaves it unexplained because it is unable to encompass religion as an oppositional part of itself.

There is no doubt that critics are dependent on the being, even the well-being, of that which they castigate and dismiss. But from this it does not follow that there is any truth in what they criticize. Religions may be inevitable and be presupposed by their opponents. This does not mean that they are not sheer error. Falsehoods, no less than truths, may be inescapable, presupposed, essential to some larger view. There are, in fact, at least two good reasons why one can take seriously the doctrine that every religion is false.

First, every religion offers testimony in the shape of its own prophetic utterances and saintly admonitions that it is incrusted with superstitions, folly and distortions. All sacred books, religious practices, and beliefs need some purging – or, to speak more kindly, some reinterpretation. Some apologists may speak as if they had nothing to add or to subtract, but the history of the religion tells a different story. Second, mystics and reformers who have spent their lives in religious activity and who are almost universally acknowledged to have succeeded better than the rest, tell us again and again that their religions, and even more certainly all other religions, are not final, that they are too restrictive, arbitrary and inadequate to allow one to rest in them as they now are. Some of these men urge us to pass through and beyond the distinctive doctrines and practices of the extant religions if the objective of those religions is to be attained. They see their own religion as at best a device — excellent in its own way, superior to all others, but still only a device — for enabling a man to come closer to his God. They refuse to keep inside their own religion in its present, limited form. They refuse to treat it as absolutely final and true. It is for them only a part of the entire truth and therefore wrong just so far as it usurps the place of the whole.

Nevertheless we cannot say that all religions are completely in error. Let it be granted that all are unsound. They could all be said to have the same disreputable causes, the same lamentable effects. The practices of all might be thought to be pernicious, their creeds foolish, the claims of none justifiable in any intelligible, communicable sense. Still, they are not unsound in the same way or to the same degree. Some are more inclusive than others, some are more in consonance with the prevalent morality, culture, and civilization, some possess virtues not characteristic of the others. And any or all might be sound when taken from within, as separate from its regrettable causes and effects. The criticisms of the prophets and the claims of the mystics can then be treated as justified observations regarding additional and perhaps more important truths that have been obscured by unessential evils and improper focusing. These men can be said to think, not that their own religions are false, but only that they are partial, incomplete, needing a supplement. The whole truth would include these religions and what the prophets and mystics insist upon. The religions would, of course, continue to claim to express the whole truth, but this would be a testimony to their incompleteness. It would not show that there was anything false in the religions, since their claims to absolutivity would be but proper expressions of their finitude, symbols of their incompleteness, not claims to be taken at their face value.

There is insufficient warrant in fact or dialectic, then, for the contention that all religions are equally and completely mistaken.

2.   The perpetual recrudescence of religion in the face of the most severe opposition and suppression, and the centrality of religious activity and belief in the lives of men and societies, make most implausible the thesis that they are all erroneous. Since the many religions are also prima facie on a footing, it is desirable to approach them in neutral terms. This double point is recognized by the philosopher of comparative religion. He tries to side with no religion, but instead strives to take them all to be true. Ideally pledged to view them as different expressions of some single, irreducible legitimate drive or search for an ultimate value, being or goal, he is usually, in flesh and blood, not as tolerant as his program prescribes. He inclines to be tolerant only of the established religions, on the one side, and the primitive religions on the other. Like the political scientist who recognizes as legitimate the claims which the dominant powers have effectively maintained for a long time, and the claims of local groups which are too small to count much in the public arena, the philosopher of religion is inclined to ignore the religions which stand in between the great traditional ones and those characteristic of primitive groups. It is hard to find a philosopher of religion who is pliable, tolerant, and broad enough to affirm that the religious drive is expressed at least as well in such minority religions as Father Divine's, the Dukhobors, the faith healers or the Druses as it is in Judaism, Christianity, Islam, Buddhism and Hinduism. However, this is only a human failing, not a failing in theory. The theory of a single religious drive — a drive on the part of man to achieve a closer relationship with God, the being who is infinitely more powerful and valuable than himself — coming to expression in diverse ways, can be extended to apply to every religion, no matter how strange and perverse its doctrines and practices may be.

This idea of a single drive coming to expression in the different religions is not alien to the spirit and intent of any one of them, though of course each would insist that it expresses this drive more adequately or in a purer form than the rest. But each could allow that the other religions are grounded in the same way it is, and that they are to be characterized in general terms similar to those which apply to itself.

Each religion is occupied with satisfying this driving need, and is so far on a par with the others. All are equally legitimate. Nevertheless they cannot all be accepted as true. "Religion" is more than a summary name for a heterogeneity of religious phenomena. It expresses a root fact behind them all, a need for a supreme enhancing power. But this is not a religious drive, and it is not expressed equally well in all religions.

Were all religions expressions of a single desirable drive, they would so far be legitimate, not in their specificity as diverse and opposed, but only in their root and source. They would be true not as religions but as expressions of a drive which, since it lacks the differentiations which mark them off from it and from one another, is not religion in any sense in which they are. The drive makes them true not so far as they make claims, but only in their status as effects of it. Even that one religion which might be said to be superior to all others because it exhibited the drive in a clearer or purer form than the others, would differ from the drive as an effect from a cause, a specialized occurrence from a common source. It would be an expression incapable of being anything other than it now is, all public as it were. The drive, in contrast, would not be exhausted by it. It, to be fully and properly expressed, would need expression in the shape of the other religions, even if these do poor justice to its richness or its goals. A drive is protean and flexible. It cannot be fully caught in any one expression, no matter how excellent, without ceasing to be a drive, a source of religions. Confined to one expression, it would be only an effect, a product, and not that which underlies all religious life.

One might, of course, speak of the drive of which all religions are expressions as of the very substance of religion. But then there would be only one religion, and this would not be identical with any religion we know. All the extant religions would, on this hypothesis, be but so many limited expressions of it, which, just because they failed to exhibit it perfectly, would not be full religions and to that extent not altogether true.

The doctrine of religious drive tends to trench on the old faculty psychology with its theory of specific appetites for religion, art, practice, and so on. Man's unity, the flexibility of his being, the interpenetration of his different interests, compel us to see the so-called religious drive as itself a specialization of some more basic concern for self-completion at the core of man, coming to expression in all activities. Religion is only one important manifestation of it. Prayer and blasphemy, indifference, atheism, and faith all specify it. It could be urged, of course, that the religious drive of a particular religion does express the basic concern of man better than any other can, but then it must also be affirmed that it does not exhaust that concern, and that that concern has other modes of expression as well, which ought to be exhibited if it is to be fully manifest. The religious drive is only a partial expression of the concern, and the manifestations of that drive in the shape of different religions must evidently fall far short of doing justice to the nature and shape of this which grounds them all.

Finally, the fact that a religion is the manifestation of a drive or of a more basic concern (even if that drive or concern be thought of as central and desirable, and religion its most adequate representative) does not assure that there is any truth in the claims of the religion. Error, no less than truth, expresses the concern and its derivative drives; cowardice is supported by the very energies which sustain courage and, as a matter of fact, exhibits the very same interests. We cannot save a religion by turning away from it to something underlying it; that way we but risk the loss of the vital religious factor in it, at the same time that we make it impossible to ground a judgment that it is true.

3.   We are left with the alternative that all religions are partly right and partly wrong. This alternative has five forms: A] all religions might exhibit some common truth more or less adequately;   B] they might be right only in what they affirm and wrong in what they deny;   c] they might be right in what they reject and not in what they accept;   D] they might be right in pointing toward some common, proper goal but wrong in being what and where they are; finally,   E] they might be right when viewed in their contexts and wrong otherwise.

A.   It is the position of the theosophists that all religions exhibit a common truth with various degrees of success. It is this common truth that the theosophists try to express. Their position is not to be identified with the previous one, which seeks a common root or source for religions. The theosophist isolates what is already explicit in the different religions; he starts with them in their specificity and tries to separate out the truth they share with all the others. Those who try to isolate a common core in particular religions instead look beneath the religions to a single drive or concern which expresses itself in the different religions in distinctive ways. Where the theosophist, at least initially, takes seriously the claims of the various religions, the latter does not. The former ignores the common intent of the religions; the latter attends to this alone. The former looks for a truth common to all religions; the latter looks for their common ground.

There is more than one theosophical society, and there will always be more than one. He who isolates a least common denominator, the common truth of all, is bound to find that others see him as only one among many, holding a particular doctrine which itself must yield some truth common to itself and all others. Also, a common element is rather jejune. A thin schema, it leaves out the juice of living religion and, in fact, rejects this as irrelevant or perverse. Its very stress on some common truth to be found in all, involves a dismissal of the distinctive affirmations of each. Actual religions are given up, then, for a philosophic category, an idle universal. To be sure, there is a nucleal core to be found in all religions. But this is no category or universal. It is a particular religion purged of its bias and thus, though concrete and vital, purer than that religion or the religion's competitors. To get to it one must return to the ultra-natural and to religious experience, and use them to guide a recovery of the essence of the dedicated community and a life of faith.

B.   The thesis that religions are right in what they affirm but wrong in what they deny has considerable plausibility. Most religions point up the values of unselfishness, humility and kindness. They proclaim the majesty of God, the supremacy of justice, the conquest of right, the worth of man, differing only in stress and selection. They are wrong only when they forget their objectives, to concentrate on a condemnation of contemporary thought and action. They can be said to be right in what they affirm but not in what they deny, right when they look up, wrong when they look down. But this answer will not do. The brute fact remains that each religion affirms some things which oppose what others affirm. They cannot all, therefore, be accepted as true in what they affirm. The thesis can be maintained only if the various religions are not compared with one another or if their oppositions to or their condemnations of one another are not treated as objectively as are their other claims. Religions cannot all be true in all they affirm, since they make up a plurality of conflicting religions.

c.   It could, on the other hand, be well argued that religions are right precisely in what they reject and wrong only in what they accept. Most, perhaps all, oppose what is wicked — the passions, the immorality of man. Though they do not clearly say what they would like to put in their place, they are quite clear and unambiguous in their rejection of some of the follies and perversions of the day. However, they conflict as surely in their denials as they do in their affirmations. It is not the case that they all reject the same things. What one disdains another sometimes accepts, endorses, insists upon. The religions provide us with conflicting denials.

D.   Perhaps the most common answer offered to the problem of how to reconcile the religions is to claim that the different religions in various ways point to some final ultimate truth beyond them all. Each on this view is true as pointing to that desirable goal, and each is false just so far as it thinks that it is already at that goal. Lessing's image is that they are different roads leading to the same mountain-top. He recognized only a few religions, but there is no reason why his view cannot be extended to apply to all. Such an extension, though, will not overcome the fatal weaknesses of the view.

This popular position does not take account of the fact that it is of the essence of each to claim that it has more of the truth now; it overlooks the fact that some religions are younger, that some have more followers, that some are more inclusive than others. Nor does it tell us about this truth which is supposed to stand outside them all. If that truth were knowable, it could be incorporated in some or all religions thereby bring them to the mountaintop, where they would be indistinguishable. If that truth is not knowable, we have no way of knowing that it is the truth, or that the various religions are approaching it. Evidently we make no advance by claiming that religions are right only so far as they point toward truths forever beyond them all.

E.   Our last alternative is that all religions are right in their limited circumstances, right in just the time and place, the civilization and the culture in which they appear. Just as a man ought to love his own mother or wife and not the others', so he ought to subscribe to his own religion and not to others, even though, in their own terms, they are not inferior to his own. Each can be said to be moving toward some higher end, perhaps one common to them all, but not as that which lies entirely outside them, defining them to be mere instruments, but rather as that which terminates, completes them, and continues to bear the mark of the fact that it was reached in such and such specific ways. They would not be different roads to some distant top, nor would they be occupants of that single top. They would be concrete, diverse and final because they in their different ways had made the top part of themselves here and now. Each could enter into the contexts which nourished the others, provided that it was willing to undergo a change in stress, pattern, and perhaps even meaning. Each would be right in making an absolute claim, for this is what it, in that situation, should and must do. Each would be wrong, though, in treating its own claims as if they had no specific cultural tonality.

On this alternative each religion is taken to specialize and make concrete some absolute truth. Each expresses this absolute with local accents and emphases, and catches it within a specific history. It asserts what is true, not merely as a function of the context in which it is found, but as a consequence of looking at what is objectively true, though from and in that context. Each religion would be wrong were it transported bodily to the contexts of others, and it is in terms of such imagined transportations that it is wrongly criticized by those others. In terms of all the other things that are accepted by people in that society, it would be wrong to have any other religion and wrong to do anything other than to claim that one's own religion was right. Each would err only so far as it failed to recognize that it deals with the whole truth within the limitations of a particular context — and this error would itself be a function of the context.

The God which a religion might acknowledge will, though individual in Himself, be one who is given meaning for this world by the religion. For the religious man, God is properly grasped only from and on the inside of his religion. But each religion should also see the others as facing the same God as it does, though vivified by each in distinctive ways. The various religions, on this view, need not be thought to be on a level. They can be judged and tested by seeing what meaning God has for them in the concrete. Do their members behave better than others? If so, then they will, as religious people in this world, be better than their neighbors. From an outside point of view, it is these religions which will be more correct, legitimate and true.

If we recognize an initial objective, a plurality of specifications and a plurality of ways of making God concrete and significant in the lives of men, we can assert that all religions are true in the beginning, true in their procedures, and true in the end, though not necessarily equally desirable as public phenomena. They will be false only so far as their claims are separated from their contexts, which is of course what must be done when they are dealt with by the other religions. Each rightly criticizes the others in the sense that it says that they, if put in its own context without change, would be wrong. Each rightly claims to have the whole truth, but this is a truth infected by the place, time, and circumstance in which it is uttered.

The absolute claims of each religion can therefore be allowed as at once reflecting a limited context, and as exhibiting the nature of the goal which the religion makes determinate. That with which it starts may be misconstrued by it in its creeds and dogmas — that is a matter for theologians to decide. The manner in which it exhibits God immanently may lead men away from a more intimate grasp of Him — that is a matter for the participants to decide. The rest of us must be content with judging it in terms of the good and evil it brings about for men.

"This," we will be told, "is a self-defeating answer. It is nothing but old-fashioned relativism in a poor disguise. Apply this theory to ethics, aesthetics, philosophy – and to this answer itself – and you will find you have lost the ability to make any universal judgments, to do anything more than express your time, place and circumstance." But there is a great difference between religions and these other enterprises. These others appeal to objective evidence and submit themselves to public discussion, criticism, and evaluation. Their claims to truth, though absolute, are not made dogmatically. They are offered to another in the same spirit and for the same reasons that they are initially entertained. A religion, on the other hand, even when it makes reference to publicly ascertainable occurrences, documents and monuments, uses proofs and accepts the outcome of analysis and speculation, regards no evidence as ever capable of affecting its claims in any way. It does not submit itself to be examined and judged by those outside it; it does not hold to its doctrines in a tentative or self-critical spirit. A relativistic answer, then, can be most appropriate to religions and yet be most inappropriate to aesthetics, ethics, philosophy – and to this answer.

"But," we will now be answered, "you have begun by saying and have too often repeated that each religion claims to be absolutely right and the others wrong, and that he who does not recognize this claim does not do justice to living religions. Yet your answer finally denies the force of such claims, since you take them all to be expressions of some limited condition or circumstance." It has not, however, been here denied that some religion's claims might be objectively valid. The point is that no one can know which, unless he has a knowledge of God and values apart from all religions. Every religion takes a risk that what it claims may not in fact be objectively true. No one is more irreligious than he who refuses to take that risk. A religious man is one who is confident that this risk is justified.

Every religion must make an absolute claim; yet each can be justly criticized for making such a claim since it has no way of knowing whether it is legitimate or not. In their concreteness, religions can and do exist in opposition. And one of them may tell more truth about God than the others. But this will be knowable only by those who already accept the religion. As not yet *known* to be true, as one of a number of competing religions, it must be recognized to make an absolute claim which is justified in terms of the circumstances in which the religion appears, but which may not, in fact, be objectively justified.

iv

THE IDEA that the philosopher has of God is not one used in religion, except as a possibility to be specified by the religion. The philosopher thus knows that religions are possible and can understand the multiplicity of religions as so many different specifications of the self-same possibility — a possibility which is in fact an idea of what God is most concretely. Each religion, by permitting beginnings to be made with it, allows for the self-same philosophic account of God. What the religions allow is actualized in a true philosophic characterization of God, and what the philosophy affirms is actualized in the shape of various relativizing religions, no one of which may be true. Each can offer a check on the other if independently developed. Those philosophers who, with Maritain, try to understand God from the perspective of a particular religion, prevent themselves from ever knowing whether or not the religion is merely a generalized version of what they have already taken for granted. Those religious thinkers who, with Bultmann, take some particular philosophic account of the nature of ultimate being as part of their interpretation of a given religion, prevent themselves from ever knowing whether or not the religion merely repeats in concrete forms what was affirmed in the philosophic account.

The revelations and miracles which particular religions offer are also to be judged in terms of what is otherwise known, or known in other ways. If they cannot withstand the scrutiny of philosophy, they must be rejected as false. Conversely, from the standpoint of a given religion a philosophy must be rejected so far as it fails to allow for the religion, its ideas and claims.

Philosophy must show how all the religions are possible; a religion should show that the one true philosophy is a generalization of it. A philosophy which fails to provide for all religions must (even from the standpoint of the religion it favors), be only an apologetic; the religion which fails to instance an independently achieved and grounded philosophy must (even from the standpoint of the philosophy it favors) be arbitrarily subjective.

A philosophy should allow for a plurality of religions; it is to be tested by seeing if they all serve as beginnings for an intellectual speculation which arrives at just that philosophy. A religion should allow for a systematic philosophy; it is to be tested by seeing if the philosophy gives an account of God for which the religion provides further details, and which are in fact encountered in religious experience, in a religious community and in worship.

Each religion speaks of God in ways not altogether acceptable to other religions. Their ideas of God are more than detailed cases of the idea of Him which one can obtain philosophically. They may, more likely than not, claim that He is and does what, from the standpoint of philosophy, is unintelligible, irrelevant, or self-contradictory. Each will of course apppeal to sacred doctrines, to history, to its prophets, martyrs, saints, to the good it has done and to the nobility of its sentiments. But since each appeals with equal passion and dogmatism to items not compatible with those appealed to by the others, they inevitably conflict. That conflict cannot be resolved by any one of them.

Religions explicitly reject the supposition that they are subject to an external test, since this would mean that they could conceivably be wrong. To be sure, there are also many philosophic systems, but each one of these is at least tacitly offered to a public community of critical objective inquirers to see if it is the ultimately true philosophy, doing justice to all reality. It sees too that it might be true and that in fact it must claim to be the true philosophy. But each and every philosophic account concedes that it might be wrong. A philosophy, because it asks to be measured by a standard of ultimate truth, can be known to fall short because of its omissions, incoherencies, arbitrary assertions, lack of self-criticism and its incapacity to provide a place for every kind of being and knowledge. It can, therefore, be known to be possibly false and possibly true. No religion though allows that it might be in error, since it does not allow that there is any way of evaluating it. It does not merely *claim* to be the true religion; it affirms this dogmatically and brooks no denial.

Because religions do not allow themselves to be measured by a standard of ultimate truth they do not allow themselves to be known as falling short of what a religion ought to be. None can therefore be known to be possibly true or possibly false, except by one who looks at it in the cold light of reason. If we wish to free a religion from the possible error that haunts them all we must cut away the specific details it adds in conflict with the details added by others, without losing the way men turn to God in act and thought, and God turns to them in justice and mercy. There is something parochial in the insistence that one can get to God only through the avenue of some such book as the Bible, the Gospels, or the Koran, or some such event as Moses on Mount Sinai, the Crucifixion, or the life of Buddha. By abstracting from these special claims one still remains within a religious situation, but it is one which has been purged of possible errors and special pleadings.

Once we look beyond specific religions with their practical concern for salvationally helpful truths, we should be able to see more clearly the reality which not only gives to our daily world some of the features it persistently exhibits but which makes both knowledge and religion possible. Behind the Gods of the various religions is an ultimate inescapable being which is irreducibly real and effective here and now, no matter what men say, think or do. This is not a mere being, a "God beyond God," but God Himself freed from the particulars added by particular religions, but not freed from an involvement with man and other realities.

v

THOSE WHO TAKE religion seriously have the choice of looking at it in the neutral spirit which this work has attempted to exhibit, or of engaging in one of its biased, limited forms. In the one case there is objectivity, catholicity, but a failure to enjoy the presence and the living search for God; in the other there is vitality, concreteness, involvement, but a failure to do justice to the grandeur of God and the universal spirit of religion. He who is without faith must be content with the former; he who is convinced that only his religion is right will be content with the latter. A fortunate few will be members of particular religions who know that there are other legitimate though limited religions, each of which exhibits in a distinctive way the fact that God is and interplays with men and other parts of this world. Each religion, including his own, will be seen to concentrate on only some of the many places and beings where God is present. He will be aware that the distinctive history, culture, activities and community of a people make it involved with God in a unique manner. On this view, no religion would be a religion for all men; its missionary efforts in fact would be directed at its own members, offering them a specialized laboratory where they were alerted to the fact that God is everywhere, but where also they were enabled to make contact with Him only some of the time or at some places. If, for this type of religious man, Jesus is the Christ, he will treat that as but a signal instance of the divine presence, which it cannot be for everyone else; others, say the Jews, with their characteristic prophets, Torah, Talmud and religious history, will find other sacramental realities more acceptable.* He will, though, despite his acknowledgment of Jesus as the Christ, be aware that, since God is a cosmic being, there are other divine manifestations. These, while as revelatory for others as his own is for him, he knows he will not be able to enjoy because he is not a vital part of their dedicated community, or their history, or their life. All religions on this view can be said to agree in that each grants that it and others have found legitimate, exclusive and conspicuous avenues for getting to God. Each will claim no more than that it stresses only some occasions when God is rightly acknowledged, and it will claim no less than that there are other occasions when God is rightly acknowledged by men who are committed in other ways. He who takes a view such as this must not, as many religious men do, merely pray for others; he must ask the members of other religions to pray for him. A sensitive religious man looks to other religions to do for him what he cannot wholly do for himself.

A religious man must also try to free himself from the limitations to which he is subject because his religion is integral to a public community. He must become free to have and practice

---

* Conversions are of course possible; but they are also rare, testifying at best to an insight usually denied to the other members of their community.

his faith privately, vitally and uniquely. Unfortunately, most men are too attached to the world — i.e., to society, community and nature — to be able to attend properly to God. Consequently, they fail to achieve a privately expressed faith or to exercise it persistently.

Everything can be looked at from a religious viewpoint. Everything can be treated as sacred. Some theologians therefore urge us not to turn away from the world. But this I think is an error. We do not start with — except only in a most primitive sense and for short periods — an awareness of the religious import of this world. We arrive at that result but only after we have succeeded in detaching ourselves from the world and attaching ourselves to God. The religious man sees that all that exists is enriched and sustained by God. He is right to do so. But it is wrong for him to forget that he cannot live this result unless he has learned how to free himself from a secular perspective, has acquired insight and strength from God, and then returned to the world, renewed and refreshed.

A religious man must belong to the world, and yet must somehow manage to free himself from it. Not until he has detached himself from it can he find his true centre. Not until he has found that centre can he relate himself to God as outside the world. Not until he has so related himself to God can he come into intimate relationship with Him. The religious man is a separated man who clings to God, and thereby is enabled to go back and enrich nature, his society and his dedicated community.

Though in the end a man must, if he is to be truly religious, be religious in private, the act of faith as a rule occurs only after he has been part of a dedicated community, and has freed himself from its conditions and limitations. It is therefore desirable for us, having examined the dedicated community, to attend now to the way the individual turns to God and gives himself to the task of finding Him, with its accompanying satisfactions, opportunities and obligations.

3. The Quest

9. Turning Toward God

THE WORLD about defies me in many ways. The most vexatious is also the most persistent. It is also the most challenging and the most subtle. The world about defies me by being indifferent to me. Relentlessly it goes its own way, heedless of my needs and presence.

I do not make the world's indifference a matter of central importance, in good part because I have learned to live with it. But I am never flexible enough, I never am dextrous enough, rarely am I wise enough to keep in perfect consonance with the ways of the world. I do not even know how to live perfectly inside the conventionalized part of the world which I, as a member of a society, accept as normative, reasonable and right. Again and again I am thrown back, shocked, disappointed, hurt, bewildered, frustrated, denied. Undaunted, I return again and again, perhaps a little shrewder, surely a little more wary, often a little more ready to find a steady and satisfying place within my society and within the larger world beyond. Sometimes I think this is how my life should be spent. But at other times I am dissatisfied. The more at home I am in the world about, the more empty my life seems to be.

Because I can never become wholly indifferent to myself, I cannot accept the world on its own terms. Indeed, a moment's reflection on the fact that it is indifferent to me, makes me see that I am of as much consequence as it is. Because I am one about which things swirl, because they are indifferent to *me*, I am aware that I am one whose center is not in the world. Precisely because I am not indifferent to the things that are indifferent to me, I know I exist as surely and at least as significantly as they do. I am ignored, therefore I am; I am ignored, therefore I am worth attending to. To be sure, I am intruded upon, but no matter how much I am affected and no matter how much I am involved in the affairs of the world, I continue to remain outside it. I have feelings, desires, needs and hopes which it ignores. To do justice to myself I must turn away from the world. Its indifference I should match with mine. I will surely become the gainer thereby since I will then recover the majesty of my I.

Everyone, sooner or later, learns to detach himself from some things. The weakening of memory, the upsurge of new desires, the zest for change, the lure of novelty lead us to loosen our grip on what we once held close. And then we find the result to be pleasurable, easy on the spirit, desirable. We are tempted to make a robust indifference a goal to be achieved. This everyone does occasionally. All of us make efforts every once in a while to detach ourselves, to sit loose from things, to hold ourselves apart. We stop to catch our breath, preparatory to taking another plunge into the midst of things, and then discover to our delight — tinged perhaps with a feeling of guilt for having yielded to an unsuspected pleasure — that there is something to be said for simply breathing.

All men rest, and all men sleep, but only they truly detach themselves who see themselves to have a position over against the rest of the world. Others merely arrest themselves, pause for a while — though even they have moments when they see that there is some value in matching the world's indifference with an indifference of their own.

Detachment is an acknowledged noble aim in the East. It has had defenders in the West. Epicureans and Stoics, so rarely in agreement, are here at one. We too have our ascetics, monks and contemplatives. And our poets, mathematicians, philosophers, theologians — indeed all those who engage in reflective or creative work — also detach themselves from the world of every day, even if it be only to attach themselves again elsewhere. No one of us wants to remain detached from everything, but no one of us is unaware that it is good to be detached from some things and at some times.

Detachment is an attitude. It can be maintained even when one is engaged in strenuous pursuits. One of the main lessons taught by the *Bhagavad-Gita* is that even a warrior can live the good life if only he would fight with detachment, accepting none of the fruits of his acts as belonging to him. He is to act like the professional hangman, doing his job but holding his self apart. The lesson has been learned by warriors in all those countries where the military has been separated from and subordinated to the civilian government. But no one can be detached regarding all things all the time, any more than he can be attached always and everywhere. What the East urges, the West practices more or less; what the West tastes, the East savors. Both are attached, both are detached, both enjoy being attached and detached, and both occasionally see value in becoming differently or more attached or detached than they now are.

He who would be religious must detach himself from the affairs of every day, from the larger world beyond, from state, from family and from church, if only in order to enable him to re-attach himself to them with more vigor and right and surety than he could manage before. It would be paradoxical if the detachment necessarily precluded a subsequent re-attachment to the world and sometimes to the very areas and objects from which one had initially turned away, or if it prohibited the use of aids from church, family, state and world. Every organization and institution concerned with man must help him to detach himself, even from themselves. They must guide and control his detachment, if only to make sure that the subsequent re-attachments occur when, how and where they will preserve the goods that the detachment achieves.

Strictly speaking, religion demands a detachment not only from all objects in this space-time world, but from all non-divine reality, from existence, ideals, and fellow-men. To say that we ought to detach ourselves from all of these is but to say that it is good to be religious, despite the fact that religion demands that we give up, at least for the moment, but possibly forever, much that we now cherish. If we eventually recover all that we abandoned in the course of a religious adventure, the religious good will prove to be the most satisfying and comprehensive of all. But if, as I think is the case, the recovery can never be more than partial, religion, though of a great value, will not offer the only life in which we ought to engage, nor will its goods be the only goods we should seek.

We succeed in detaching ourselves only for moments, and then only with respect to some things. No one becomes religious merely by detaching himself. Such detachment is only one step in the process of a conversion from a concern with the worldly to a concern with the divine. However, the more persistent our avoidance of involvement with worldly matters, and the larger the area from which we stand away, the more completely can we attain a state where we can live on terms more satisfactory than those that the world seems to provide. By altering our attitudes toward the world, we free ourselves from the alien, the irrelevant, and the external. We cleanse ourselves, become more unified, and whole. It is good to be detached even if we never become religious.

The act of detachment is promoted by subjecting men to sudden arrests, by forcing them to call a halt to their usual ways of thinking, acting and speaking. Changes in posture, place and tempo help loosen their chains. So do activities different from those usually pursued.

The act of detachment purifies. The purification is celebrated by both real and symbolic cleansings. It is one of the major tasks of circumcision, baptism, ritualistic baths, changes in linen, incantations and sacrifices to at once detach and clean. But these and similar devices, while freeing men from an involvement in the world, also tie them to some part of it. They purify one side and qualify another. Quite soon these agencies cease to provide effective means for achieving a purifying attachment, and instead, encourage an involvement in the world sometimes greater than that which had prevailed before.

If a man could take an agency for detachment to be part of himself, defining it as an outermost limit which bounds him off from the world, he could, through its aid, achieve a full, unalloyed detachment. The agency would then be for the man what his heart now is — an organic part of him. Such a result men try to achieve through the endless repetition of a gesture, word or prayer, by fingering a rosary, and by a meticulous conformity to a ritual. These, by helping keep attention confined within narrow limits, provide opportunities for cleansing agencies to be and to operate. In the end, though, the effort is question-begging and self-defeating. If this or that alien item could, with warrant, be made part of our being, we could with equal justification substitute or add others. Since the world's ruthless indifference is manifested in and through each and every item in it, it would be less arbitrary and more courageous to follow the materialists and naturalists and suppose that a man ought to identify himself with the nature or course of the entire universe. But, as Spinoza saw, to become one with the whole universe it is necessary to become indifferent toward oneself, and that act presupposes a prior detachment from all that goes on every day. If we are to escape the bondage of the world completely, we must either identify ourselves with the whole of it, or turn away from all of it. In either case we must detach ourselves from every item in it — and therefore even from every item that is part of a dedicated community.

We always risk becoming attached to the agencies by which a detachment is accomplished. And if we become attached, we so far lose control of ourselves. The loss could be turned into a gain, if the agencies were extensions or expressions of God himself. Sometimes clergymen or theologians speak of prayers, religious ceremonies and rituals in this way. Were they right, a man by using these could at once detach himself from the world and attach himself to God. Nothing could be neater; nothing could be swifter. Unfortunately, this desirable outcome presupposes the successful performance of some rather difficult acts. At the very least one will have to distinguish in the prayer or other agency a divine and a secular component. And that is not easy.

Unless one is to identify the spirit with the letter, a religious with a secular object, one must always distinguish, in every supposed religious agent, the secular vehicle from the holy meaning it contains, sustains or reports. No one can attend to the meaning unless he first thrusts the vehicle aside. The vehicle could conceivably have been divinely instituted. It might be the best possible vehicle for carrying a religious truth or message.

It might be the only avenue through which God's intent will be known. Still, whether it be book, prophet, saint or miracle, it will have a secular dimension from which we must turn away if we are to know what is being conveyed. The vehicle must be confronted if a message is to be heard, but at the same time it must be pushed away if the message is to be understood.

To be sure, if certain words, books or men are divinely chosen to be vehicles for a divine expression, they will, like saints, have distinctive inherent virtues, or like prophets, have distinctive bestowed ones. But this is only to say that the vehicle itself allows for a distinction between itself as divinely designated and itself as merely part of this world. The most holy of books is printed, glued and bound, bought and sold; it falls apart and is sometimes burned. Temples are built by men working — we hope — at union wages, spending energy to subdue stone and wood. We can suppose that the divinity which supervenes upon the whole seeps through and ennobles even the grossest parts, thereafter making them divine. But the holy books and buildings will still decay and crumble in the same ways and at the same rates that other books and buildings do. They too have a side from which we must cut ourselves off, at least for the moment, if we are to know what divine message they carry. And from what carries none, we should all the more cut ourselves off, in order to avoid being treated indifferently by it.

Christians are one in believing that our involvement in the world reveals a fault in each of us; the Hebrews find fault with Man. We are miserable sinners, or human, all too human. Every religion makes related suppositions. Each supposes that the religious state is most desirable. Each, therefore, supposes that any state other than the religious must be rooted in what the religion takes to be wrong, wicked or evil. But history and politics, art and ethics, science and philosophy make similar claims. No account of what men ought to do will ever be satisfactory which does not find a place for all these claims, revealing each discipline to have a dignity denied to the others. Be that as it may, to suppose that detachment is now necessary only because men fail to do or to be all they ought, suggests that they could conceivably be so properly involved in the world as never to need to be detached from it. But this is not true. The world goes its indifferent way when men are pious and good, and when they are not, and sooner or later will frustrate and will eventually destroy them. It also overlooks the fact that a dedicated community, like every other group, is governed by conventions, caught in traditions, burdened with worn-out procedures, and moves with a rhythm and rationale of its own. We ought to detach ourselves from the community as well as from nature no matter how well attuned we are to them, and no matter how much they benefit us. Our true centre lies outside them and cannot be found unless we turn away from them. We must undo our relationship with our own community and all else in the world, if only to enable us to find ourselves.

The Buddhist sees all involvement, any involvement, as evidence of our failure to crush the craving of desire toward existence, and for success. Detachment – he calls it "right view" – is the first of his four noble truths. He sees clearly how difficult it is to achieve this state for any period and to any great extent, and subjects himself to long periods of arduous self-discipline. He does not deny the indifference of the world, but only the necessity that we be involved with it. Though the Christian and the Hebrew also, on behalf of their religions, regret our involvement in the world, they do not suppose that we ought to aim at escaping from it forever and in every way. All are agreed, though, that to be religious one must be converted, the first step of which is to hold ourselves away from the world with which we are in fact involved, and with which we will remain bodily involved no matter what we believe and what we accept as our own. They do not clearly say, and apparently do not clearly see that since no detachment is complete and steady, no man could be completely religious all the time. Nor do they clearly see and say that detachment is only one of a number of essential conditions which must be met before a man can be religious.

A religious man is a converted man who follows up a detachment, first by a retreat within himself, then by an advance toward God, and finally by an acceptance of an assessment of himself by that God. Most of the men we call "religious" are not religious in this sense. They belong to a religious community which presumably has itself gone through similar stages, signalized in various acts in which men are expected to participate and which, it is hoped, will lead them then or later to go through the required stages on their own.

A community or organization tends to detach men from the world only to attach them to itself. This result it must constantly combat. It cannot suppose, without becoming an idol, a grave obstacle in the way of religion, that a religious man need do nothing more than act as it prescribes. It must point its members toward a God outside itself and them. This means that it must help men to free themselves not only from things in the world but also from itself.

ii

     I can succeed at times in meeting the world's indifference by detaching myself from it. I am not successful for long, or over large areas. More disheartening, the world pursues me. It is intrusive and insistent; I am constantly subject to its brute power. I suffer because of it. Pain, sickness, hunger, thirst tear at me, cut into my vitals. I am distracted, pulled this way and that. Quickly I learn how to shrink before its onslaughts. I try to learn how to soften its blows, and to anticipate its intrusions. I make myself learn something of its activities; I learn how to act effectively on it. I try to master its patterns and to channelize its energies. I must somehow transform, regulate and control it. Even when I turn my mind to other matters, I must see to it that my body keeps apace with it. Long before I take seriously the need to detach myself, and in between my successful acts of detachment, I habituate myself to so act that the world's cudgelings will be reduced. It is my hope that I can learn to deal with it through instruments which redirect or at least hold it up for a while.

We live today in the age of the engineer. All of us are trapped inside the patterns governing production, communication and transportation. It looks as if we would lose more than we could gain if we detached ourselves from this engineered, well-regulated scheme of things, particularly since this will not prevent it from continuing to intrude on us. If we are affected by the world, whether we detach ourselves from it or not, it would seem better not to turn away from it, but instead to spend our time and energy in trying to know and control it.

We ought to avoid making ourselves into nothing more than sensitive beings ruthlessly intruded upon. We ought to know the course of the world. This is worldly wisdom. It would be foolish to dismiss it. But since it offers no protection against the world and therefore does not negate the need to be detached, it would be equally foolish to rest content with it. The most one could urge on behalf of our remaining within our well-controlled engineered world, is that the gains which a detachment from it might provide are more than balanced by the reduction in suffering which our control will produce. Still, a reduction is not elimination, and some of our saddest sufferings no external power can control or reduce. Death awaits every one of us. Humiliation, confusion on all fronts, insecurity, worry, unsatisfied appetite, insatiable desire, distraction, weariness of spirit hound us all — even those of us who are well-adjusted, wise men of practice. No, the enemy is already too far inside the ramparts of each of us to allow us to spend all our energies on what is external to us. We would be foolish indeed to try to live merely as public men, no matter how smoothly the public engines run.

Because I know that it is I who feel, precisely because the world affects *me*, I know that I am greater than it. Let it throw me down, let it break through my defenses, if I do not take account of it, what is it but meaningless clang and bustle? Without me to feel it, it is not only brute but senseless, flat, a lock-step of monotonous causes and effects. I feel, therefore I am; I feel, therefore I am sensitive; I feel, therefore I am self-aware, a throbbing centre who gives what is acting on it a meaning, an importance, and even a sanction. A world which affects me is a world *I* make valuable.

Important though I now see myself to be, I still am subject to the world in ways I do not want to be. I am not strong enough nor wily enough to avoid its onslaughts and its dictates. It satisfies me little to say that without me it is meaningless; with me it is sometimes terrible. Would it not be better then to make myself numb, insensitive? Not unless it would be better for me to cease to be myself, to become just a part of a meaningless procession of causes and effects. The anodyne which saves me from all woes can be nothing short of death. No, *I* want to conquer. To make myself insensitive is to cease to be; it is to give up. It is to yield not merely some things, but *everything*, to a meaningless power.

The act of detachment I must follow with an act by which I successfully meet all that challenges me. I must not simply retire before the world. I must retreat from it strategically, by treating all that intrudes on me as insignificant, touching only what is not an essential part of me. And it is right that I do this, for I had wrongly identified the areas, where the outside world impinges, to be genuine parts of myself. When I retreat from those areas I move further back into myself. If I can go back in far enough, I may be able to continue to remain sensitive to what is outside me, but without any longer allowing it to be central for me.

No matter how successful a retreat may prove to be, I am not content with it for long. Though I like being at a place where I am not longer dictated to, there nevertheless is much in this world I find pleasurable, worth having, and worth having repeated. If I retreat, it must be only to get to a point where I can somehow adequately deal with what had challenged me. Each of us, all the time, the sybarite no less than the ascetic, retreats to a private point where all that is can be effectively possessed.

No one remains so caught in what the world offers him that he does not detach himself from it and retreat from its effects on him. But none retreats so far but that he knows from where he came and to where he should return. All men retreat so as to be in a better state than they were before. Each moves to the point where *he* can enjoy whatever there be, and can advance on it eventually on better terms.

Why retreat from anything but the unwanted? Why not retreat from all pain and suffering, but remain where the pleasures are? Unfortunately, both occur in the same places, usually intertwined. Why not analyze them then? Let's divide and thereby conquer. Wars are won in skirmishes; advances are made by regiments; victories are achieved through a succession of battles. Ought we not follow this lead, and master region after region, isolating the desirable pleasures? Such activity requires that there be a self which enjoys and keeps the gains together. But if this be so, why need one retreat at all? Why might not that self directly concentrate on pleasures? It might.

But this would not obviate the need to retreat, for to be pleased is still to be bound, to be a creature of others — in a word, to suffer.

To live a life of pleasure we must deny ourselves at times; we must put an edge on our hunger and thirst, punish ourselves some. And then we will find that we are precipitately let down. Pleasures pall; all end in aridity. Nor are pleasures possible except so far as we are externally sustained. To concern ourselves with pleasures is to become insensibly but firmly attached to the instruments by which they are produced. Yet these, we have already seen, ought to be put aside. Why not then wait to see what pleasures come, and take our fill of these? We could not do this without once again opening ourselves to intrusions which may prove to be most disagreeable.

Is this not true only of intense pleasures? Though Don Juan must follow conquest on conquest without cessation, might not a less violent occupation with love produce a more persistent joy? I think not. Pleasure is essentially climatic; it must have its contrasts, its negative moments if it is to have any value at all.

What difference does this make if the result is good on the whole? Because pleasures pluralize, disperse, divide. They make us lose ourselves. The best we can do is to put aside those pleasures that demand a high price in advance or subsequently, or which preclude our having desirable pleasures. Let us then stay with the pleasures which divide us least, the harmless ones. But this means we must become undistracted, unified, and self-centred. Only when this state is achieved, will it be possible to know what pleasures are good for us. We must retreat from pleasures as well as pains, if only to find those pleasures which it is desirable to have.

It is not good to lose oneself forever, even if it be in pleasures. We must retreat from pleasures no less than from pains. But, it might well be urged, even if it be good to retreat from them, it is not good to retreat from everything. There are goods of the mind worth pursuing. By all means let us give up a life of pleasure if we are thereby enabled to spend our energies in reflection, study, speculation or inquiry. Knowledge distinguishes men from beasts. There is a bracing, ennobling satisfaction to be obtained by giving ourselves up to the pursuit of science, metaphysics, history or some similar rigorous discipline. It is a satisfaction which must never be wholly denied, unless we are to deny the very powers which set us off from all other beings. And if we do not use those powers we will surely lose an opportunity to master both ourselves and what lies beyond us.

Unfortunately, our thoughts, more often than not, are agencies for attaching us to the world. They do not keep that world at bay. Not all our ideas are equally viable; some are confused and others confuse us, and the best of them are oriented away from us. Truth, after all, is a relation tying our ideas to what lies outside them. Our ideas therefore do not, they cannot of themselves offer an adequate answer to the world's indifference or intrusions.

The intellectual life is a life of frustration. The thinker is often bewildered and beset by error. His is a life of solitude, incomplete, distorted, streaked with prejudgments. There are satisfactions, deep and long-lasting, but they never go the length of meeting all external challenges or all the needs of the individual. Also, no matter how complete and comprehensive an intellectual achievement be, it will be expressed in abstract terms and thus will lack the texture, the rush, the finality of what exists. Each discipline, moreover, demands a life's devotion before it yields its most precious goods. To do justice to it, the pursuit of other disciplines must be hobbled or denied.

The thinker lives a partial life at best, fragmented, abstracted and unreliable. Creative spirits — poets, composers, choreographers — fare no better. They too are distraught, dispersed. To avoid being creatures of what is not themselves they too must retreat until they stand outside the multiplicities they themselves produce.

Retreat is not a means by which we annihilate ourselves. It is a means by which we find a place where we can maintain ourselves. Nor is it inconsistent with action. It does not require us to wipe out ideas, destroy knowledge, disdain all pleasures. But it does demand that we turn away from these to reach our selves, behind all their divisions, behind all distinctions. Without distinctions, to be sure, we could neither speak nor think. Yet we must retreat behind all distinctions. In terms of the distinctions, that at which we will arrive will be Nothing. That Nothing *is* like white light, not like night. It exhibits no distinctions, only because it transcends all distinctions, because it is richer than any set of distinctions could be.

To be successful a retreat must move away from where distinctions occur and are germane. It must find the silence which is at the root of speech, the one that is at the heart of the many, the axle which is at the centre of the wheel. There is a vast library telling us how best to do this. The oldest methods tell us to control our breathing, to concentrate on sacred sounds and great events. These are surely more hopeful agencies than drugs and drink. Drugs and drink edge us toward stupor. They do not bring us to a centre. They encourage vagrant images, the creatures of a disturbed body and mind. The challenges we constantly face cannot be overcome through the use of such poor props as drug and drink, and the dim wits these promote.

The Buddha urged men to retreat to "nothingness" itself. He sometimes spoke as though he himself were truly nought, though if he were, there would be nothing *he* could do to reach that dead centre. To reach it he would have had to have a self, real and powerful. But whatever the supposed terminus, the practices which are recommended can at best be only instruments enabling us to reach the point where the retreat is carried out by ourselves, in privacy, alone. We must retreat no less from the agencies which promote a retreat than from the more evident forces that intrude upon us.

Retreat is the second of the steps that must be taken by one who would give up a purely secular life for a religious one. Even those who convert from one religion to another must first find the authentic centre of themselves before they can properly attach themselves to the new religion. But if retreat be a part of the act of becoming religious, does it not depend for its success, perhaps even for its possibility, on God's help? Without grace, there can be no salvation, we are told. Now of course there is a deep and inescapable sense in which nothing can occur without God's help, if God be that being to which everything, by the very fact that it is, makes reference, and if He be that being who, if He be anywhere, must be everywhere. But the doctrine of grace — natural, irresistible, habitual, prevenient, efficacious or otherwise — wishes to say something more than this. It asserts that, overlaying the nature which man intrinsically has, there is a supernaturally produced glory that enlightens the mind and assists the will, thereby enabling a man to participate in the goodness which is God. But then either God alone makes a man be religious, or a man will, by disposing and preparing himself properly, guarantee that God will so act that God will be loved by him — which is the Pelagian supposition which even Thomists make. (When a Thomist says that a man must cooperate with God, he may of course intend to say that God alone is truly active and that men merely allow Him opportunity and occasion. But this view not only goes contrary to the Council of Trent, which denies that God alone is the active one, but it also supposes that God is not really omnipotent, merciful, capable and willing to enter into and to conquer everything.)

Whether God's aid be necessary or not, the fact is that without a retreat by a man from what otherwise would be dispersive, there is no position from which he individually can concern himself properly with God. And in the end this is perhaps what the doctrine of habitual grace, a permanent, intrinsic, supernaturally bestowed quality of the soul, comes to. It allows one to say exactly what the Hebrews, who have no such doctrine, also say: a man always has the ability to believe and worship. And in the end this is perhaps what the doctrine of prevenient grace, which moves the will to incline toward God, also comes to, since it allows one to say exactly what the Hebrews, who have no such doctrine, also say: a man always has the ability to get ready to believe and worship. In both cases, however, the ability requires that a man first find his own centre by retreating from the periphery of his being where his intent, feelings and ideas are possessed and pulverized by the world.

Whitehead goes too far when he says, "Religion is what the individual does with his own solitariness." This is protestantism, rather on the low-church side. It overlooks the role of the religious community, of religious ritual and ceremony. It is hard to reconcile with the existence of religious history and religious works of art, since these are public not private in nature, no matter what their origin be. A religious community, as we have seen, relates a man to a being outside it and himself. Only if God were wholly immanent in a man could he be religious solely by doing something with his solitariness. But it is also true that no man is religious unless he does something privately.

For some philosophers men are inescapably solitary. These thinkers then ask how a man could come to know or encounter the external world. But they could not have asked the question with any propriety unless they had somehow managed to retreat far from their bodies and even their ideas. This means that the answer that they seek was present at the beginning, but that they turned their backs on it. Nothing is easier than to be part of the "external" world. Even a stone manages it. We, as mere bodies, like stones, are cosmic realities. When we retreat within ourselves we do not lose our hold on or our place in the cosmos. We merely reach a position from which we can come to know what that cosmos is like, and what else there may be besides.

I retreat to a place where external realities can no longer intrude. Unfortunately, it is a place dictated by them, travelled to at a pace and with a success which they partly determine. Because I started from a place externally defined, moved back an arbitrary distance, and along a route in part conditioned by where I started, by what I was involved with and by the power it exerted against me, I am still oriented toward the world. Wherever I stop in my retreat is only a resting place, not my true absolute centre.

I ought not to have allowed my backward movement to be determined by what is not myself. So long as I permit this I can only be one who momentarily rests beyond the world. Again and again I will slip back into that world, and again and again I will have to retreat from it. I have no fixed place at which I can stand so long as all I do is move back into myself. I will then arrive nowhere, but merely stop at some distance from where I started in order to retreat further, or again.

I am conditioned, therefore I am; I am subject to arbitrary dictates, therefore I am one who insists on himself. Because I am acted on by realities which have no regard for *me*, I can look at them as being irrational, trivial and absurd. I know that I have a value that they lack. The world from which I flee is nothing more than a world which I can evaluate as not being all it ought to be for me. But if I am to find a place which is my own, and not merely a place which the world does not own, I must learn to be more positive. I must assert myself.

I once acted in ways which made an act of detachment

desirable. I had insisted on myself in ways which made it desirable for me to retreat from the world. I must now assert myself so as to possess the place to which I retreat.

I must assert myself. If I do not I will sink into passivity, and thereby make myself even more open than ever to determination by what is alien and undesired. I will evidently undo all I had done if, after detaching and retreating, I do not assert myself. Indeed, I must expand, fill out the entire region over which I fled. To be myself I must radiate out, be myself throughout the area I retreated from. More. I must subjugate what lies beyond me. I must impose my terms on it, and thereby expand in and through it. Nor can I stop my advance until I recover not only all the territory I once abandoned, but all that lies beyond it. But if I expand so far, do I not become involved in the world's blind contingencies once again? Was it not because I was so involved with other beings that I sought to be detached from them? Why then should I now try to encompass all of them? And if I stop short, will the world respect my self-restraint? Will it not defy me again and again?

I actively dislodged myself first here and then there. But now I advance in principle, paying no attention to details. My retreat was by painful steps, but now I progress in a single conquering leap. I characterize, evaluate, impose categories on what lies beyond to make myself the master of all I survey. I assess the world as contingent and insensitive; I disdain it as too crass, too stupid, too limited to do justice to my needs and nature.

I control the world from my hidden centre by means of my ideas. I am its master. Victory is mine — or so it seems for one vivid moment. Quite soon I see that I have actually gained nothing. My supposed victory over external reality in fact contains within it a double defeat. If I encompass the world through my ideas, I thereby hide the world, as it is in and of itself, from me. I have it on my terms, but my terms are precisely those I ought not to impose, for they prevent me from seeing what it is on which I impose them. I must not make myself into a Kantian who turns the substantial, real world into a thing in itself which he by definition precludes himself from knowing. When I insist on myself I ought not place a veil of ideas between myself and what else there be. We all impose ourselves — and we should, but in such a way as to enable us to reach and really master the world.

The second defeat which an imposition of conditions by me would involve is even more complete. I assess a world which is my other. But it cannot be my other unless I am its other. "Otherness" is a symmetrical relation, in which each term qualifies the other. Each makes the other a creature of itself. By treating what faces me as my other I raise it up to be my equal. More, I acknowledge its rootage in a reality independent of me. If it is my other, and I am its other, there is in each of us something which sustains the relation of otherness between us. If we are not to be one another's others, hopelessly creatures of one another, dependent upon our dependents, we must have beings of our own. But then I cannot claim to have altogether conquered it.

Each of us has its own integrity; each has its own power, its own value. The relation of otherness connects us. But need the connection be so intimate that each loses itself? The question is badly put. If each of us has a reality unrelated to the other, there would be no way, being at one of them, that we could ever reach the other, ever know what it was like or even that it existed. We would in effect become Kantians twice over, adding to a world of unknowable things in themselves, ourselves who are equally unknowable.

I assert myself; I keep no core away from everything. I take the initiative, dictate to the world, spend myself in categorizing, assessing it. I have a being of my own, but it is no idle thing in itself. This seems to be the very truth which Kant intended to affirm. But the converse must also be acknowledged. Other realities, because they accept my categorizations of them, have already made contact with me. They are not, any more than I, hidden things in themselves.

Why not affirm that I accept the world as an object of my assessment, and that it in turn accepts my assessment of it? Perhaps the world that is not I is but myself caught hind way to? The I that is not the world would then merely be the world negated. The view is in root Hegel's. It is so brilliant that it deserves to be true. But it cannot become so until it is considerably modified.

A being on which I impose myself is distinct from one

which accepts me; the first is receptive, the second is accommodative. The I which assesses is distinct from the I which is accepted; the one is active, the other is passive. In one part we have an active I assessing a receptive reality, and in the other we have a passive I accepted by an accommodating reality. In each part I unite with an other, but in the first I am mirrored by, in the second I mirror my other. Hegel's solution thus breaks in two.

To be free of the world I must be able to control it fully or negate it completely. I cannot do the first. Can I do the second? I know very little about myself. Nor am I sure what I am to do if I am to negate the world successfully. How can I negate all the others unless I somehow can be absolute? Yet I am assessed by others as surely as I assess them; at my very roots I seem not to be absolute but relativized, and thus not to have a being all my own.

If there is something for me to negate, I am. But were I nothing more than one who negates them, I would be a function of them, dependent on their presence for material with which to deal. If I am to be more than something for them — and this I must be if I am to be — I must have a nature of my own. If I sustain relations to other beings, I have a nature independent of those relations, enabling me to ground those relations at my end. Since I sustain the relation of otherness, I must be something more than the other of the rest.

Because I am other than whatever else there be, severally or together, I must have a being over against them. There must be more to me than can be caught in the expression "not these." I am more than one who is the other of the beings which are together with me, whether these be viewed as spiritual, necessary, contingent or indifferent. I am an other *of* them only because I am an other *for* them; i.e., I other them because I *can* other them. And I am an other *for* them only because I am other *than* they; i.e., I can other them because I have a being distinct from theirs.

If something new were to come into existence, I would be an other for it, but only because I already have a being of my own, apart from the relation I can have to it. Because I am unique, ultimate and unduplicable, other than, I can be an other not only of and for the things in the world, but also of and

for possibilities, space, time, men — indeed of and for everything.
Let anything come into being. I know that I will not be it.
I will continue to remain myself, unaffected by its, or any other
being's coming or going. I will never be one who merely negates
it, for I am more than a function of what is exterior to myself.
I do negate it; I am an other of it. I also can negate it; I am an
other for it. And I am an other for it only because I am more
than a negator; I am other than it.

Since I continue to be even when this and that thing pass
away, I must have a being independent of them. But then either
I am an unreachable, unrelated thing-in-itself or I am related to
something which is not as inconstant as the particular things
about me. The first alternative is self-contradictory. If I know
that I am unreachable and unrelated, I already, through knowledge, reach it and relate it to myself. Only the second alternative
is possible. This has two wings. Either I am always related to
"some thing or other," or I am always related to something
over against each and every thing. Since I am a substance, I must
be sustained and thereby related to something more powerful
than an abstract "some thing or other"; to be able to be other
than things I must be an other of a being at least as substantial
as I. Because of it I can sustain a relation to them, and am
knowable apart from them.

My initial attachment to the world revealed me to be an
other of that world. My detachment shows I am an other
for it. I see now that I am able to be an other for it because
I am other than it, and that I am other than it because I am
related as an other to something else.

What can this be to which I am related when I am other
than the world? It cannot be another man, for not only is he
part of the world from which I turn away, but his privacy does
not endure through the exact time span that mine does. When
I am, he may not be, and when he is I may not be. Nor can this
which I seek be eternal ideas, a permanent space or some similar
reality, for though these allow me to continue to be even when
other men pass away, they lack internality, vitality, genuine
subjectivity. My persistent other is at least as inward as I.

Is there something which has sufficient permanence and
internality to enable me to be other than every thing else?
I think so. The traditional name for it is "God." Can this be

whatever is the object of an ultimate concern? I think not. Tillich says that the "ultimate concern is the abstract translation of the great commandment: 'The Lord, our God, the Lord is one; and you shall love the Lord your God with all your heart and with all your soul and with all your mind, and with all your strength.' " He also says (in a world where there are Hindus, Buddhists, Jews and Muslims) that our ultimate concern is with the "New Being in Jesus as the Christ." And in the very book where he writes "Whatever concerns a man ultimately becomes god for him; and conversely, it means that a man can be concerned ultimately only about that which is god for him," he also says "A heavenly, completely perfect person who resides above the world and mankind" *is not* "a matter of ultimate concern." These assertions are not easy to reconcile. More pertinent to our inquiry is the fact that like many other modern theologians he speaks often as though an ultimate concern and its object were inescapable, and that as a consequence all men are necessarily religious. There is something amiss, though, in any defense of a precious good which says that even those who explicitly reject it or deny its existence nevertheless accept or possess it.

Not every man is ultimately concerned. Some spend their lives attending to trivialities. Some ultimate concerns, too, are not religious concerns. There are worldly men, attached to non-religious goals, who refuse to look to God. There are others who try not to assert themselves, being content to remain outside the fray as long as they can; there are also those who occupy themselves with secular tasks or with creative enterprises. None of these avoids all contact with God. But they do not concern themselves with Him; they have only the dimmest awareness and the slightest of interests in what enables them to stand over against all else. Nor is every concern for God religious in intent or in act. Men can concern themselves with God but not take account of the fact that He takes account of them. It is possible also to obtain an idea of God (we have already seen) by moving back into ourselves and emerging with an emotionally-toned unity for whatever there be. But we do not thereby become religious.

It is possible to detach oneself and retreat from the world, to affirm oneself and refer to God, and still not be religious.

Even one who is concerned with attaching himself to God need not be religious. God and he must meet, somewhere inside himself and also somewhere beyond. The religious man is receptive to and accommodates himself to a divine assessment and acceptance. But it is not easy to be receptive to God and to accommodate Him — it is not often attempted.

There are, of course, millions of people who are pious, reverential, worshipful, who pray, sacrifice, believe. It would be wrong to say that they have no religion. But if they also *are* religious, it is only because, as members of a dedicated community, engaged in religious practices, they willingly but almost unconsciously go through the various stages by which a man is so turned away from the world that he actually turns to and accepts the decisions of God. No one of them is, and no one of us can be, fully religious for long stretches. A man's religious attitude varies in degree, depending on just how thoroughly he detaches himself, how far back he retreats, how much of what he affirms of himself he refers to God, and whether he has a faith that God will be mercifully just to him.

No concern, not even an ultimate concern, not even a concern for God makes a man religious, unless we take desire for attainment, will for fact, promise for performance. We refuse to do this in art, in science, in philosophy; we refuse to do this in ethics, in politics, in history; we refuse to do this in business, in work, in games. Why should we not refuse to do this in religion?

Everyone has creative moments. All have moments when they inquire systematically. Everyone occupies himself with some issues in ethics, politics and history. All attain some results in business, work and games. But few have enough of these moments to allow them to be termed artists, thinkers, leaders or athletes. Similarly, though all men have religious moments and can have religious interests and achieve religious results, these are usually too minor, too episodic, too inchoate and ill-defined to make the men be truly or fully religious.

Teachers tend to encourage backward students in a given enterprise by telling them that they already are participants. The slower, the less confident, the more inept are sometimes praised more highly than others are. Enthusiastic teachers in a

world indifferent or antagonistic to the enterprise, understandably give these pupils higher marks than they deserve. Religious
teachers exhibit these failings more than other teachers do,
with little noticeable benefit to their students, their religion,
or their God.

My ultimate concern is to be as I ought to be. The satisfaction
of that concern will, I think, eventually prompt me to attend to
God. But if I tried to attend to Him, without regard for what
I am, I will only long for him. I will seek, but I will never find.
Religion is not the wail of a man hopelessly lost, forsaken,
crying in a wilderness, offering himself up without reserve to
some remote and perhaps non-existent God. It is not evidence
of a persistent, inescapable failure, nor a fruitless pursuit of an
absconded being. It reaches. It heals. It unites. It helps answer
the question: what ought I to be? Eventually it will help me
know what I ought to do.

iii

APART FROM THINGS, men, possibilities, space and time,
there must be a being which makes me be other than they are.
It must be at least as private as I am. It must be as persistent
as I. And it must allow me to assess things and still have being in
reserve. This is God. Since He enables me be other *than* things,
He must be an other *for* me. But if He is an other for me, I
must be an other for Him. And if we are others for one another,
we can be others *of* one another, be involved with one
another. I evidently escape involvement in one direction only
because I am ready to accept it in another.

My basic problem is to elect in which direction I should turn
for my involvement — toward the world or toward God. I
rarely provide a deliberate, clear-cut solution to this problem,
or remain with any one solution for long. I take myself quite
often to be one whose business is only with space-time things
or with men, even after I turn from them and spend some time
affirming myself. But they do not adequately answer to myself
as at once persistent and private.

Only if I allow myself to become involved with God can
I avoid being involved in the world, and conversely. The more
deliberately and resolutely I set myself to avoid being tied to

things, the more surely and persistently I must be related to Him. Actually I point in both directions most of the time. Or, what is the same thing, I am as a rule only partially other than things and only partially other than what is outside them. If I am to belong to the world, I must become more involved in it than I had been. If I am to stand over against the world, I must be more ready to become involved with the God who is outside it.

By making myself an other *for* God I become that which is other *than* the world. By making myself an other *of* God, I can be steadily other *than* the world. Conversely, by making myself other *than* the world I make myself an other *for* and can make myself an other *of* God.

Were I merely to refer to, but never terminate in God, I would never acquire the status of being an other of Him. Yet the degree and manner in which I take the position of being other *than* the world is measured by the degree and manner in which I take the position of being an other of God. I am able to be steadily other *than* things only because there is a God of which I am an other. The way in which I am involved with Him and thereby possess the character of being an other of Him, determines the way in which I stand away from everything else.

Otherness is a symmetrical relation. If I acquire from something the role of being its other, it must acquire from me the role of being my other. I am the other only of, for and than what has the status toward me of an other of, for and than me. My other and I are indissolubly linked. We mirror one another. If I give myself to it, it accommodates me; if it insists on itself, I yield to it. My other and myself are reciprocals.

If a man puts primary stress on his self as that which endows God with the status of being an other *of* it, he sees himself as self-defeated. If instead he puts primary stress on God as a being who makes his self be an other *of* Him, he sees himself ennobled. Taking both together he is a subject tensed between defeat and glory. If he puts primary stress on his self as that which endows God with the status of being an other *for* it, he sees himself cherished. If instead he puts primary stress on God as a being who makes his self be an other *for* Him he sees himself disdained. Taking both together he is a substance synthesizing acceptance and rejection. If he puts primary stress on his self as that which endows God with the status of being other *than* it, he sees himself as insignificant. If instead he puts primary stress on God as a being who makes his self be other *than* Him, he sees himself as existing forever. Taking both together he is a being spanning time and eternity. Taking all of these together, he is a soul representing all else, and stretched between the infinitesimal and the infinite.

It is sometimes said that the religious man recovers his true self. It would be more accurate though to say that for the first time he allows his soul to flourish. The child surely does not have a soul more certainly than a man; it is too muddled, distracted, too much a prey to appetite and whim to be one who lives in or close to its proper centre. When then could a religious man have acquired a soul? Surely not before he was born, or before he was converted. From the start he too is immersed in the world about and must, to find himself, detach, retreat and assert. His self is there to begin with, but to begin with it is so intermixed in alien affairs that he is not yet all he ought to be. He acquires a soul before he becomes religious, but not before he is attached to God.

There is no soul except so far as there is an involvement of the eternal in the affairs of the self; there is no immortality except so far as the self has become that which is other *than* the things in the world. My immortalized being contains my self evaluated as more or less good, depending on how that self stands away from the world. My soul contains an assessment of my self as more or less concerned with what is not worldly. I have a soul and am immortal because I am at once involved with what is both not my self and not the world, and this is involved with me.

I unite myself with God, the other of and for me when and as I am other than the world. The more surely, the more fully I do this, the more surely and the more fully will I have a substantial, permanent soul. But I cannot do this except so far as God exists. He must not only be an other of and for me but also other *than* I.

What is other than I stands apart from me; it has an independent being, a reality of its own. When I am involved with it, I either face deceptive illusory signs of it, signs apparently produced by me, or I face partial revelations of it. I then either create what I face, or I grasp something of what is itself eternal and private. But if I created it all, how could it be an other of or for me? The nature God has in Himself and as other than I, is not altogether alien to the nature He has relative to me, since He owns, grounds what He offers to me.

Those theologians who speak of God as unknowable, absolutely transcendent, forever hidden, who take every piece of evidence to be evidence of the reality of a being radically different from that evidence, are indistinguishable from naturalists. Having lost that which makes them souls, they can do nothing but leap — but they know not where nor with what success. These theologians have no right to say that man is the "image" of God. They cannot determine from what they face, anything about the way in which God is over against things, any more than they can determine from the way He is involved with men, what He is like over against them. No one of course knows God exhaustively, but then nothing is known exhaustively. We may distort His nature when we involve ourselves with Him, but distortion is not sheer falsification. God is transcendent but only so far as he is immanent too, and what He is like as transcendent is fore-shadowed in what He is like as immanent.

I need no faith to affirm that God exists, if by God I mean only that which grounds what is other of and for me. Such a God must exist if I do, an ensouled being with a conscience, judged and justified, representative of whatever else there is, absolutely other than God. If I wish to avoid saying more than the minimum, I must say only that God exists, eternal and private, able to be involved with me. If I want to go beyond these statements I must have faith.

I do not need faith to be confident that God will act in terms of the evidence I present of the way and the degree in which I turned away from the world, and the way and the degree in which I identified myself with what I then confronted. His unity assures that in His depths He will act relevantly to what He does correlative to me. I do need faith, though, to be sure that He forgives and redresses — or less anthropomorphically, that the evidences I present regarding my concern for what is eternal and good are used to bring about what is eternally better. I need no faith to know that if I cling to Him I will be able to withstand the world more effectively than I ever did before. But I do need faith to be sure that whatever answer I give will be assessed and completed, and the result accredited to me.

I need faith if I am to accept as right the value which God

puts on what I do. If I have such faith, I am a religious man. If I have not, I have at best been converted from one who lost himself in the world to one who not only has found himself but is aware that there is more to reality than himself and the world. If I allow myself to be guided by revelation and testimony, or if I follow the teachings, practices and commands of a dedicated community, I can readily take advantage of momentary turns and longings to express the faith that my redeemer lives. If I am ready to do this, or if I occasionally believe that merciful justice will prevail, I am sometimes said to be religious. But I am then religious in somewhat the way a student painter is an artist. Conversely, like a mature artist who belongs to no school at all, it is possible to be religious without accepting any revelation or without belonging to a dedicated community. Sometimes it even may be better to act counter to what the community demands, particularly when it is about to over-regulate its most religious members.

I need no faith and therefore no religion if all I wish to acknowledge is the existence of God and the fact that He takes account of me. But I need religious faith to enable me to accept the evaluation which He puts on me. In either case I must first make myself into one who is other than what daily defies me. I must turn from the world and look to God, if only in order to be able to have a soul and thus a reality of my own over against all else. After having made this turn I ought to return to the world. Inevitably I am forced back, if only to meet its challenges to my peace and my continuance. It is only there that I can fulfill some of the duties I there assumed. I ought to come back too to realize my promise as a creative being. And I owe it to God to come back so that I can make His intent viable and effective outside Him. But it would be best not to return until I had reached Him through faith and prayer, for only then will I have become acquainted with Him, and know something of what He would have me be and do.

10. Faith

I WOULD NOT be able to attach myself to God were any one of four states of affairs possible to me. I would not attach myself to God:

— Were I completely involved in the affairs of the world. *But were I completely involved in the affairs of the world I would not be one who could become so involved.*

— Were I able to stand away from some parts of the world, be other than them, solely by becoming involved with other parts, i.e., by becoming an other of those parts. *But were I other than some parts solely because I was an other of others, I would not be self-identical except so far as I continued to keep myself in one position and was related to what was unchanging. But I am unsteady and the world is everywhere in flux.*

— Were I able to stand away from the world by becoming involved not with God but with existence or an ideal. *But were I not involved with God I would be only an adjusted part of a contemporary world, or an obligated being, but not also, as I in fact am, a private subject.*

— Were God wholly immanent in me. *But were God wholly immanent in me, He would not be other than I. God enables me to be other than Him and therefore to be an other of and for the world. Because of Him, I can be something by myself and also be involved with the world.*

ii

I KNOW that God has a being in and of Himself, because He is involved with me. Because He is involved with me, He must also be transcendent. Those who do not allow that God is in any sense involved with them, must allow that apart from faith He is completely unknown to them, and might, for all they know, not be at all. But then they cannot know how they can be private beings with souls and consciences, capable of interplaying with the world.

There are some theologians who think the only agency by which one can make contact with God is through faith. They find no hope in reflection or speculation. They disdain philosophy. For them God is forever hidden to those who are not religious. It is not easy to isolate their reasons. Apparently they think that men cannot know God, not because He is indeterminate or unintelligible, but because He is so completely determinate and perfectly intelligible that nothing but an intellect, purer than any a man could have, would be adequate to the task. Our intellects are impure, tinged by the emotions, directed inevitably toward the world, unable to look at that which is intelligible through and through. Since we lack an adequate intellect, they think, God must remain unknown to us unless we have recourse to faith. Though they do not suppose that the faith will reach God as He is by Himself they think that it gets closer to Him than the intellect could. And since God is the only object of worth on this view, any occupation with some other topic than God, they also hold, must be intrinsically without value.

The view rests on a number of suppositions, no one of which is plausible. It supposes that without faith no one concerns himself with God, or that if he does, he cannot know anything about Him. But if God is an ultimate reality, anyone who makes evident the indispensable and universal conditions governing any reality must provide at least a partial picture of the nature of God. We cannot in fact avoid having an accurate, though not necessarily complete, grasp of God so far as we succeed in understanding the real nature of any thing.

Only one who held that God was intrinsically unintelligible, that a partial grasp of Him was no grasp at all, or that nothing could exist apart from Him, could make plausible the supposition that it is impossible to provide any knowledge of God. But none of these points can be sustained. If God were intrinsically unintelligible, we would not be able to know whether He had any value or not, and could not therefore claim that we, in failing to deal adequately with Him, fail to deal with that which has supreme worth. If a partial grasp of God is no grasp at all, no one, no matter how mystical or religious, could reach Him, for only God Himself can grasp His entire nature completely and perfectly. Finally, if nothing could exist apart from God, the universe must be part of God, so that anyone must inevitably, in speaking of that world, be speaking of a part of God.

To defend faith it is necessary to grant that we have some knowledge of reality, that that knowledge reveals something about the nature of God, and that it points to the fact that there is more to know by non-intellectual means. Knowledge must be acknowledged to be valuable, if for no other reason than that it makes evident the desirability of supplementing what we grasp intellectually with what we can garner by an act of faith.

The second supposition the view contains is that what is other than God has no value of its own. But if, as these theologians believe, God is good and the creator of all there is, what He has produced must also be good, and a knowledge of it should be desirable. If the universe is God's product, then a study of that universe must inevitably be concerned with what is valuable.

To defend the second supposition, it is necessary to say that the value which things other than God possess does not belong to them in themselves, but only as reflections of God's concern for, or approval of them. But to this two replies can be made. First, it is better to make something intrinsically good than something intrinsically valueless. A perfect and good God would therefore produce the former and not the latter. Second, if all things were intrinsically valueless, there would be nothing in them which would warrant the election of some and the rejection of others. There would be no real difference in value between a virtuous and a vicious man, health and disease, knowledge and ignorance, philosophy and faith. But then God could have none but an arbitrary, unreasonable reason for approving of one intrinsically indifferent thing and condemning the other. We would have no warrant for saying that God approves or disapproves of philosophers, civilization, science, or prayer. We could not say that He did not want things to have an intrinsic value of their own.

To defend the value of the object of faith, it is necessary

also to defend the values of other objects which the object of
faith makes possible. Only one, who (as I do) goes along with
Aristotle, and denies that God created the world, could escape
from such an obligation. But then he would not claim that all
value was in or originated from God. Let us however for the
moment grant that there is no value at all in the universe. The
third supposition behind the view that God is the object only
of faith is that a study of the universe would therefore be valueless. But this confuses the value of the known with the value of
knowledge. In some cases knowledge is good, in others bad, and
in still others indifferent, and this whether or not the objects
known are themselves good, bad or indifferent.

It is good to know the good, if one is good or can make
proper use of it. It is of value to the saint and the student to
know in what direction the good might lie and how radically
it differs from the evil which might happen to mimic it. But
knowledge of the good is bad if used for bad ends or in bad ways.
The devil, it is said by those who presumably know, can quote
scripture to his purpose, and the fanatic certainly can quote it
to his and our ruin. A knowledge of the good, finally, is indifferent so far as it is a knowledge which does not enter into the
being and activities of the knower. Teachers of ethics and
theology are rarely conspicuous for either vice or virtue. They
know more about the good than most, but their knowledge
makes little difference to what they are or do. On the other hand,
to know what is bad is good for the judge and for the doctor
and for anyone else who is concerned with and capable of pre-
venting, controlling and correcting evil. Such knowledge, however, works havoc on the minds and lives of the immature and
unstable, and is almost without value for those who are indifferent to the welfare of others. Finally, it is good to know the
nature of the trivial if one's purpose is to make life more pleas-
ant, but it is bad to know the trivial when it obscures insight
into higher values. And it is neither good nor bad to know the
trivial if we do not allow it to have an effect on whatever else
we might know or on anything we might do.

From the hypothesis that the universe has no value it does
not therefore follow that there would be no value in knowing
it. There would, in fact, be great value in knowing a valueless
world if such knowledge made possible a better life, and an

awareness of the existence of still higher values elsewhere. Granted that the universe contains nothing of value, it still is good to know what it does contain and what it only appears to contain, and good to know whether or not there are evidences of God within it. But to know the difference between the real and the apparent, and to discover what the universe contains and whether it offers evidences of the existence or activity of God is one of the tasks of philosophy and not of faith.

Caution would dictate a modification of the original contention so that it reads: "Since the understanding of any good requires a grasp of the highest good, without faith all knowledge, because necessarily distorted, is valueless or bad. The intellect must move only within the confines which faith prescribes; otherwise it will stumble into folly."

If faith be understood to be not a special mode of reaching God, but an adherence to specific dogmas defended by a church, this last view would express a claim to the effect that only the knowledge possessed by one of the true "faith" was right. Let us suppose that there is someone who is willing to go this far. What evidence will he offer that he has the true "faith?" Will it be evidence that anyone could grasp, whether he be an atheist or pledged in another way, or will it be evidence which has strength only because it is supported by the very "faith" it attempts to support? If the former be the choice, he acknowledges the power of the intellect to understand, even though it be unillumined by that "faith." If he adopts the latter, he admits that he can have nothing to say to another in defense of his view, except that he believes as he does.

If, however, by faith we mean not the acceptance of some dogma or creed, but a mode of reaching God in a way not open to the intellect, it is possible to assume a more plausible position held by numerous mystics and religious men, some of whom acknowledge no particular dogma or creed. These men claim to have reached God and to have learned from Him secrets of the universe which are hidden from the mere intellect. They claim to see the world in a way no one else can, and that what they grasp, alone accords with what is really so. But these men, like everyone else, were at some time ordinary mortals. By their own account, their merely human power was not adequate to the task of enabling them to escape from the limitations, errors, distortions and falsehoods which they and everyone else suffered. Nothing except the act of God's reaching down, plucking them out from a multitude and presenting them with the required power and vision, could have made it possible for them to attain the stage of knowing what is really so. At its strongest, this view confesses that we can have no reason now for suspecting the truth of what our intellect reports, and no way of evaluating what we know apart from faith, so long as we have no faith to guide us. We must await the time when God will reach to us as well, and thereby make evident how mistaken we had been. The mystic and the devout man confessedly can prove nothing to us and we nothing to them, if by definition they hold as basic what we cannot, and conversely. They cannot say we ought to have faith, and make this contention plausible to us who have none. Instead they must admit that their God allows men to wallow in error and folly until He apparently arbitrarily and miraculously saves them. They must hold that even our logic is wrong, that our most evident certainties are tinged with error, and that an intellect, which sees the possibility or need of faith, cannot even to that degree be right. They therefore tacitly grant that their God created or allowed the bad, the deceptive, and the foolish to be the order of the day. Such men speak of a universe which the rest of mankind does not and cannot know, and in a way it cannot understand.

If we define knowledge to be valueless or necessarily false, we make impossible a defense of faith, preclude the possibility of appreciating its results as public and open, lose an opportunity for non-believers to distinguish true from false believers, and define God as having provided us with an intellect which is less powerful, accurate and autonomous than it might have been.

Religious experiences are too common to permit one to dismiss offhand the possibility and importance of a knowledge of God acquired by nonintellectual means. One can readily admit that, as a consequence of such knowledge, the entire universe and all its details take on a new and refreshing look, despite the fact that the knowledge, systems and daily lives of religious men do not seem to be radically different from those of others. But if one is to avoid cutting himself off from all discourse and defense, he must concede that what he knows without faith is close enough to what he knows with the help of it to enable him to compare the two, and thus see the value of ennobling a secular

Faith

knowledge with the results of religious insight. And so far as
it is philosophy alone among secular subjects which explicitly
deals with first principles he must grant that, if philosophy is
not the most important of subjects from a religious point of
view, it is more relevant to it than any other secular study. The
object and achievements of a philosophy should, even for a man
of faith, be recognized to have some value. It is one thing to
show a preference for porterhouse; it is another to throw all the
sirloin to the dog.

Only this far need one go in order to meet the criticisms
sometimes made by some men of faith. But we must go further.
In fact, we cannot stop until we bring faith and its object under
philosophy as special illustrations of ultimate philosophic truths,
and this without denying faith its autonomy and validity. It
was perhaps an awareness of this necessity to go further that
has led some to deny the value of philosophy outright. If this
be the case, a double blunder was committed — the blunder
of denying the truth and the blunder of not seeing that the value
of faith and the transcendence of God are supported, not de-
stroyed, by being brought within the scope of a philosophy.

The object of faith, if at all intelligible, existent and valuable,
must conform to the conditions which define the intelligible,
the existent and the valuable. The laws of logic, the truths of
being and of value, are illustrated in the act of faith as surely
as they are in every other act. If faith — and God — did not
illustrate the truths of philosophy, they would not be intelligible
in any intelligible sense, existent in any sense in which things are
existent, or have a value in the sense in which anything else has
a value. They could not, therefore, be known or preferred by
any rational being.

Faith can be reflected on as well as lived through, known as
well as used. It is a legitimate object of philosophic thought.
Indeed, unless we make a philosophic study of faith, we will
fail to know just what can be claimed on its behalf and what
cannot.

iii

GOD MAKES IT POSSIBLE for men to be other than He. He
affects and is affected by men. And in Himself He takes account
of them. These truths we can affirm though we have no re-

ligious faith, since they are consequences of what we know
speculatively, and are also presupposed in our achievement of
the state of being an other of, for and than the world.

Words in the field of religion are not used in constant ways
today. And sometimes religions differ significantly on how certain key terms are to be used. The meaning of "religious faith"
divides Protestants from Catholics radically. But we can come
close to the core common to both and to other religions if we
take faith to tell us that an eternal power ennobles us. Such a
faith is had by anyone who, in giving himself to God, recognizes
himself thereby to be made more worthy than he had been. The
religious man believes that God, in accepting him, frees him
from what is defective and false.

We need religious faith if we wish to reach God, the transcendent reality who is other than all else. We need it too if we
wish to ground the claim that God loves us, that He forgives
us and heals us — or to use the language of the East, if we wish
to ground the claim that our finite selves will eventually be
nihilated and we will thereupon be ennobled by becoming one
with a distinctionless ultimate reality.

We speak of having faith in man. Sometimes we say that we
have a faith in reason or a faith that all will turn out well. Religious faith is different from all of these. A faith in man, reason
or the course of the world is mainly trust; it involves little or
no certitude. Each is independent of religious faith though perhaps supported by it. Unlike religious faith such faiths are not
inevitably justified, not necessarily satisfied.

We speak too of a faith that a particular religion is true.
Such a faith usually presupposes religious faith; it is more a
matter of participation than of belief. He who has faith in a
religion is loyal, whereas the man of religious faith is hopeful.
The one acts, the other finds. Where the one is untroubled, the
other is confident; where the one is at rest, the other still seeks.

It is sometimes said that a scientist has faith in the order of
nature, a philosopher has faith in the power of reason, a man
has faith in his wife or partner. But these men would be more
correctly described as believing in something. If we wish to say
instead that they have faith, we should add that this faith is
not religious. A religious faith is directed toward a being who
is not only other than ourselves but is more than a principle

or ground for science, philosophy, a happy marriage or a satisfactory partnership.

Religious faith combines within it many factors. Together these make up an attitude of belief that one is eternally cherished and is so far of great value. It contains elements of hope, of conviction and of confidence. All of these are oriented toward that which makes it possible for a man to be forever ennobled. If that fact is not overlooked we can profitably analyze these components out of faith and remark on their distinctive powers.

Each one of us occupies a tiny portion of a vast space-time dynamic whole. We find ourselves ineffective again and again. We return again and again to the challenge which existence offers, buoyed by the hope that it will not now destroy all we cherish. We support that hope in a double way. We back it with an assurance that we can subjugate the world, and with a reliance on our ability so to participate in the course of the world that we make ourselves effective. The assurance is behind our mastery of the arts which creatively present us with the texture of existence and thereby enable us to enjoy existence even where it is tragic and punitive. The reliance is behind our participation in history, where we interlock with nature to produce a humanized way of holding on to the past and of prescribing to the future. Both the assurance and the reliance are partially justified by the achievements of technology. But no matter how efficient we are, no matter how creative and effective, existence in the end defeats us. If we are to prevent it from making all our efforts add up to failure we must have our basic needs satisfied, or we must be so empowered that we can deal with existence with an effectiveness we never had before. The second alternative is taken by religious men to be a special case of the first; they believe that there is a being, a place and a way apart from the world enabling men to achieve all they ought.

Each of us has obligations. We are ethically required to do good everywhere. But we never come near doing this. We are guilty beings; men who do less than they ought on behalf of an ideal. Despite our failure, we return again and again to the struggle to realize the good, supported by the conviction that it will be realized somehow. We support that conviction in a double way. We dedicate ourselves to bring the good about.

and we are faithful to any enterprise or organization which promotes this result. Because we are dedicated we are ready to engage in an ethical life, and because we are faithful, we are ready to act in common enterprises. Our dedication and our faithfulness are themselves partially justified by our efforts on behalf of whatever promotes peace and prosperity, self-confidence and courage. However, we never altogether free ourselves from guilt. No intentions go the length of producing all the good that need be achieved; no organization brings about only good. We cannot escape guilt unless the good is realized on our behalf, or unless we are forgiven. But we ought not to be forgiven if the good is not somehow produced; forgiveness requires that the good which we ought to have realized, be divinely realized for us.

Each of us, finally, is occupied with the task of becoming a complete man. But we are limited beings, facing a multiplicity of actualities. They defeat us, reduce us to impotence, and sooner or later bring our span to an end. We would despair were it not that we have a confidence that, puny though we are, we have a dignity denied to all other space-time beings. That confidence we back in two ways. We have a trust in our ability to conquer other actualities through the use of a distinctive human power, and we commit ourselves to face them on our own terms. The trust provides one of the motivations for our pursuit of knowledge, since by knowing a thing we possess it in some form. The commitment leads us to act with resolution, to make our wills effectively over-match the threats other actualities embody. And when we together forge a human realm over against the rest of the world we make good in part both the trust and the commitment. Yet we suffer and die, whether we are knowledgeable or not, whether or not we have dealt effectively with other actualities. We cannot meet the challenge of other actualities successfully except by having all the fruits of such success ascribed to us, or by having everything reduced to the status of an instrument for us, thereby enabling us to be actualities benefitted by whatever else there is. The religious man believes that one or the other or both results are produced by his God.

We have a religious faith if we believe that we will possess all we ought, do all we ought, and be all we ought, and this despite the fact that we discover again and again that our acts are futile, that we are guilty and impotent. Faith contains a hope that good will be preserved, an assurance that existence will be blocked, and a reliance that we will be divinely empowered. It contains a conviction that we will escape guilt, a dedication that we will live in terms of God's intent, and a faithfulness toward the life He prescribes for us. It contains a confidence that we will somehow conquer death, a trust that we will truly know what we and others are, and a commitment to continue to live now and later in terms of the excellence which God embodies. Because of faith we think we have a power greater than that possessed by all existence, that, despite all iniquity, we are assessed with merciful justice, and have a nobility which cannot be matched by subhuman beings, severally or together.

iv

HOW CAN ONE acquire religious faith? Can we know that the faith is justified? Might not such a faith be only an expression of a longing never satisfied? Perhaps its object is no more than a fantasy? How can we become worthy of the benefits faith promises? Why does no man of faith ever grant that his faith has been betrayed? Is the admission that one's faith has been betrayed, identical with the act of abandoning faith? These questions demand an answer.

A faith which brings about perpetually satisfying results is eminently worthwhile. The freethinker asserts that men have faith precisely because they want those results. He thinks men want to be forever protected, to feel loved perpetually and to be radically purified. But reflection, says the free thinker, shows that all these objectives are illusory. He does not though agree with those therapists who claim that even if these objectives are illusory the faith is justified, provided only that it results in peace of mind. The freethinker wants truth, and has no interest in errors even where they heal. Faith on either view, is a grandiose strategy in self-deception. Is it, in fact?

Though it is often said that it is easy to deceive oneself, and particularly with respect to what one ardently desires, there are many who, though they spend their lives engaged in religious activities, seem to manage to have faith only occasionally, and then only for short periods. If a man of faith deceives himself, he does so after he has made strenuous efforts to believe, which are then only partially and momentarily successful. Evidently he finds it hard to achieve what has been termed a "state of self-deception." To this it might be said, "All the sadder for those who succeed, all the better for the rest of us." And to the observation that those who strive most seriously are often most anxious not to be deceived, it might be replied: "The unconscious is incredibly wily, able to deceive the most alert and critical." Let it be so. We will still have the problem of knowing how this faith is obtained. Are we tricked by the unconscious into deceiving ourselves? Then we are puppets, and of nothing less or other than what was once called an evil spirit or the devil, except that it here operates to bring about a faith instead of to destroy one. A genuine freethinker must, even more than a religious man, insist that faith comes about in some other way. He abandons his principles if he says that there is a bad unconscious, an evil spirit or a devil which maliciously leads a man to believe in God.

No religious man maintains a steady position or a steady relation to God. Complete confidence and unswerving assurance are quickly followed by sickening doubts, abrasive questions, hesitations, and fearful moments of emptiness or regrettable denials. The religious man again and again gropes about, feels lost and alone. At one moment caught up in a spirit of happy submission and self-abandonment, at the next he is on the verge of disbelief and despair. In turns he is certain and doubtful; he is also certain and doubtful simultaneously. His certainty is streaked with suspicions that he may be deceived both by others and by himself; his doubt is criss-crossed with flashes of assurance that he is and will be divinely sustained and ennobled. He can be called truly religious only if he deliberately maintains his faith over against the corroding despair of recurring disbelief.

Though mystics often speak as though they had no question about the success of their ventures, their experience, too, like every other, is blurred and confusing. The mystic constantly moves back and forth from a too intimate to a too remote relation to God. His certainty follows fast on the heels of an uncertainty, and this on a certainty and so on. He wants to move to the mystery which hovers on the edge of the community, to make contact with it as an individual. If he succeeds he will dispel some of the mystery which confronts the religious man, but he will never dissolve it entirely.

Many defenders of faith look at it in the very same spirit as the opponents of faith do. Instead, though, of making men puppets of an unconscious they make them puppets of God. God's grace they hold is the source of man's faith. That grace is irresistible, and those who are fortunate enough to be subject to it become men of faith. Those who have no faith are barren ground in which God's grace has not found rootage. But why should one suppose a divine "irresistible" grace to be so feeble? What kind of God is this who leaves some — perhaps most — unbenefitted and presumably damned, and for no distinctive fault? Why does He help you and not me? Are you not as base, as corrupt, as unworthy as I? And why suppose that all of us are absolutely powerless, that we cannot ourselves move toward God, but must be lifted up by Him? It would be better I think to accept the Hindu idea of Karma and take those who are without faith to be suffering from some wrong committed in a previous life. We would then at least have a reason why some are benefitted and others not. But in the end this answer also will not do, since it pushes us back life after life in search of that one in which we were free to turn away from a faith somehow already possessed and exercised. That initial faith is not accounted for by Karma.

A more traditional doctrine is that God's grace is a necessary, not a sufficient condition for faith. Man has the power, it is said, to respond or not to His grace. Putting aside the question as to whether Aristotle is not right in supposing that God has more important things to think about than man and his limited concerns, we are faced with the question of how weak man could have sufficient power to withstand a divine grace. And how odd it is to suppose that he exercises that power to deny himself a great good. How odd it is to suppose that anyone who was confronted with divine grace would want to reject it. How odd it is to suppose that a merciful God would boggle at a man's hesitation, reluctance, confusion or even willfulness.

"But," it will be said, "though a man can do nothing without God's help, he has a free will, permitting him to accept and reject anything whatsoever, even the highest of goods." God, on such an account, is thought of as inciting a man to deal freely with the grace that is being offered him. Is the incitement constant and universal? If not, God's acts will once again be arbitrary and niggardly, occurring at some times and not others, and then benefitting only some of us, regardless of anything we are or do. But if the incitement is constant and universal, we would not be able to distinguish it from a native state in all men. Perhaps what is intended is the view that were a man to freely engage in an act of faith he would be sustained by God? That I think is true. But instead of accounting for faith by grace it leaves the occurrence of faith unexplained, to tell us merely about some of its consequences.

Might not the faith be elicited when we face something surprising, something which does not fit inside the usual patterns? I think not. An arresting object would not elicit faith unless we took that object to be an instance of a divine revelation. But then the object must first be approached from the perspective of faith. We would have had to have the faith to begin with. A surprising object can support a faith; it does not provoke or promote one.

If we have a religious faith we are turned toward God, and are receptive to His presence, alert to His signs and message. To a man without faith, bibles are books, miracles are oddities, and prophetic admonitions are the gnomic utterances of deluded men. If a man, on turning the pages of some religious book hits upon a passage which makes him not only abandon his previous course of life but makes him give himself up to the worship or service of God, he is one who reads with the eyes of a man of faith. Without faith he would read as others do, and as he perhaps might have done many times before — unheedingly, seeing nothing that is of religious import to him.

Men sometimes acquire faith when they despair of the world. In great distress, suddenly cut off from the possibility of success in some central endeavor, or faced with a loss of what they most deeply cherish, they still hope. If they believe that the hope is not in vain, that what is hoped for will eventually come to pass, if not here then elsewhere, they are expectant men, religiously hopeful. They do not yet have faith. To have faith they must be convinced that they are now and will also be somewhat benefitted. They must be confident that what they feared is and will be at least partially but in any case divinely mastered. Faith, to some degree, is always satisfied, always justified, always rewarded, and is expectative of the remainder. It is a seeking which already contains part of what is sought, which seeks for more of what it in its seeking already has. In the act of faith there is some of the substance hoped for; in faith one hopes for more of what one already has.

A man of faith does not blindly long. He is not one who in despair turns desperately, he knows not where for an answer that may never be given. An act of faith is one by which some part of the good that is needed and sought is bestowed and enjoyed, and the remainder promised. It is not possible to one who is completely immersed in the world. To be completely immersed in the world is to be involved with the changing, the contingent, to be subject to alteration. Fortunately, no one is perpetually in this state. If he were he would have no way of accounting for his conscience or self-identity; he would never have a moment in which he was truly alone, over against all else, and he would of course be always precluded from knowing that the answers which he and the world offer are redressed and completed on his behalf.

Nor is faith possible to one who is completely sunk within himself. A perfectly self-contained man is a self-sufficient man. He looks neither alongside nor above. But there could not be such a man, unless a man could manage to live without appetites, without needs, without interests, without expectations, hopes or fears.

Faith is not possible to one who completely despairs. But no one can despair utterly. If one could, it would be possible for him to have an unmovable belief that he is and will always be defeated with respect to all that is.

Faith is not possible to one who is completely dissatisfied. But if nothing satisfied, everything would be equally bad or indifferent. Such a man would be unable to make any decisions, to express any preferences, to acknowledge anything as being achieved, and thus as providing a ground or a measure for what he is still to do. He would either be entirely sunk within himself or be in utter despair. But neither of these we have just seen is really possible.

Nor is faith possible to one who does not have a distinctive free belief in something real. Such a belief differs from the belief that we will die, both in its origin and in its consequences. Most of us have reluctantly come to believe that we will die. We make that belief our own because we see how like we are to other men who have died. We are forced to believe it, and it rarely gives us any satisfaction to do so. But no man is forced to believe that he will be mercifully judged, that all that he rightly cherishes will be preserved and perhaps even ennobled. Such a belief is free and carries with it the joy which a free exercise of any power does.

The belief that peace will be here tomorrow and forever after is also a free belief and one that brings much pleasure. But though satisfying, the belief in peace is not satisfied. It differs from the belief ingredient in a faith by its failure to find a fact to support it. Because faith relates a man to God it is partly satisfied. Faith already tastes something of the final satisfaction which it seeks.

Faith relates a man to God, but only so far as the man has withdrawn himself from a world which he continues to remember, which he continues to cling to, which still remains pertinent to him. The belief he has that there is a final assessment of himself in relation to all else is a free belief and a relevant one. It is not gratuitous. If it were it would be wholly unwarranted, unrelated to anything that he knew or anything else he believed. It would be an exercise in fantasy supported by a rejection or suspension of what he normally accepts or claims. But no one can reject or suspend all his normal acceptances or claims all the time. No one can spend all his time in sheer fantasy. When a man turns away from the world he cannot forget entirely what he accepted there.

I can believe *in* someone or something apart from and even in the face of obtrusive facts. I can tear up a written promise which I am convinced will be kept, and put my trust in the man. What I do then is not to abandon what might evidence my belief, but on the contrary turn to the source of such evidence. I believe in the man, ready to take what he offers me for belief. When I do this I may be foolish, my decision may be impractical, unwise, naive; I may have believed too much. But to have a religious faith is always to fail to believe enough. He who rests with the satisfaction of knowing that he is or will be ennobled will then and there have lost his religious faith. Religious faith requires that he be satisfied while exercising it, but not wholly satisfied, not content, not at rest.

Religious faith is a belief *in;* but it does not become this until it has acquired some of the virtues of a true belief, a belief *that.* A true belief is met by a fact; it is an honored claim, an attitude supported, a certitude justified by what is the case.

The reward of good acts is the acquirement of virtue, the habit of acting properly, the readiness to face a new situation in the spirit which we acquired from having acted well. True beliefs, similarly, leave behind them the certitude of having been truly believed, and build up in us a confidence in the agencies we have been using.

Faith has a certitude to it, the very kind of certitude which is characteristic of true beliefs. We cannot say that that certitude is bestowed on faith by its object, without begging the question. It must then have been acquired, either directly from true beliefs, or indirectly from an attitude which those beliefs promote. Both cases occur. We bear the marks within us of the fact that we acted or knew in a certain way. We continue to bear those marks even when the objects of the doing and the knowing have passed away. We then find that we approach some new experience in a spirit which it does not itself generate. We may even mistakenly say that we had once before had the experience, because we now deal with it in the terms we used before.

The relations of true beliefs to their objects could be produced in many ways. The beliefs might issue from us in the form of questions which are then answered with appropriate objects. This is apparently something like what Tillich has in mind when he speaks of the method of correlation between existential questions and their final answers. True beliefs might be elicited by objects when we confront them in certain ways — which is something like what Descartes had in mind when he spoke of the "natural light." Or the relation might be produced by our facing the objects of belief when sane and well-adjusted. This is the way we ordinarily look at the matter. In all three ways our true beliefs are related to the source of their certitude.

Men can and do transfer to faith the certitude of true beliefs. Take away the certitude from the faith and the faith will be-

come indistinguishable from longing, a hope deferred. But faith
is a hope already satisfied to some degree. Deny that the certitude
of faith is derived from true beliefs, and you deny yourself an
empirical ground for an account of the way in which religious
faith comes about.

Faith has the certitude of a true belief. That certitude is
not native to it. Faith has a certitude which once adhered to
true beliefs that now, for the moment, are being ignored. It
inherits the certitude which true beliefs entrain. Were this all,
a man of faith would have a certitude without any facts to
justify it. He would have a belief indistinguishable from a true
belief, but his belief could well be false.

The belief ingredient in faith outstrips the evidences, but not
foolishly. If I believe that it is raining now because I see it is
raining, I gain nothing if I continue to maintain that belief but
refuse to look out the window. Since it might have stopped
raining, I in fact will lose the opportunity to see if my belief
can still be maintained. I would be foolish. Faith is not foolish,
for it is not satisfied with the certitude it has inherited. It has
the certitude of a true belief, but in addition it looks to its
object to warrant that certitude. Faith is satisfied and dissatisfied at once; it seeks and is answered, it is answered and
continues to seek. The satisfying certitude that it embodies is
related by it to a not yet mastered reality. That reality is faced
as that which allows the faith to have a certitude of its own.
Faith rightly possesses the certitude it inherits from true belief
because it terminates in that which justifies the certitude.

A faith entirely unsatisfied is no faith at all. To have faith
is to feel oneself enriched, ennobled, altered for the better, presumably by that in which the faith terminates. And so far as
the faith is satisfied, it rightly possesses the certitude it inherited.
Faith consequently always has an inherited and rightly possessed
certitude.

God is accepted by faith to be faith's proper and satisfying
terminus, when and so far as the faith is satisfied. To have faith
therefore is to truly believe in God, to face him as the warrant
for the very certitude which faith inherits. Faith's relation to
other true beliefs turns the satisfaction which God provides in
faith into evidence that faith's certitude is warranted; the satisfaction which God provides, in turn, makes faith's inherited
certitude a certitude rightly possessed.

Were there no God, the satisfaction felt in the act of faith would be self-generated. Whether this is the case or not, faith cannot know. But a knowledge that God exists, obtained without recourse to faith, eliminates this possibility, for it shows not only that God exists, but that He can enrich the act of reaching toward Him. It always remains possible of course that though God could enrich the life of a man of faith He in fact never does so, and that this enrichment must therefore be the result of man's own act. This would mean that faith was self-certifying but not that it was unjustified. It would require one to suppose that God does less good than He might, and that men have a power to enrich themselves in a way that God can conceivably enrich them. These are less plausible suppositions than that God does all the good that He can, and that men cannot do what He can. In any case, they do not involve a questioning of faith or its products but only of the source of the goods which the practice of faith involves.

Faith, to begin with, is unfocused, ill-defined, half-unconscious. Quickly it becomes overlaid with fantasy, mythology, creeds. When a man decides that he will not lend himself to illusions, errors, or dogmas, he too readily says to himself that he will no longer keep his faith. But sooner or later, well or poorly, he comes back again, armed with a certitude that God is, and thus that what ought to be cherished is eternally cherished in fact.

The question, how does one acquire faith, is evidently misstated. We can ask how a faith can be weakened or strengthened, how it can be impoverished, or enriched, but not how it can be obtained, if by that we mean that we once were entirely without it. There is never a moment when we do not have a tincture of faith, hardly a day when we do not have flashes of full faith; hardly an hour when we do not lose some part of the faith we had. Again and again we turn away from the world with an inherited certitude directed to what then remains over, and again and again we turn toward the world with a combined confidence and longing which vibrates with but still departs from faith and what it confronts.

True beliefs make faith possible, and faith in turn allows us to credit true beliefs with an unquestioning assurance no confrontation of fact would produce. Though we ignore the particularities which make our beliefs true, we inherit the certitude which true beliefs provide; though we lose our faith again and again, we inherit the assurance which the faith acquired from its relation to what is other than ourselves. And just as the world will yield further goods, particularly if we continue to approach it in terms of an assurance inherited from faith, so the object of faith will yield further goods, particularly if we continue to approach it in terms of a certitude inherited from true beliefs.

We face non-religious situations not with faith but at most with resolute determinations to continue to suppose something which is essential if we are to conduct some enterprise there. No such resolution need be — perhaps cannot be — transferred. Different resolutions are tied to different contents. If I resolve not to smoke I do not also resolve not to drink; the strength of the one resolution is not carried over into the other.

Each resolution must be made afresh. If all a man wanted was to suppose that there is a good God, so as to be able to deal with various problems in effective ways, all he need do is to suppose it. There is no reason why he cannot hold on to that supposition as resolutely as he holds on to any others. But a resolution to suppose that there is a God, we now see, falls far short of a faith that there is one, or of a faith in one.

v

CERTITUDE IS INSEPARABLE from faith, and that certitude is derived from true beliefs. "Of course faith has a certitude to it," it might be said, "of course it derives that certitude from true beliefs. All the worse for it. True beliefs have a certitude because there are objects which make the beliefs be true. Those objects can often be predicted and confronted. The beliefs are then verified. There is evidence for them. We can therefore show why they are true; we can therefore distinguish them from beliefs that are mistaken, false, unwarranted. But precisely because there are no possible ways in which one can see if there is an appropriate object which would make a religious faith true, faith evidently has a certitude it ought not to possess. Faith deludes; it is an usurper, a pretender, a bearer of a claim it has no right to make."

There are defenders of faith who think that such an argument — toned down a bit — expresses no objection to faith. They would in fact present a similar one themselves, and on behalf of faith. According to them a faith needs no evidence. They have faith in that which they do not understand, in that which they have no reason to believe. But it is hard to see how they can then say that they believe in God and not in the devil, in something that exists rather than in nothing at all. These men are not strong friends of religion.

The objection, it is to be noted, avoids the mistake of saying that a faith could not *possibly* be true. This would require a demonstration that there could be nothing answering to a religious faith, that there was no God or that He had no relation to us. Such a demonstration is not possible. God not only exists but is known to be in relation to us by virtue of the fact that He is known to be immanent in us. Not even the apparently cautious objection that there might *possibly* be no God, or that He might possibly have no relation to us, that the certitude which accompanies faith might conceivably be unjustified, can be maintained. God is the ground of Himself as having the role of a relative other for us; He is also in us in the shape of a power making us a relative other of Him. And He is in us as well in the shape of the satisfaction a faith enjoys.

One can of course say that what is here being referred to in the name of God is only mankind writ large, the whole of existence, or the good. But, as was remarked before, no one of these can ground an other which is the correlate of a private individual self. No one of these can therefore be the object of faith. Faith starts from us as private subjects, and terminates in the ground of that with which we are related when we retreat from the world.

A faith which rested with the acknowledgment of a God who is merely our other would content many philosophically spirited "natural" theologians. They speak of an absconding being, a Nirvana or of a God beyond God — realities which are free from the limited characterizations that mark the contentions of particular creeds. Their views are metaphysically tempered, religiously acceptable, and avoid over-commitment. One could hardly claim less than they do without giving up the defense of religion. And those who claim more seem to slip in unwarranted additions and into regrettable prejudice. Natural theology, on this view, is minimal but inescapable theology or religion. Few men are content with so little. But might one not go on to say that it is one of the functions of particular religions to add to this minimum? If so, their special revelations, prophesies, omens, and witnesses could be said to convert the minimal faith that there is an ultimate assessing being into a particular faith which might claim for example that He judges all, and perhaps loves and hates, forgives and punishes. Natural theology would then be nucleal theology, to be enriched in multiple ways by the different religions.

The position is not altogether clear. It is difficult to know whether reference is being made to a faith *that* without a faith *in*, to a faith *in* without a faith *that*, or to a faith *in* which is additional to a faith *that*. The first of the suppositions is made by these who say nothing more than that God is the object of faith. But if God is also taken to have an inwardness and if He justifies our having faith, one must hold as well that He is a being *in* whom one can have faith. But this is the last supposition. Some men though seem to want to make only the second supposition. They would like to treat every particular description or event, every specifiable truth, name, historic occurrence or claim to be part of a myth. Apparently they believe that one could have faith in God without a faith that God is anything, or that He does anything. But since God provides faith with the warrant to possess its inherited certitude, this view also sooner or later turns into the third. Only the third seems tenable.

If we were to detach the faith that God exists from a faith in an existent God, the faith would be indistinguishable from a mere belief, from a rational faith that God exists, one of the irreducible realities that make up the universe. But a religious faith *that* God exists is inseparable from a faith *in* Him as warranting the desirable certitude that we have, and perhaps other goods as well. When and as God is acknowledged to exist He is also accepted as at least the ground for a certitude that He exists. The man of faith does not then simply believe that God exists, and that He therefore will act as existent beings do; he takes God's existence to involve the production of a desirable quality in himself.

The certitude enjoyed by the faith *that* God exists is underwritten by God. It is that underwriting, *in* which we have faith. To have faith is then to enjoy a good consequence of

God's existence. It is to face God as a ground for some present good.

Could we, when we confronted ordinary matters of fact, face these not only as objects which made our beliefs true, but which made the truth adhere to our beliefs, we would not only believe that those objects existed but would also believe *in* those objects. But we do not believe *in* them. We believe in the power of our minds, our methods, our memories. These are the agencies by which the truth is possessed by us and we as a consequence are enriched.

A faith is always expectant, always tinctured with hope. It cannot be exhausted in the acknowledgment of an existent God with the consequent production of a certitude that He exists. We have a growing faith when we are certain both that God exists and that He makes still other goods possible. Were this not the case, there would be only the certitude which is produced whenever one is overwhelmed, forced to believe by some power or authority. A fearful or a credulous man will believe what is said to him because it is said by a powerful person, official, teacher or institution. He will not necessarily expect that there will be other things for him to accept. He accepts only what he must, when faced with the authoritative force. He is submissive, not necessarily expectative. But a man with a growing faith is a *faithful* man. His is not only the certitude that God exists but the certitude that God is the source of other goods besides that of the enjoyment of the certitude. He is a man for whom God's existence means not only that he now enjoys a certitude but that he will continue to enjoy it. He thus faces God as the source not only of something that now is the case but of something that will be the case. His faith in God involves a desirable certitude that God will continue to exist, at least as the justification of such certitude and the source of other goods.

The man of faith experiences his certitude as more and more desirable. As time goes on, the more satisfying is the certitude that his faith embodies. He experiences the continuance of God, who made the certitude rightly attach to his faith, in the form of a qualitative enhancement of that certitude. The hope which the faith had initially is so far justified. But there is, so far, no warrant for the hope that he will continue to be satisfied or benefitted in other ways as well. A hope is always expectative.

So long as it exists as hope, it cannot be fully satisfied. But it is possible to have it satisfied in part, and to provide reasons why one can expect that there will be further benefits to come. May one justifiably hope that God is the source of still more goods? I think so. If we have faith we are related to a being who ennobles everything. But only a special form of faith, a growing faith grounded in a revelation of some kind, assures us that God will provide us with additional goods in the course of this life.

To know that further goods will be provided, a man must know something of the being in which he hopes. We now know that God is absolutely other than all else. He stands over against the world and me. He also ennobles us by making us integral to Himself. Every being in the universe is accepted by God in the guise of a preserved part of an ennobled reality which God has made into a constituent of Himself. The hope that God is the source of further goods is therefore justified. But there is as yet no justification for the hope that there will be more goods provided by God in this life.

The Hindus and Buddhists seem content with this outcome. They apparently hope for nothing more. God for some of them is identified with all reality, and as such provides a final though not necessarily personal, conscious or deliberate assessment of all that is. If a man becomes one with God he must then make himself one with that totality. Jews, Christians, Muslims and to some extent even the Buddha himself take a different approach. They see themselves individually or as a people to represent all else. They take themselves to be men who can so hold themselves over against the rest of the universe that they can retain the certitude appropriate to the existence of things there, and who speak or act as though they have been divinely assigned the role of lords of the universe.

The western man of faith has the hope that God will accept him as such a representative. If God does this, then, despite the fact that each man is contingent and fallible, he will be accepted by God as a cognizing, ethical man of faith who had detached himself from the world in fact while mastering it in idea or in intent. He will be an "image" of God.

For westerners God provides a final assessment of the degree to which they have made themselves or have been made into distinctive, full men. Their hope is different from that of the Hindus and Buddhists. But all are justified. All of them rightly take God to be the source of further goods than that of enhancing the certitude of faith.

Different religions are in part functions of the kind of beings men take themselves to be in the eyes of God. Orthodox Jews insist that man's representative role must be carried out by a people, and carried out along the lines of well-formulated rules. But their view is not so far in principle different from that of less orthodox Jews, or from that of the Christians and Muslims. All of them take men to be God's image, and the lords of the universe. Calvinists seem to hope for nothing more; a man for them is finally assessed for being whatever kind of man God initially elected him to be. But most westerners go further. They hope that God is not merely related to them, but that He also concerns Himself with them to the degree at least that they have faith in Him. They hope for further goods in this life, and for a final assessment by God of what they have made of themselves in the course of time. They do not really know whether this hope is justified. They, together with those who hope for more — e.g., that God will forgive — must hope for revelations. These alone can provide the assurance that further goods will be granted in this life. But the acceptance of revelations presupposes faith, and cannot serve to justify it.

vi

FAITH IS an achievement. Its direction, its strength, its degree of satisfaction and its element of hope are functions in part of the manner in which a man has succeeded in detaching himself from the world, retreated inside himself, supplemented his self, and turned to a steady loving other, existing outside himself. He who becomes converted expects to find himself radically altered and his rewards correspondingly affected. He who remains within the confines of a given religion shares something of this expectation so far as he sees that he can give his faith greater clarity, better focus, a changed import. A man's hope that God will subsequently benefit him in ways God does not benefit him now, is justified because it refers to what God must do to take account of an altered man. But what is then hoped for are different goods, not necessarily goods additional to those already bestowed.

A man looks to God to enable him to overcome all the dangers and qualifications to which man is subject. Though he is in the end impotent in the face of other actualities, for he must die, he hopes that he will somehow live on. Though he fails to do justice to the ideal good to which he has obligated himself and is therefore guilty, he hopes that he will be forgiven and thus be innocent once again. And though he finds that he is ineffective in his perpetual struggle with existence, he hopes somehow to escape a life of futility. God for him is the being who provides him with the answers which he could not get in other directions.

God does not, however, provide the full answer nor the only answer to the questions which are faced by man. He does not really protect man from death, guilt and futility. At most he replaces the effects of these with others, and thereby adds new dimensions to man's being. To reduce the dangers of death, guilt and futility, men must engage in knowledge and action, ethics and politics, art and history. They are then ennobled in a way and to a degree that they are not in religion.

The religious man knows himself to be defective, one who has not yet succeeded in being all he ought to be. His failure is made good in the other areas, but in a non-religious guise, and thus not in the way the religious man desires and needs.

An individual man might spend little or no time or energy in the exercise of faith and still be able to benefit from religion, if only he were willing to accept as his own the goods which men of faith obtain. This is constantly done, though perhaps less conspicuously at the present time than in previous ages when religious men were so much to the fore. On the whole we today tend to think that religious men benefit from the enterprises which others pursue in other directions and that they give little or nothing in return, but this is just as much an illusion as the belief of previous generations that all benefits issued either directly or indirectly from religion.

Religion is a basic discipline offering a man answers to all his basic needs, but it can do this only by giving indirect and transformed versions of the direct answers which other basic disciplines alone provide. It must be supplemented by these others. Without religion a man will not achieve the maximum value he should have; but if he were religious and nothing else, he would die sooner than he need, do less good than he can, and be less effective than he in fact is.

Those who find this conclusion unsatisfactory will either have to be content with living narrow incomplete lives, where much is neglected that ought to be done and to which much of the good in the world is irrelevant, or they will have to find other ways by which they can benefit from the existence of beings who have other perspectives, and are engaged in other disciplines. Two alternatives seem plausible: one might devote oneself to the production of something that was excellent not in one but in multiple dimensions, or one might produce what is excellent in one dimension and accept as part of its meaning and value whatever dignity it has in other dimensions.

It is possible to engage in political work which is religiously endorsed, or to paint a great picture having great historic import. In these cases an excellence achieved from one direction is found to be excellent from another. If now we could produce in one perspective what is excellent in all, we would, despite specialization and bias, have produced truly monumental work; while pursuing one limited life, we would in fact have achieved a complete one. Unfortunately, no one is sure just what would be excellent from all perspectives. And if we knew what this was, we would be up against the fact that circumstances would force us again and again to attend to what is less than monumental. Also, we would still be left with the question as to just what our own perspective should be. Are all perspectives and all disciplines of equal value? Does not each have a flavor of its own making a distinctive difference to us and what we do? If we approach excellence from one of them will we not lose what is obtainable only from another? Suppose your elderly mother asks you to say your prayers. It is one thing to obey her because filial obedience is demanded by your religion, and another to pray because you want to please her. In the one case religion would ground an ethical act; in the other an ethical act would ground a religious one. These are distinct and perhaps incompatible; a choice between them is arbitrary at best, inevitably involving some loss.

A better alternative keeps in focus the fact that a man must give himself to one of many different disciplines and adventures, and can never do full justice to what all the others demand. But he can be willing to accept as part of the meaning and value of what he now does whatever meaning and value is accreted by his achievements in other areas. He can hope that what he does excellently will be found to be excellent from other perspectives as well, but he will make no claim that this is so. He will obey his mother on ethical grounds alone, but hope that his religion will endorse his act; or he will pray for religious reasons alone, but hope that this will please his mother. In the first case, he would be an ethical man sustained by a religious hope — which is perhaps typical of most men who, though they devote themselves to non-religious tasks, think of themselves as truly religious men. In the second case he would be a religious man sustained by an ethical hope — which is perhaps how many of the clergy think of themselves. Since what is religiously excellent would not be the primary concern of the first nor what is ethically excellent the primary concern of the second, it is unlikely that all that ought to be done will be done in either case. In both, one would have to depend on others to do what is excellent in their areas, and hope that the results will be added to one's own. In the end then both must recognize that a man must do what he can in a given area and trust that what he necessarily neglects will be done by others, and accredited to him. It is never enough to say that one will attend to worldly affairs confident that God will make all things right eventually. Unless one can share in the resulting excellence, that excellence will not help satisfy one's need to be completed through the direct or indirect doing of all that ought to be done.

The most a religion can do is to enable man to be as excellent as man can be in the light of his eventual final assessment by God. All other desires — for survival, effectiveness, virtue — are answered more directly and adequately by those who give themselves up to other enterprises to the same degree that the religious man gives himself up to religion. A full man is never solely a political, an ethical, an historic, or a religious man.

vii

THERE IS a difference between the faith which a member of one religion has, and the faith characteristic of another. The different kinds of faith are inseparable from basic decisions as to what a man is and ought to do with reference to the world in which he lives. Sometimes those decisions are culturally determined; at other times they help determine the culture. This is not to say that religions are merely social products or instruments, for they are in part conditioned by the men who practice them in the private recesses of their being. Nor is it to deny the possibility of a man converting from one religion to another, since men can make decisions in opposition to what is habitual or accepted.

There can never be a single religion of mankind, so long as men make themselves into distinctive types by virtue of the way they define themselves in relation to the world, fellowman and their final assessor. They may of course at some time all subscribe to one single creed; they might even all follow the same rituals; they might all work in harmony. They would then be part of one single religious community, but they would still, within that community, decisively make themselves into distinct types of men. The reduction of creeds, rituals and works to a single, authorized type would undoubtedly affect the kinds of decisions men make, and would affect the kind of natures men will in fact have and exhibit. But since religion is also a private matter, depending for its existence on what men do with themselves over against a world and in relation to God, the men will in the end be religious in different ways.

A living religion is inseparable from a certain type of life that is being culturally allowed and encouraged. It falls short of what a pure faith can attain; it ought therefore to see itself as in an endless process of improvement, guided by what it has learned from a neutral study of God and religion. The neutral study lacks the drive and lure of any of the religions and will never by itself satisfy men. But it is indispensable if religion is to become more than the practice of men who disdain and sometimes try to destroy one another because they show their love for God in different ways.

Only he has a right to criticize any or all religions who knows what man can and ought to be, for only he is in a position to judge whether or not the followers of a given religion have distorted that nature or have unnecessarily limited it. Such knowledge, though it does not ignore what can be gleaned from biology, psychology, anthropology and history, must in the end be speculatively acquired and expressed within a comprehensive philosophic system. The religions defend themselves, usually by referring to their miracles, revelations, sacred books, noble figures and worldly achievements. But these offer confirmations for the truth of a particular religion only for those already convinced of it.

viii

"THIS IS PRECISELY what is wrong with all religion, and all discussion of faith," we will now perhaps be told. "Faith is essentially dogmatic, irrational, maintaining itself even in the face of contrary evidences. Children are born blind, crippled, dimwitted and with short life spans. Innocent men are injured and killed. Evil prospers, while virtue is disdained everywhere. Do such facts make the religious man abandon his faith? No. Sometimes it seems as if his faith is not even shaken. What value has a faith to which no fact is relevant? At most one can take faith to be a way of postulating that something desirable will be divinely produced, and treat this as a guide or beacon in one's life. Better perhaps, it could be viewed as a way of postulating a desirable and possibly defeatable hypothesis that God sooner or later strengthens the righteous. But nothing more."

This common and often persuasive barrage of perplexities and answers rests on a number of assumptions, rarely examined. They are in fact unwarranted. To be sure, if God interferes with the course of the world, then, since He is good and powerful, one cannot avoid being perplexed by the presence of the corrupt, the destructive and the hurtful. But few religions suppose that a good God must prevent or eradicate these. Some say that these evils do not exist, others that they testify to wickedness in men. One can take them to be the outcome of an expression of God's justice, or to somehow add up to good on the whole. In the end recourse can always be had to the formula that God works in mysterious ways His wonders to perform. But it is better to say, I think, that God, though He qualifies and affects, does not interfere with the course of the world.

Nor need one suppose that all evidence is public evidence. The faith men have is private, and it results in benefits to man. Each man can himself decide whether or not he actually receives an increased strength, peace, joy, control as he continues in his faith. Should this increase not be forthcoming, he should doubt that he actually has a religious faith. There is relevant evidence, then, but it is not public. And it is evidence having to do not with whether a faith is a rational act, but only with whether or not it is present.

There are reasons, though, that one can offer on behalf of faith. The supposition that faith is an irresponsible act, a daring risk of one's will or mind, outrunning all possible thought, is not justified. He who exercises a faith may do so without reflection, but it does not follow that reflection may not justify what is then done. The nature of faith, the kind of role men can have with respect to God, the way in which God deals with what is other than Himself, are all intelligible and can be understood by anyone willing to pursue dialectic wherever it may lead.

It is also being supposed that something is gained by reducing one's claims to postulates and hypotheses, which will then serve either as programs for a life or as suppositions which could be faced with some countervailing occurrence. But postulates and hypotheses are intellectual products. If accepted as programs, they are supplemented by acts of will, and then only in order to serve the end of making a certain kind of life coherent or possible. A faith, in contrast, involves the entire man — mind, will, emotion and tendencies to act. It is already part of a distinctive type of life. If one decides in the light of some hypothesis to live a certain way, or to look for and to attend to certain types of occurrences, one gets ready to commit oneself. But men of faith have already committed themselves to live in a certain way, usually without antecedent intellectual reflection. Faith is no hypothesis, nor a consequence of a decision to use one.

The man of faith is committed to act in the light of what he has gained in virtue and confidence, matters which make no reference to the occurrence or reason for existent evils. Those evils are not produced by God. Not all of them are consequences of man's wickedness. They offer no evidence that faith is unjustified or betrayed. To be aware of evils and the fact that they cannot be part of God is to be aware that there is a great difference between God and the world; it is to be aware too that the goods which He produces are spiritual in nature. The evils need not be treated as tests divinely forged or as obstacles deliberately placed in man's path by a stern divine interrogator or disciplinarian. They can be taken to be means for redirecting faith, thereby enabling it to be strengthened.

Nevertheless a grave problem does face one who seeks to understand the nature of faith in relation to what goes on in this world. Religious men are constantly challenged by the world. What gives them pause, though, are not the occurrences which conflict with what faith promises, but those which are in consonance with it. Any situation which is excellent on the whole tempts a man of faith either to immerse himself in the world, or to become idolatrous and suppose that God's being is exhausted in some limited matter of fact. The more wonders there are, the more wonderful the daily world or any non-sacred world seems to be. Only if one can look beyond the wonders to the ultra-natural or to the supports of experience, can one escape the thrall of the everyday. But this usually can be done with persistence and clarity only when supported or directed by faith. Only if the wonders are treated as divinely sustained can one hope to block the tendency to live with them as part of some non-sacred world. But to take such an approach is already to have acted as a man of faith. The temptations that beset a man of faith can be met only by more faith.

Without faith a man would not attend to God as constantly or as perceptively as he can. As a consequence he would present God with less than God can use, and would therefore now and later have less worth than he could have had. God of course could make up any deficiency; but still, the less men offer Him, the smaller the final result will be.

A religious man is vitally engaged with God. He is directed toward God in faith and has God as part of his soul. He is sure that God exists and that God is good, that all beings are divinely assessed, and that God inevitably adds to whatever good there is whatever good He can. His attitude is one of adoration. It is this which he expresses in his worship.

11. Religious Language

WORSHIP IS EXPRESSED adoration, whether by individuals or by communities. It usually has one of three forms. Men exhibit their appreciation of God's majesty and of their own insignificance by their use of religious language – this being understood to include prayer, hymns, dogmas, creeds, myths, as well as gestures and postures. By living in terms of an ideal which reflects the nature and demands of God, worship is also expressed in a quasi-ethical form. By participating in the rites and sacrifices of a dedicated community worship is carried out in a third, a ceremonial way.

The ceremonial form of worship has already been touched upon in the discussion of the dedicated community, and need not detain us now. But the first and second have hardly been mentioned, though they have a broader range and a greater importance, since they relate to the distinctive expression of an attitude of adoration not only in but also outside a dedicated community. They are the topics of this and the next chapter. The present concerns itself with some of the main features of religious language and prayer; the next is devoted to a consideration of a life of service in which one lives up to ethical commitments, altered in the light of God's presence and commands.

ii

A RELIGION is both epitomized and exhibited in a language. The language is at once a many and a one, touching each individual and uniting all in a single bond. Whether used to affirm truths, to exhort, to report, to categorize, it is the language of a dedicated community only so far as it is integral to that community and thereby expresses it. If the community uses the words of a secular society, it makes them conform to its own needs, structure and meanings — in effect changes them into the words of another language. In daily life, in a philosophy of religion, in a theology and in a philosophy we can assert that God is love, that He forgives sinners, that He is perfect. A community might dress these up, vitalize them in psalms and prayers. Whether it does or not, it uses them in a new way, to express a present (and a hope for a consequent) union of man and God.

A religious language could be taken to have been produced by God. The language of prophesy, revelation and ecstasy is sometimes so viewed. Or it could be thought to be entirely man's creation. But we can understand no language which is completely discontinuous with the language of every day, nor can we make use of a humanly created language for religious purposes except so far as it has a meaning and value, reflecting the presence of God. Like the community it is the product of both God and us. It has a being of its own which is to be enjoyed apart from any function it might have in saying something true. It is rooted in but can be used apart from the community; it not only binds together the individuals in a community and relates them, as together, to the God beyond the community, but it enables them individually to relate themselves to that God.

Religious language has its own distinctive terms and its own distinctive grammar. It is primarily sacred. To misuse it is to blaspheme. 'God' for it is not a proper name or a noun, but a form of address, a salutation, an expression of reverence. Our logics and analytic techniques are unable to do justice to religious language. At its best, when expressing the togetherness of God and man, that language is a forceful and transformative agent offering a means for punctuating the activities of the community.

A religious language not only binds together the members of a religious community but can be used to admonish them, correct them, judge them, rule them. It can also be used on behalf of those who do not belong to the religion. It can be taken to express God's commands; to be as it were an articulation of Him. It can take the shape of a petition or express one's love of God. Each of these has been called prayer, but a prayer, strictly speaking, though it has all of these within it, is more than any of them.

Prayer is a form of speech addressed to God. Whether or not there is a subsequent response elicited from God, the prayer is answered when it is uttered. Prayer is a seeking of God by one who has already found him, and indeed who then and there possesses him. All prayer is answered in the sense that it embodies God, and through this embodiment directs and guides men. The answer does not preclude, but in fact demands that both God and man remain outside the prayer. A living vital union of the two, prayer comes to be and passes away with the coming to be and passing away of its utterance. A prayer could have a private form; it could be silent. It could even accompany a mystical act of self-abandonment, but in its normative form it is communal. It may have the form of a complaint, an argument, a despairing cry; it may express hope, and it may sound like a mere petition. But it will not be a genuine prayer unless and only so far as it unites men with God.

To provide continuity and stability to the community, the time, place and character of the prayer are usually prescribed. When the individual prays he may function as part of the community, or he may stand away from it. In the latter case, he still is part of it if he uses its prayers in the way prescribed by the community. If he instead forges his own prayers he is so far engaged in a private act.

The prayer is a union of God and man, a new reality in which both have a role. Each is absorbed and transformed in the prayer itself. The prayer in turn has a meaning and a being outside both; it has its own logic, its own rationale and career. As an articulation, it is an agency which is offered by men to God, enabling Him to be multiplied in meaning and works; as a single unity it offers a means by which men can be together with one another and with God.

In the end a petition is a plea to be properly related to, to have an excellent form of togetherness with God. Every prayer contains such a petition in a double sense; it asks that men be related to God in a more significant way than they now are, and it asks for something specific here, or now, or elsewhere, or later. As the first it asks for a closer contact; as the second it expresses what it means to achieve such closer contact.

A prayer exhibits the commanding power of the divine and the subjugation of man. It should itself provide a condition for a closer union with God, and may properly ask for a sustaining force to enable one to do what is right. This has degenerate forms in the petition on behalf of success in worldly affairs, and in magic where there is an attempt to direct or use divine power to further one's own aims. At its best a prayer petitions only that "Thy will be done on earth." Something is then asked of oneself and of God; nothing is asked for oneself. It is hoped that what is desperately wanted is in consonance with what the divine power will perform. The fact that the divine "will" operates apart from man's solicitation or activity does not change the fact that in the prayer His "will" is seen to supplement man's.

A petition in its meaning and substance can express a submission to the being and intent of God. Such a petition might be made on behalf of others. It may be expressed as a request for this or that worthy result. It may be addressed to surrogates, agents, representatives of God. It may be spontaneous, in the form of a series of exclamations. Such petitions but sharpen or specify the request that the divine will be done.

The best of prayers expresses an acceptance of God as the excellent being who will lovingly assess us finally. By means of it we shift the centre of our interests and activities so that they constitute facets of His being. The prayer gives men to God just so far as they give themselves to the prayer.

A prayer is a vital juncture of God and man, coming to be and passing away at every moment. It releases men from finite conditions, at the same time that God enables the men to live in more accord with Him. Though God is always immanent, prayer makes Him be as intimate as it is possible for men to have Him be.

In the attempt to hold on to the results of prayer, men have tried to regulate its expressions, and have tried to engage in it continuously. But they then made its performance mechanical or monotonous, and sooner or later have had to yield to the needs of the body, the weakness of the mind, the aridity of the soul and the pressure of circumstance. Also, there are other uses which language has in a dedicated community. It is used not only for prayer but to express the rules and regulations by which the members of the community are to live with one another and in the world beyond, to state creeds and dogmas, and to sustain rites and ceremonials.

iii

LANGUAGE as expressing rules has to do with the carrying on of the work of the community rather than with the truth of its claims. Such language offers a structure for the community. It may help close off the community from other groups or it may vitalize the community, enable it to function as an organic whole.

Creeds and dogmas are solidifications of beliefs, summations of history, concretions of myths, sharp formulations of truths to which the members of the community are supposed to adhere. The dogmas tell us what is being claimed to be true, the creeds tell us which dogmas are to be accepted on faith. Either may be minimal and largely implicit. Both express the community in its authoritative role, whether this authority be conceived to be derived from a higher authority or to be self-defined. They tell us in general what is the definitive source of revelation, what is traditional and acceptable, and what is not. The members of a community have their loyalty to the community expressed in the form of their acceptance and use of the language which the authority makes intrinsic to the community. Those who do not accept the authority are heretics, pagans, atheists, non-members.

In prayer language exhibits an agglutinating power. In dogmas and creed it has an authoritative role. It lacks these features when it is part of a ceremonial. It then functions somewhat as a syncategorematic, as a kind of tissue interconnecting the more significant elements of the community, a kind of convention regulating the order in which things are to occur. When prayers, dogmas and creeds are viewed as parts of ceremonies, there is a stress on the way in which the language is expressed rather than on its content or use.

Every language has a life of its own; it grows and decays, changes and fractionates in multiple ways over the course of time. Religious language is no exception. All religions regulate it so as to preserve some kind of identity with the past. The language can be regulated by a supervising body or by the re-writing of the various sacred books or prayers. We blaspheme when we use its terms in another context — an indication of the fact that they are not loosely added to the religious community but are integral to it.

Religious language also has a mystical side. It is a language of love for one another and for God, expressing the fact that the community is made up of interdependent beings who together are dependent on a being beyond them. It may express this fact in a myth, a vivid portrayal of traditionally endorsed ideals, exhibited in the religion's great past and decorating its final end. The myth achieves particular shapes in stories, festivals, dreams; it is punctuated by individuals and incidents, thereby becoming more assimilable by the multitude. The acceptance of it determines an outlook in terms of which the major values and basic divisions in work, status and interest are defined.

Initially and apparently always, myths have a religious tonality. None is ever merely secular. All report what men take to be the qualification which their tradition-grounded ideal future receives from God, and with which they interplay to constitute themselves a people lured and limited. The myth anticipates what would be the state of affairs were men to achieve the religious good they seek.

Expressing a juncture of the temporal and the eternal, the myth is the community idealized, made vivid, and then presented to the community as a desirable objective to which it should attend and seek to exemplify. It presents a pattern which the people is expected to realize if it is to achieve its divinely selected destiny. Though this has been made the topic of such historians as Spengler and Toynbee, it is not primarily an historical matter. We come closer to its meaning when we attend to Augustine's *City of God* which stands before all men, but has a different shape at different epochs. It is conceivable for example that mankind might permanently accept the myth of Christianity; if it did the myth would have a nature which persisted and which in fact would have to be presupposed in any history of mankind, but which itself was not necessarily grounded in such a history.

The myth characterizes man in terms of values relating to his status in relation to God. It defines an ideology which tells men how they are to be interrelated and how they are now to act if they are to do what God requires of man. It offers a relation between the is and the ought, the juncture of mankind with an ideal qualified by God, the meaning of a "spiritual" group with its distinctive nature, career and language.

iv

RELIGIOUS LANGUAGE is sometimes said to be metaphorical. But this it is only if some other language is literal. What language would this be? Ordinary daily language? This is shot through with metaphor. Scientific language? This is either purely formal, a species of mathematics, or it is a refined form of commonsensical language, sharing in its metaphors or adding others.

A metaphor brings together two literal meanings. "God exists" is a metaphor therefore only if "God" and "exists" have literal meaning. And this they have. "God exists" is literal in religious language, thereby making the secular uses metaphorical. Common sense, science, metaphysics, art and religion all have a right to be called literal; from the perspective of any one of them the others are metaphorical. When we move from a non-religious language to a religious one, the terms undergo a change in meaning by virtue of their new affiliations and the fact that they are now part of a community in which men are united with one another and with God in a distinctive way. He who tries to understand the nature of religious discourse by following the analyses employed in common sense, science, mathematics and the like is bound therefore to deal with it in alien terms. Is this not a way of encouraging obscurantism? No more than an acknowledgment of the distinctive nature of poetic discourse need promote obscurantism. The point is missed when one tries to make the religious assertions be "true" in a sense similar to that in which scientific or common-sense statements are true. Religious discourse is constitutive of a distinctive domain; its "truth" is inseparable from its being. An examination of the language of a religion consequently will never tell us what the religion is, or even what its words mean for it. A full-bodied religious language is an articulate form of togetherness rooted in the dedicated community.

When men speak religiously, they either make individual

use of a common language, or they manifest their religious sentiments and insights in words which have primarily an expressive rather than a communicative or binding role. They nevertheless are still able to worship effectively, i.e., to evidence their reverence, awe and love of God.

12. The Religio-Ethical Life

A RELIGIOUS MAN may ignore the dedicated community. He then risks a loss of objectivity, and can readily slip into ecstasy, sentimentality and self-delusion. A religious man may keep focused on the dedicated community; but then he risks being parochial and tends to substitute ritual for vital acts. To keep free of these extremes it is desirable for him to supplement his faith and prayers with service. He then carries out, in daily life, the demands of ethics so far as these reflect the presence and requirements of God. If the service is held apart from faith and from the worship of a dedicated community, it degenerates into "social gospel," where the love of God and the love of the dedicated community are both minimized, where not extinguished, to make room for good works which could have been produced by purely secular men.

God is served directly by those whom He commands. But it is very hard to know whether the voice one hears is one's own or God's, or some mixture of the two. That is why most men think of serving God by following out the injunctions of some sacred book or of their community, or by imitating the life of a distinguished religious hero of the past. Such service, however, can easily become service on behalf of some particular religion or belief. The surest and in a sense the richest service one can render on behalf of God is one in which divine demands are filtered through an absolute ideal. We attend to that ideal when we are ethical; if it is qualified by God, we are then religiously ethical. It is the religiously ethical man who most truly worships God through service in His name.

In religious ethics one attends to an ideal qualified by God. The primary acts of intent and performance, characteristic of

227

the secular, are carried out as before, but for a different objective. A man's virtues, his character, his attainments are still to be judged in terms of his readiness and success in living up to his duties, but the import of these duties, the particular stresses they involve, will be different from what they are secularly.

God imposes a qualification on the ideal. Through prohibitions and injunctions, known by reflection, revelation or model men, He makes it yield goals which men are to realize. The ideal is thereby backed by a command. The command makes this or that goal desirable, giving it an insistence that it does not intrinsically have. A secular morality assumes the shape of a religious morality when it recognizes this additional divinely grounded insistence on a limited form of the ideal, or goal.

Liberals try to find in the injunctions and prohibitions of their particular religions some kind of rationale, but to the degree that they succeed they abandon a religious ethics for a secular one. What is divinely commanded may not, from the position of a secular ethics, be ethically warranted. But this does not imply that God acts capriciously or perversely.

Goals are usually imposed on men by their societies, which at the same time mold the men, with the consequence that the goals have an appeal for them. Faced with such goals they exercise their freedom solely in order to select one of a number of possible means to bring about the appealing goal. A religious morality adds to the specifications and insistence of goals. The goals are thereby commanded. Men then face goals as making demands, and not only as having appeals. It makes no difference whether a man has been secularly trained to accept the commands, or whether he has had them religiously sanctioned first, he is religiously moral only so far as he tries to live in consonance with them.

Preference is the free determination of what is now to be done to achieve a goal. Since religious goals are commanded by God, a religious freedom of preference will be exercised with respect to the means to be taken to reach commanded goals. We are free of course to prefer religious to secular goals, but this is only to say that we can have a goal beyond either, for which their goals are means.

Goals, though socially approved, though imposed by a society, may not have the form which that society, for its own good or the good of its members, ought to allow. If the goal is what the given society ought to allow, it is a part of a morality; if it is what *any* society ought to allow, it is part of an ethics. Though there are thinkers who deny that this distinction is legitimate, it is necessary to make it if one is to account for the fact that societies are condemned by their members again and again because those societies urge men to behave improperly. Since any one and perhaps all societies may fall short of what a morality or an ethics requires, every religious community could conceivably be without justification, not only in what it urges, but in merely functioning as a community. But on the other hand, any community, and thus a religious community, might endorse and function in full consonance with what morality and ethics demand.

In secular morality there is something in the goal that makes its acceptance desirable for a socialized man; if he is not adequately focused, or is confused about what is adequate to his basic needs and constant nature, he will tend to take as desirable what is only an object of his present desire. In religious morality one accepts the goal because one wants to live in consonance with what God requires. The goal here is not an apparent good, as it can be in secular morality — though of course one may be mistaken as to just what it is that God endorses. Divinely commanded goals ought to be attained because the outcome is endorsed by God; secular goals, though urged by a society and accepted by men, may be goals that ought not to be attained.

Anything, it would seem, could conceivably be a means to an accepted goal, contributing to its achievement sooner or later, even when it seems to be the case that the accepted means have long been known to make such a goal impossible. Men constantly deceive themselves and accept as means what at best only remotely contribute to the attainment of the goals they endorse. They give different weights to their goals, and can, by loosely holding to an accepted goal, allow themselves to prefer a means to which they are strongly inclined but which has minimal contributive value for that supposedly desired goal. In religious morality the means which are of importance are primarily inclinations of various sorts, rather than particular acts or things. And one can take anything whatsoever to be a means to a divinely sanctioned goal, provided that one then varies the way in which the goal is accepted and is allowed to operate in one's self.

Any secular goal can be treated as a means to a further goal, for there is nothing in a goal which makes it final. A religious goal, though, either has a finality bestowed on it, or it is commanded as a means to the realization of some further goal. In either case, the religious goal bears the marks of a divine insistence, and the acknowledgment of what is insisted on makes one aware of a sovereign power still beyond. Even when a man accepts what is approved by society, he must, to share in a religious morality, see this as qualified by the divine, and to point beyond itself to the being who is able to impose that and other qualifications on that and other goals.

The goals we accept in secular morality are desirable; there is something in them which is germane to us. A religious goal, in addition, demands obedience. It is accepted because it is taken to be insisted on by God. We may be mistaken in believing that it is; the only evidence that we have that we are not mistaken, apart from a revelation of some kind, is to be found in a directly confronted insistence, not traceable to ourselves or society, or to anything other than God. Without this we have no warrant for supposing there are religiously sanctioned goals.

A secular goal is usually some state of affairs of which we are a part, some object we wish to have, some outcome we want to bring about, though a secular goal expressing some state of mind or being is of course possible. A religious goal is one which always expresses a prospective state of being or mind, divinely endorsed. It is possible, of course, to have as a religious goal some desirable state of affairs, object or outcome. But the religious goal will then contain the assurance that its realization will relate one to the divine being who insists that it be realized.

A society, once having imposed itself in the guise of some intrusive goal, may allow a man to realize the goal outside of and even in opposition to the society. Societies have sometimes encouraged men to stay with their families or to live in solitude. Indeed it is one of the functions of a good society to produce men who will be engaged in such non-societal activities as reflection, artistic creation, self-mastery and worship. Sometimes, to be sure, a societally endorsed goal requires men to be more closely involved in society than they had been before, but this demand is not a function of the insistence of the goal.

The realization of a societally endorsed goal, even when it leads one to turn away from the society, has the endorsement of a society; but the acceptance of a goal endorsed by God is inseparable from the effort to attain a greater intimacy with Him. A religious goal requires a man therefore to be even more closely related to God than he was before. He is not only to be occupied with realizing a goal but with being better related to the power which insists on that goal. In doing what he is asked to do, the religious man consequently relates himself more intimately to the insistent power beyond.

In religious morality a preferred inclination is made insistent because the insistence of a commanded goal has been added to its native insistence. Consequently, the secular thinker sees nothing in the religious situation except a regrettable acceptance of some among many equally respectable goals, while the religious thinker sees nothing in the secular situation except a regrettable acceptance of limited questionable, because solely secular, goals. But each morality has its own rights and its own distinctive achievements.

The religious goal, which has the dignity of being com- manded by God, accretes a further dignity by being accepted by one who is in consonance with God. The inclinations which are endorsed are thereupon made into a means for what, through the divine insistence, has a status superior to other respectable determined goals. As a consequence the religiously moral man is one who is effective while obedient, geared to bring about what had been divinely endorsed. The inclinations which he pushes aside may still have considerable power. Since rejected inclinations continue to insist on themselves, they will come readily to the fore as soon as he relaxes his grip on the goal. These inclinations are acknowledged by theologians under such names as "the evil principle," "the devil," "original sin," "self- centredness."

A religiously commanded goal can promote the acceptance of an otherwise regrettable act. This is the point overlooked by some of the defenders of Abraham and his attempted sacrifice of Isaac. The killing of an Isaac is an alternative that must be rejected, and no goal that endorses this is to be made our own. One can still continue to wish to be obedient to God, but this obedience should be understood by an Abraham to involve a change in the meaning of the words uttered or heard, and of the acts recommended or criticized.

Is this not what anyone can do with any onerous command?

Yes. The alternative which a command makes preferable can always be rejected as undesirable on some higher grounds than that offered in a religious morality. But this is only to say that obedience to this or that divinely sanctioned moral goal is not beyond questioning.

To be sure, no one can rightly claim to know better than God what it is that He wants, though one can claim to know better than society what is good for society. Society can misjudge needs and ends; God does not. We can rectify society; we cannot rectify God. Only an arrogant, only a presumptuous man could suppose that he, by ignoring or rejecting divinely sanctioned goals, could in fact do what he was divinely intended to do. If a religious man disobeys what he thought was divinely commanded, it can then only be on the ground that he has not been faced with a genuine divine command, or that he is preparing himself to be able to obey. One may justly reject what is in fact urged by the society in order to promote what the society needs; religiously, one can reject only what is not being divinely urged at this time.

He who puts aside a divinely sanctioned goal in order to identify himself with another goal, must, if he is to be religiously moral, show that this latter goal is a means to a fuller divine obedience, that it is in fact what the other goal merely claims to be. Abraham was too uncritical, too naive and too insensitive. He need not have taken the voice he heard to be the voice of God; he need not have so quickly supposed that he heard God command him to kill Isaac. But granted that this was what he heard, he should have understood it to tell him that Isaac was not his to do with as he would. Abraham should have said to himself that if he treated Isaac with affection and justice he would be preparing himself for the day when he could obey God excellently by giving up his hold on his son. The killing of Isaac is a goal which merely claims to allow Abraham to show his obedience to God. A greater obedience would be shown by Abraham by his working to make Isaac a man able to live apart from him, and eventually able to be a man worthy of giving himself in love to God.

Not all men are religiously moral, not all attend to goals which have a divine sanction. From the perspective of a religious morality these men are disobedient. They differ radically from those who turn away from some religiously sanctioned goal in order to obey some other. Religiously viewed, the latter are perhaps mistaken and at most presumptuous, but the others are wicked, corrupt.

In the religious situation a man tends to exhibit a rather constant degree of obedience. If the degree is slight it may not suffice to enable him to do more than attend occasionally to a divinely sanctioned goal. But if the degree is great it will enable him to follow inclinations which otherwise would be resisted.

The means required by divinely sanctioned goals are not necessarily sustained by God. Consequently the pursuit of divinely sanctioned goals may require a turning to a world over which God has insufficient influence. Such a turning could conceivably be demanded by the divinely sanctioned goal, but whether it be demanded or not, the divinely sanctioned goal will require the use of means which are structured and which operate in ways no obedience to God need help us to know or master.

ii

A SECULAR MAN faces an ultimate end which is pertinent to himself and all other valuable realities; it has a place for all of these, and he is obligated to realize it just so far as he here and now reduces the value of any of them. What he reduces is, in principle, thereby compensated for. The religious man also faces an end he has a duty to realize. Though the end may be one to which he is committed by what he did in a secular context, it is not a religious end until it has been divinely approved. And he has a duty toward the divinely approved end even when it is one which the particular losses, for which he now is responsible, do not force into primary focus. For the religious man, duties, defined by ends, come before obligations, which are defined by the losses in value that he produces.

In the religious situation only one ultimate end is obligatory. Whatever we do obligates us with respect to it, and not to any others. It is externally endorsed as being superior to other possible ends, even those which seem to require much less work on our part in order to make good the losses we brought about. We are committed to the end not merely because we thereby justify what we do, but because we find it possessed of a dignity which owes nothing to such commitment.

In the secular situation an end is chosen solely because this is required by the losses produced; in the religious situation an end is chosen because it is divinely approved. We are free to reject or accept the religious end. If we accept it we justify whatever it be that we are doing. The religious end makes good the losses for which we are responsible, but it is not chosen solely because of that fact. It may make good other losses as well, with which we have not yet been involved; it may have an excellence beyond that needed to make good any and all losses in value.

The religious end has a divine warrant. Not to live up to that end is not only to fail to do one's duty; it is to be disobedient. It is not only to lose a sanction for some previous act, but a proper relation to God, the being who specified some end as the source of our duties. A divinely sanctioned end, even when the loss of value is small, may entail duties that may prove difficult to meet. Unless God actually comes in and lifts us up, empowers us in new ways, we will then find that an end which He endorses, and which makes good the loss in value which we are now producing — and other losses as well — is beyond our power to realize. A religious man supposes that God will then make good all his failures. If He does, and if He accredits the result to him or allows the man to accredit it to himself, the guilt which is a man's because what should have been done by him was not done by him, will no longer exist. He will be guilty for not having done what it was his duty to do, but he will be forgiven in the sense that he will be allowed to accept as his own the divine doing of this which he had not done. Divine forgiveness at its most complete is the divine performance of what ought to be done and the accrediting of the result to men, or the allowing of it to be accepted by them as their own.

The story of Abraham and Isaac could be understood as illustrating this truth. Abraham will then obey God, acutely aware of the enormity of what he was about to do, but confident also that the good which should have been done to Isaac will be divinely done and accredited to Abraham. But it would have been easier, wiser and safer for Abraham to suppose, as I have already remarked, that he did not hear correctly or did not properly interpret what he had heard.

For a religious man, only that alternative is the best possible which is in consonance with a divinely sanctioned end. Having freely committed himself to adopting a divinely sanctioned end, he is a sinner if he takes any alternative but the one which is directly compensated by the sanctioned end, and which can promote that end to the highest possible degree. Though free to disobey, he is still not free to accept the divinely sanctioned end and at the same time take any alternative whatsoever, except at the price of giving up his knowledge, habits and character, and abstracting himself from the existent circumstances.

A man remakes himself in the course of his acceptance of alternative and end, each supporting the other. He always acts out of character in the sense that whatever he does is a free act outside the control of what he had been; yet he always acts in character, no matter what he does, for not only does his character affect his decision, but his character is partly constituted by the decision. At the same time that the religious man constitutes his character, he determines the nature of his obedience. The habit of obedience to some divinely sanctioned end promotes the formation of character just as a secularly approved end does. But the divine sanction helps determine the kind of character which is being formed.

In a religious situation we start with an end to which we are devoted, in part because it had been divinely sanctioned. That end may be quite different from what our acts require. It may not be supported by what we thereafter do, not because it fails to make good the losses for which we are responsible — for it, like every other end, necessarily does this — but because the kind of acts in which we engage are different in kind, situation, opportunity from those which are required to realize a divinely sanctioned end.

The realization of the divinely sanctioned end may require considerable effort even where there has been little loss in value, for it is not an end which merely recompenses for damage done. The wisdom which teaches the secular man to do as little damage as possible so that the end to which he is committed is not too difficult for him, can therefore be utilized by the religious man only in part. The end to which he is committed may require much more radical activity than he can himself summon, and often more than was entailed by his previous behavior.

Religious morality is rooted in the assumption that what a man must subsequently do is possible for him to do — or that it will be done by God and accredited to him. The two ideas can be combined in the view that God will give "superhuman" power to men, enabling them to do what they normally could not do, provided only that they really dedicate themselves to the divinely sanctioned end and do all they can in preparation and in act to bring that end about.

The fixity and the nobility of a divinely sanctioned end means that every failure to live up to it is a testimony to an added burden that we have, but not a ground for our adopting (as it is in secular morality) a new end which justifies the new loss. Our commitment is in principle fixed because our end is desirable regardless of what we had done and will do. In secular morality we are forced to give up one end for another, particularly when it is the latter and not the former that can be realized. But in religious morality we have only one end and must cling to this no matter what we do, while hoping that the losses which are not sanctioned by it will nevertheless be made good by us through God's aid or by God himself.

God qualifies the ethical ideal in such a way as to guarantee values at present not realizable. Without such a guarantee, men would use up, reject and ignore some valuable things, and would not know how to compensate for what they failed to realize. The losses in value, and the associated prohibitions and rejections, are linked by God to a reevaluation of what is being urged. He who realizes what is divinely sanctioned, as a consequence, will bring about all the values which would have been realized had the losses not occurred.

iii

IF WE ARE to judge religious communities or ourselves justly, we must make use of an independently known ethics, secular or religious. We measure the communities and ourselves by a secular ethics when we wish to see if what is done is good for man or other actualities. We measure them by a religious ethics when we wish to see if what is done is in consonance with what God demands. Conformity to the demands of a religious ethics may not make one necessarily in consonance with secular ethics. This, infanticide, human sacrifice, cannibalism, and holy wars make abundantly clear. (If we deny that these can ever be sanctioned by a religious ethics, we will in effect be affirming that religious ethics is but a form of the secular, endorsing and condemning part of what it does.) Yet a religious ethics has rights of its own. If we are to avoid falling into provincialism and yet want to determine what is a higher and what a lower religion, we must, among other things, have recourse to a religious ethics.

A religious ethics involves a guarantee that what cannot be done, and perhaps even what in fact is not done by man will be done by God. The qualification which God imposes on the good is the guarantee that it will be realized somehow, no matter what men do — by having men empowered in ways they had not been, by having God interfere with the ways things behave and what is achieved, or by having God himself make good what men have failed to do.

A religious ethics may demand that men make sacrifices, which is to say that they deny or reduce the values of certain things for the sake of achieving the desired good. Men sacrifice usually as a way of getting to something else, but the sacrifice of the religious man may not promote the achievement of any desired good except that of being or doing what is divinely demanded. Sometimes he sacrifices that which is most precious and which no act on his part could ever make good. Sometimes he sacrifices the best of things — say, the first born, the unblemished, the distinctively marked, that which is first encountered in such and such a place. In these cases the divine qualification of the good consists in defining these sacrifices as efficacious. A genuine religious sacrifice then is not a destruction or forfeit of the valuable for the sake of attaining a community with God; it is the making something sacred, the dedicating of it.

A religious ethics urges man to give to others and to God what is most precious to himself, thereby ennobling himself, the others and God at the same time. Since love is a way of possessing what is other than oneself, and thus a way of becoming complete by the addition of what conditions oneself, a man can be urged, in a religious ethics, to love fellowman and God. In loving them he makes fellowman and God a gift of his experiences, of what he obtained through his flesh and finitude. He is perfected by an act of identification, and all are perfected by his contribution.

The secular sacrifices and loves men exhibit are ethically justifiable only so far as they involve a genuine improvement of themselves and others, an improvement which otherwise would not be possible. Secularly we ought to love our neighbor because he is intrinsically lovable, and not because he is loved by God or because we are commanded to do so by God. But a religious ethics asks us to love our neighbor though we do not find him lovable. The asking is a way of making us alert, of making us see that our love must be extended beyond the scope of what in fact happens to elicit it. Secular ethics defines love to be a desirable state, but religious ethics directs one to a specific object and thus makes it possible for that state to be realized. Religious ethics says that one is to adventure and love where nothing lovable is being discerned, and this because the ethical good has been qualified by God, the being who knows what beings intrinsically are.

In a religious ethics, goals, ends and the ideal are qualified by God. They possess insistencies additional to those characteristic of secular objectives. No substitute for a secular ethics, religious ethics nevertheless provides one with standards of measurement and behavior appropriate to men who live in a world, taken to be under the aegis of an ethically alert God.

But how can God be ethically alert? If he were, why is evil everywhere? More, we rightly object to some practices and beliefs of religious men. No one would endorse those practices and beliefs were it not that he has already convinced himself that their obtrusive, regrettable features can somehow be explained away. One might claim that those who engage in them were granted special dispensations by God, that their beliefs and practices serve a particular divine or ethical purpose now hidden from us, or that they were not really condemnable. No one of these answers faces up to the fact that we have an independent secular ethics which shows the evils to be regrettable and the practices and beliefs to be wrong. And we will beg our question if we make the religious ethics all-inclusive or beyond all criticism. It would be much better to insist that though these evils, practices and beliefs are secularly bad, God subjects them all to a re-evaluation, correction and supplementation.

iv

AT THE ROOT of every man is a most complex need. Each seeks to be loved and to love, and yet to be free. The need was once completely satisfied — in infancy.

Perhaps even the most unwanted of infants has its moments when it feels that it is being loved for itself, without reserve, that it is being accepted completely. Each has moments when it responds spontaneously as a single being. Some men, understandably, try to recover this joyous state. Some even try to return to something like infancy so as to recapture the love of some adult to which they can respond without constraint. Others are content to symbolize the infantile state. Their world is primarily an extension and projection of whatever made possible the idyllic world which they once occupied. But most men instead seek to satisfy their need to love and be loved without blurring or compromising their adult interests and values. They have mastered the lesson that even the most spoiled child soon learns: no one is ever loved as much, as often, and the way it wants to be loved.

The love we would have we do not get; the love we would give we do not express. Very early we are all faced with denials, demands, obstacles; we are opposed, rejected, admonished, directed, disciplined, trained. As we grow older we face the double problem of finding someone who will love us without crushing, and who when loved will not rebuff or withdraw.

Cats and dogs and other pets offer an answer to the problem, but only for those who are content to forget that these either have no real free selves to give or never give themselves wholly to anyone else. Infants and children are better objects and agents of love than any animal could be. But they do not know enough to love an adult properly, or to know what he intends with his love. The infant needs the love it receives, and what it returns is all it can give; but what it needs is less than what an adult can give, and what it returns is less than what an adult needs.

And as the young begin to grasp the meaning of the love they receive and can give, they grow older, and grow away.

All men seek to be loved for what they truly are. No man wants to be loved only for the good he has done and the good repute he publicly has. These are too exterior, too impersonal, too transitory, too fixated to do justice to a man's full nature and promise. At best they are only indices of what a man is in root.

Men have different rhythms, experiences, problems and powers. They do not, they cannot, love to just the degree that the love is needed by or is acceptable to another. They can, to be sure, be rather constant in their affections, but love is too vital, transformative and penetrating to be sustained for long, kept at a constant pitch, or even varied in consonance with the appetites and powers of others. Every lover is at once too niggardly and too demanding; every lover is at times too rough and at times too gentle.

Everyone seeks while he awaits, retreats even when he advances, fears as he gives himself, withdraws as he submits. The love one offers is not altogether acceptable; it is the love that is withheld that is wanted. Yet he who would give without question would go too far, since he would jeopardize his own and the other's freedom, just as he who would receive without question would not go far enough since he would not give himself and would fail to identify the other.

The religious affirmation that there is a God is one with the affirmation that all beings are loved for what they are, by a single, constant lover. God alone always loves without compromise or hesitation; only His love is absolutely appropriate to the beings that receive it. He alone never withdraws, never falls short, never over-reaches. Only God loves without hesitation or fear. Only He loves adults as completely and as well as they were loved when they were infants.

The infant is loved when asleep and when awake. But when asleep it does not respond. The love it accommodates is at a minimum. Only when the infant is awake can it respond to the love freely given, and thereby make possible the expression of still more love for it. Non-religious men are like infants asleep. They are not unloved by God, but they are loved only minimally. To receive greater love they must become religiously awake, which is to say, they must pray and worship. It is that love which finds its expression in service.

Every man at every moment is faced with the decision as to whether or not to be religious. This he can be only if he freely accepts God as his lover. The love should not be thought to exclude judgment. Nor need the judgment be taken to be personal or conscious, or to preclude mercy and forgiveness. The religious man in adoration and in devotion presents himself to God for assessment, and deals with what else there is in the light of what he takes God to be, do, and demand.

As part of his response to his acceptance of God's present and eventual assessment, the religious man gladly helps the poor and the unfortunate, the weak and the downtrodden. Eventually he must turn back to the world and see all within it as divinely enriched and subject to an eventual divine transformation by which maximum good is produced out of them all. He will act as a representative of God, doing all he can to cherish what is excellent and to transform evil into good. The greatest religious service he can do for another, however, is to pray for him. This does not preclude his helping him; indeed, it places help within the desirable context of a divine sustaining love. Since prayers are framed in a particular language and reflect the limitations of a specialized religion, he will not be a complete religious man unless he not only willingly prays for others but asks them to pray for him. To all, in humility and hope, he should make one request: "For the love of God, pray for me; alone I can not do enough."

INDEX

INDEX

254

Objectivity, 39, 66
Obligation, 17, 69, 71, 140, 142, 159, 166, 187, 195, 212, 233
Obscurantism, 225
Observation, 14, 25, 69
Obstacles, 123, 125, 239
Occurrences, 80, 125, 128, 130–32
Omens, 205
Omnicentrality, 38
Omnipotence, 93, 96
Omnipresence, 101, 173
Omniscience, 96
One and many, 116, 137, 173, 219
Organization: 113; social, 67
Organs, sense, 70
Other: 60, 78, 92, 177, 206; absolute, 11, 185, 210; for, 178, 182–84, 187, 194; God as, 98; of, 178, 182–84, 187, 194; persistent, 179; relative, 11, 207; than, 178, 182–84, 186, 187, 193, 194, 195
Otherness, 78, 177, 178, 183
Otto, R., 60, 64
Ought, 68, 182, 225

Panpsychism, 28n
Pagans, 223
Pain, 25, 39, 41, 42, 46, 64, 142, 168, 170
Paradise, 93
Part and whole, 68
Participation, 40, 101, 106, 107, 111–13, 116, 121
Particulars, 32, 58
Passivity, 46, 176, 178
Past, the: 111, 125; and future, 125, 135; and God, 134; and present, 123, 126, 130; and religion, 129, 135; being of, 123; effect of, 130; encounter with, 129; preservation of, 123, 129
Peace, 113, 196, 202
Peirce, C. S., 18, 26, 27, 28, 73
Pelagianism, 174
People: 116, 211; chosen, 140; religious, 64
Perception, 14, 24, 79, 85, 86, 88
Perfection, 78, 79
Peripheral, the, 45, 49, 52, 60, 61, 62
Permanence, 179
Persistence, 78, 182

Personality, 104
Perspectives: 41, 56, 109, 213; religious, 10, 159
Petitions, 3, 220, 221, 222
Phenomeno-analysis, 8
Phenomenology, 25, 30
Philosophy: 56, 162, 166, 181, 188, 195; aim of, 109; and common sense, 15; and faith, 193; and God, 109, 110, 121, 155, 191, 193; and religion, 9, 145, 154, 155–57, 193; language of, 17, 30, 220; mystery for, 109; speculative, 29, 88, 108, 215; task of, 15; test of, 156
Piety, 121, 181
Pity, 105n
Places: 128, 175; sacred, 58, 61, 102
Plato, 17
Pleasure, 13, 42, 64, 170–72
Plurality, 74
Poetry, 41, 144, 162, 172, 225
Politics: 17, 24, 68, 110, 113, 116, 118, 166, 181, 212; and ethics, 118; and religion, 213
Positivism, 80
Possessions, 41, 63, 170
Possibilities, 17, 68, 83, 179
Postulation, 39, 217
Potent, the, 61, 62, 63
Potentiality, 25
Power: 35, 45, 47, 48, 60, 197; hidden, 25, 66; irrational, 15, 168
Practice: 14, 26; and experience, 20; men of, 169; religious, 4, 145, 181, 238
Pragmatism, 25, 27
Prayer: 3, 60, 100, 116, 149, 158, 165, 181, 186, 213, 219, 220, 227, 241; and community, 221; answer to, 221; best, 222; components in, 165; effect of, 222; logic of, 221; nature of, 221–23; regulation of, 222; request for, 241
Predicates, 94
Predictions, 90, 128, 129, 206
Preference, 201, 228, 229
Present: and future, 125; and past, 126, 130; being of, 94; historic, 123–25, 129; kairotic, 126–27; magnitude of, 124, 127
Prescriptions, 21, 27, 72, 73, 118